Painfully Correct

By
Paul Aaron

Published by JHW Publishing Co.
First Edition, 2011

ISBN-13: 978-0-9847865-0-3

Printed in the United States of America

For uninformed current and future voters.

CONTENTS

PREAMBLE

This book contains everything you need to know about being *Painfully* Correct, but were afraid to ask.

Disclaimer:

- The following may be challenging for Democrat ideology.
- The following may be difficult for the rationally impaired.
- The following may be difficult for those having a hard time dealing with reality.
- The following may not be suitable for Liberals, discretion advised.
- Liberals, I'm here to burst your 'fairy tale version of the world' bubble.
- A note to the Humane Society – pets were capriciously mistreated, neglected and psychologically abused while I was busy writing this book.
- The building where this book was written is not wheelchair accessible.
- If you need the book written in brail or in a different language, you're sh!t out of luck.
- If the truth hurts, that's your problem. Live with it!

If you have been voting for Democrats and their ideals don't reflect your views, or if you finally realize you would like to continue to live in a nation that still has freedom and liberties, maybe it's time to change party affiliation. If not, and you are insulted by some of the following comments, great!

viii

PART 1

POLITICIANS, ETC.

Al Gore (D), Vice-President of the United States 1993 – 2001, Democrat Presidential Nominee 2000

Copyright 2010 The Associated Press/Dita Alangkara

All Bore.

An Inconvenient Bore.

An inconvenient whore exposed him as acting like a "crazed sex poodle".

The first android in office.

1

An escaped mannequin.

Chad.

A horse's ass.

He is uniquely unqualified.

He said, "Can't tell a leopard by its strips."

He's got that Al Gore rhythm.

His speech pattern sounds like he is talking to a group of dogs, whose heads are turned sideways.

The Alpha Male, ha, ha, ha! If anything, he is the Alpo Male.

Dread the thought, but if Gore had become President, he could have been referred to as President Dimples.

He is an erectile dysfunction, a 'limp dick.'

He has a Clintonesque propensity to lie.

He authored *Earth in the Balance*; it more appropriately should have been titled *Earth by the Unbalanced*. He is left of balanced.

He claimed he "invented the Internet".

He claimed he discovered the problems at Love Canal.

He claimed he and his wife were the inspiration for the novel *Love Story*.

He claimed he authored the Earned Income Tax Credit.

He infers he identified Global Warming.

2

In 2000, Gore claimed he has always supported Roe v. Wade, yet in 1977 he voted for the Hyde Amendment, which says that abortion "takes the life of an unborn child who is a living human being," and that there is no constitutional right to abortion.

In 1993, Vice-President Gore cast the Senate tie-breaking vote that imposed taxes on Social Security benefits of the elderly and disabled.[1]

In 1996, he was involved in an inappropriate fund-raising event at a Buddhist temple in California.

In 1997, he rationalized there was "no controlling legal authority," when illegally making fund-raising calls from the White House.

In 1998, famously stingy Al's tax return revealed that gave just $353 to charity.[2] Liberals are notorious for spending taxpayer's money, but not their own.

Gore just kept asking for a recount of the 2000 Florida election ballots, adnauseam. He must have been one of those kids that always yelled "do over". Bill Clinton's mother didn't teach Bill to tell the truth. Al Gore's parents didn't teach Al to lose gracefully.

According to Lewis Smith of The Times, in 2007, after a school governor had accused the government of brainwashing children, a British High Court judge ruled that Gore's film, *An Inconvenient Truth*, was littered with nine significant inconvenient untruths and can only be shown in schools on the condition that it is accompanied by guidance notes to balance Gore's "one-sided" views. "It is a political film." Some of the claims were wrong and in "the context of alarmism and exaggeration." The claim that sea levels could rise by 20 feet in the near future was dismissed as "distinctly alarmist."[3]

In June 2009, two American female journalists were convicted of grave crimes and sentenced to 12 years in a labor camp in North

3

Korea. Al Gore was to be sent as an envoy. An appeal to North Korea should have been, please do a swap, and keep Gore.

A Southern Baptist, this country bumpkin's family grows the demonized tobacco plant.

His father was a liberal anti-Vietnam War critic. To help his father's re-election campaign and to help the anti-war movement by getting his father re-elected, Al enlisted in the Army, but Al senior lost his House seat anyway.[4] It seems his motives have always been calculated and insincere.

While in Vietnam, Al had a bodyguard, the most dangerous weapon he carried was a typewriter, he left after three months.[5]

Al said of Van Jones, Obama's former Green Jobs Czar, and admitted Marxist, "I love Van Jones. I love his work. ... I love his mission."[6]

Part of the cosmic joke being played on Al is the school that bears his name. The Carson-Gore Academy of Environmental Sciences, is located above an abandoned oil field that has terribly contaminated soil from underground storage tanks.[7] And he settles for second billing, a reoccurring theme in his life.

Runner-up Al never makes it to first place. He didn't complete law school; he came in third for the 1988 Democrat presidential nominee; he was Vice-President under Bill Clinton; he came in second for the 2000 Presidential bid; he shared the 2007 Nobel Peace Prize for Intergovernmental Panel on Climate Change; and he was runner up for *Times'* 2007 Person of the Year.

It is ironic that there is usually an Arctic Blast when Gore goes places to lecture on Global Warming. God is making a joke of Environmentalists who think they can affect the weather. You can tell that God doesn't like this Devil's messenger, because He keeps playing tricks on him. You can tell when ol' Arctic Al is coming to town by the drop in temperature.

In the 2010 remake of the movie *The Day the Earth Stood Still*, a stoic Al Gore type robot was instructed to kill all humans because they were harming the Earth. That is an accurate depiction of what environmentalists really believe. The Earth is what is most important, and because humans just pollute and hurt it, they must be eliminated.

The Environmental Evangelist.

There have been Limousine Liberals, now there are Gulfstream Green Elitists. Just refer to Al as a Gulfstream Greeny.

What is his carbon offset to his frequent use of private jets, limousines, SUV's, and owning multiple very large homes?

In 2006, Gore's electric bill was more than 20 times the national average.[8]

Critics have claimed he has a conflict-of-interest for pressing members of Congress to pass legislation to curb emissions for the added benefit of self-enrichment from his green technology investments.[9]

Cap and Trade is a risky scheme.

Regarding man-made climate change, Al is not a scientist, as a matter of fact in the two science classes he took in college he scored a C+ and a D; he is a politician and a profiteer. I have "high confidence" that he would cripple the U.S. economy just to get rich from the diabolical Cap and Trade scam.

He is ethically disoriented.

A climate profiteer.

A carbon billionaire.

An inconvenient truth is that Wikileaks revealed that the Obama Administration was cutting off foreign aid to countries that opposed the Copenhagen Accord that was the focus of the 2009 U.N. Climate Change Conference[10] that Al Gore supported.

President Klaus of the Czech Republic gave a speech at the 2008 International Conference on Climate Change that conveyed his insight comparing environmentalism with communism:

> "I have spent most of my life under the communist regime. ...in the former Czechoslovakia. ... Future dangers will not come from the same source. The ideology will be different. Its essence will, nevertheless, be identical - the attractive, ... at first sight noble idea that transcends the individual in the name of the common good, and ... its proponents ... right to sacrifice the man and his freedom in order to make this idea reality. ... Formulated in ... my recently published book ... *What is Endangered: Climate or Freedom?* My answer is clear and resolute: it is our freedom. I may also add and our prosperity. The insurmountable problem as I see it lies in the political populism of its exponents and their unwillingness to listen to arguments. They, in spite of their public roles, maximize their own private utility function where utility is not any public good but their own private good – power, prestige, career, income, etc. I am afraid there are people who want to stop the economic growth, the rise in the standard of living, though not their own, and the ability to use the expanding wealth, science and technology for solving the actual pressing problems of mankind, especially of the developing countries. This ambition goes very much against the past human

experience which has always been ... to better human conditions. I am also afraid that the same people, ... in their own megalomaniac ambitions, want to regulate and constrain the demographic development, which is something only the totalitarian regimes have until now dared to think about or experiment with. The global warming alarmist ... call for a radical decrease in carbon dioxide emissions. It can be achieved only by means of a radical decline in the emissions intensity. ... We know, however, that such revolutions in economic efficiency ... have never been realized in the past and will not happen in the future either. To expect anything like that is a non-serious speculation. What I see ... is a powerful combination of irresponsibility, of wishful thinking, ... with the strong belief in the possibility of changing the economic nature of things through a radical political project. As a politician who personally experienced communist central planning of all kinds of human activities, ... climate alarmists and their fellow-travelers in politics and media now present and justify their ambitions to mastermind human society. The climate alarmists believe in their own omnipotency, in knowing better than millions of rationally behaving men and women what is right or wrong. To give adequate instructions to hundreds of millions of individuals and institutions. We have to restart the discussion about the very nature of government and about the relationship between the individual and society. Now it concerns the whole mankind, not just the citizens of one particular country. Discussion about socialism or communism. It is not about climatology. It is about freedom."[11]

Al?

<u>William J. Clinton (D), 42nd President of the U.S. 1993 – 2001</u>

Copyright 2010 The Associated Press/J. Scott Applewhite

The Lying King.

A bold-faced liar.

A habitual liar.

A chameleon.

An adulterer.

A rapist.

Hillary's husband.

Monica's boyfriend.

Monica Lewinsky:

- She's looking for Mr. Right-now.
- Coined a new term, receiving a Lewinsky.
- She is a Fellatio Alger story.
- Instead of E.T. the Extraterrestrial, she is E.Z. the Extramarital.
- She kept the dress with Clinton's baby pudding on it.

Clinton just gave lip service, one intern returned the favor.

ClintonCigars@Monica.orgy

He brought new meaning to the word "is".

Clinton would say what he got on Monica's dress depends on what the definition of Giz is.

When Clinton was first running for President and was interviewed on TV about Gennifer Flowers, it was obvious that it wasn't plausible to make up a twelve-year affair. So voters should have realized that if he betrayed his wife and daughter, he would betray us too.

The definition of "mortified" had to be his young daughter knowing the entire world was aware that her father had been cheating on her mother for decades.

Commander in Heat.

He was monogamously challenged.

He habitually attempted horizontal encounters.

He was always on the lookout for a sex care provider.

He is morally impaired.

The Clinton Administration was like a Soap Opera, every week there was a new unbelievable scandal.

When Clinton first became President, he claimed, "This will be the most ethical Administration in the history of the country." His list of scandals include, but are not limited to: Travelgate, Tailgate, Filegate, Whitewatergate, Chinagate, Indonesiagate, Golfgate, Troopergate; violation of the oath of office, abuse of power, Obstruction of Justice, Contempt of Court, witness tampering, lying to a Grand Jury, lying to the American people on TV, he was Impeached, Disbarred; he received Campaign Contributions from Communist China and criminals; he is implicated with Vince Foster's death, and Ron Brown's death; and then there's Paula Jones, Monica Lewinsky, Juanita Broaddrick, Linda Tripp, etc.

- Whitewater began when Bill was Governor, and it cost the taxpayers of Arkansas $60 million when Jim McDougal's Savings-and-Loan went broke. The Clinton's were partners that improperly benefited from a land deal. There were 15 convictions or guilty pleas.
- Filegate was when Bill's Administration improperly went through 900 FBI files on Republican officials to compile a potential enemies list.
- Indonesiagate, featuring the Lippo Group, with long-standing ties to Bill, had funneled $452,000 through a couple of modest means.
- Vince Foster, a former Hillary Clinton law partner who became a White House lawyer and was a central figure in Whitewater, Filegate and Travelgate, died of a gunshot to the head under very suspicious circumstances. See the movie *Absolute Power* starring Clint Eastwood.
- Travelgate, the Clintons fired career staffers to make room for Clinton cronies in the White House travel office.

- Paula Jones, an Arkansas state employee when Bill was Governor, sued him on sexual harassment charges in a federal court case for dropping his pants and asking for oral sex.
- Juanita Broaddrick filed a sexual assault and rape charge.
- Young White House aides were hired despite FBI background checks that found recent use of hard drugs.[12]
- Chinagate, Clinton said China will likely replace the USA as world leader; it is just a matter of time. In 1997, Clinton allowed China to control the Panama Canal by leasing the ports on each side of the openings. As a globalist, Clinton promotes "multipolarity", the doctrine that no country should be allowed to have a decisive advantage over others. He appointed anti-nuclear activist Hazel O'Leary to head the Department of Energy. She leveled the playing field by giving away our nuclear secrets. She declassified 11 million pages of data on U.S. nuclear weapons and loosened up security at weapon labs. Federal investigators later concluded that China got our best secretes. Defense contractors willing to sell technology to China poured millions of dollars into Clinton's campaign. In return, Janet Reno stood down while Bernard Schwartz's Loral Space & Communications, Lockheed Martin and Hughes Electronics helped China modernize its nuclear strike force. Clinton's top campaign contributors for 1992 were Chinese agents; his top donors in 1996 were defense contractors. Clinton received funding from Chinese agents including James Riady, who owned the Indonesian Lippo Group, John Huang and Charlie Trie. When Clinton took office in 1993, China presented no threat to the U.S., Chinese missiles couldn't hit the broadside of a barn. Few could reach North America. China can now hit any city in the USA, using state-of-the-art missiles with deadly accuracy.[13]

This is treason!

11

Commerce Secretary Ron Brown served as Clinton's front man in the Chinese dealings. When investigators began probes, Brown died suddenly when the airplane he was sent on, suspiciously crashed, killing 35 people. The military aircraft was not equipped with either a cockpit voice recorder or a flight data recorder. The itinerary was changed four times before the flight began. The stop in Dubrovnik, Croatia was not listed in the change. The pilot of the flight "was known for very thorough mission planning and briefing." It was not reported that there was an emergency call from the pilots before the crash.[14] It seems like a murder plot.

The most dishonest, corrupt and treasonous President in U.S. history.

On December 19, 1998 Bill Clinton was impeached for lying under oath to a federal grand jury and obstructing justice.

Clinton being impeached for lying about Monica was as relatively minor a crime as Al Capone being convicted of income tax evasion. They were both so slick, it was all you could prove.

A perjurer.

Clinton should have been a two term President, one term in office followed by a term in prison.

Bush is charged by his moral convictions; Clinton is convicted on moral charges.

The Moral Crisis in America was fueled by Clinton's indiscretions. People on the edge of truth, justice and marital fidelity were given an excuse by example to make the wrong choice. The youth were influenced by Clinton, concluding that oral sex wasn't sex, and as a result, incidents of that skyrocketed in young teenagers. He morally corrupted the youth and the country.

Trickle-down immorality.

Clinton defenders said his crime didn't rise to the level of an impeachable offense; Clinton didn't rise to the level of the Office of the Presidency.

Reagan did what was best for the country; Clinton did what was best for Clinton.

Clinton's re-election was most revealing, it exposed: who defended a liar, an adulterer, and the hypocrisy of the feminist movement.

Nancy Reagan got heat for buying China for the White House; Now Clinton is getting heat for China buying the White House. - Rush Limbaugh

A stranger to the truth.

Cartoon: Clinton and O.J. sitting in a golf cart. Caption – O.J. is looking for someone with a wicked slice and Clinton is just looking for a good lie.

Clinton and Michael Jackson should be on the TV Game Show "What's My Lie" or "To Tell the Truth".

He was morally handicapped.

Truman observed that the buck stops at the President's desk. A Clintonesque response would be, Hey, I never saw the buck, somebody else must have gotten that, I didn't know about it till I read it in the newspaper, I was short changed!

Clinton said in 2003 that he learned there are some things you should not do just because you can. It's a shame his mother didn't teach him that when he was 5 years old.

He proclaimed the beginning of "a new covenant". A covenant with the Devil!

The reason Clinton wouldn't let Doctors examine him, is so they wouldn't find the 666 on his body.

With Nixon it was said you had to count the silverware, when the Clintons left the White House the citizens wanted a full inventory preformed.

Slick Willie's Used Cars – would you buy a used car from Clinton?

Fish rot from the head down.

The Left kept telling the Republicans to just move on after Clinton's Impeachment. Then an organization was formed named MoveOn.org. The ironic thing is, they 'just can't seem to move on'. They are the worst at continually rehashing the past.

The Lincoln bedroom was used as a dorm room for the Electoral College.

A self-serving politician.

He is morally challenged.

Letting Clinton speak at Reagan's funeral would be like Benedict Arnold speaking at George Washington's funeral.

If Clinton was in George Washington's situation, instead of, "I cannot tell a lie, I cut down the cherry tree." Clinton would say, "I never asked anyone to lie for me, it ax-saw-dently got cut down."

Clinton didn't inhale marijuana; right.

Ross Perot purposely created a situation so George H. W. Bush would not be elected president, and that is the main reason Clinton was able to win the election. Clinton did not have a majority vote; he was elected by 43% of the voters in 1992.

The Mad Bomber. This is a list places he had bombed during his Presidency: Somalia, Yugoslavia, Bosnia, Haiti, Croatia, Zaire, Liberia, Albania, Afghanistan, Iraq, Yemen, and an aspirin factory in Sudan.

Whenever Clinton was around our military, they were ordered to not have any bullets in their guns. He is the only Commander-in-Chief to have done that. It goes along with the Left's distrust of the military.

The Democrats and feminists never denounced his actions.

In college Clinton reportedly was a member of SDS, Students for a Democratic Society, whose goal is world communism.

As a student, he protested against the USA while visiting Russia.

In 1993 he signed into law the Motor Voter Bill. He had Richard Cloward and Francis Fox Piven there in attendance. They co-authored the 1966 article *The Weight of the Poor: A Strategy To End Poverty*, which describes how to overburden the Welfare system to collapse the American government and bring about socialism, it is known as the Cloward-Piven Strategy. They based their strategy on the U.S. Communist Party strategies from the 1930's.

In 2001, he commuted the 40 year sentence of Weather Underground's Linda Sue Evans, who killed three police officers in 1981.

Clinton was referred to as the first Black President. Yet during the blood-bath in Rwanda, where 860,000 Africans were slaughtered in 100 days, he did nothing.

In referring to his endless string of corrupt escapades, Clinton would often say, "Can't we just put this behind us and get on with the business of the American people." Can't we just put you

15

behind us with a new president and get on without the soap opera. Clinton would often say in his speeches, "We can do better than that." Well Bill, regarding your Presidency, we can do better than that.

Clinton's Cabinet

Motley Crew.

The Clinton Crime Family.

James Carville = Joseph Goebbels, Corporal Cue ball. He suffered from severe follicle regression.

Janet Reno, Attorney General. She can't help that she is as homely as a mud fence, a dyke, and couldn't get a date with a million dollar bill strapped around her waist. She is aesthetically challenged.

The Department of Obstruction of Justice.

Madeleine Halfbright, Madeleine Notsobright.

Joycelyn Elders, Surgeon General, her quote "masturbation is something that … should be taught." I don't think teenage boys really need instruction in that subject. How would you grade the ambidextrous kids?

Secretary of State, Warren "who cut the cheese" Christopher.

Laura Tyson, National Economic Advisor. A ditz that couldn't figure out how to open a box of Cracker Jacks.

Harold Ickes, White House Deputy Chief of Staff. He appeared to be the most conniving sleaze bag imaginable and not someone you would want to allow to have an influence on our country.

Robert Reich, Secretary of Labor 1993 – 1997.

What is this!

He is vertically challenged.

Actual size.

Place your opened hand under his nose. This is what the picture is supposed to look like at the bottom of the page.

Copyright 2010 The Associated Press/Donald Stampfli

17

Which group did you feel more comfortable with protecting your country and family's safety, this group or George W. Bush's capable cabinet with Donald Rumsfeld, Gen. Colin Powell, Tom Ridge, John Ashcroft, and Condoleezza Rice?

Hillary Rodham Clinton, Secretary of State 2009 -

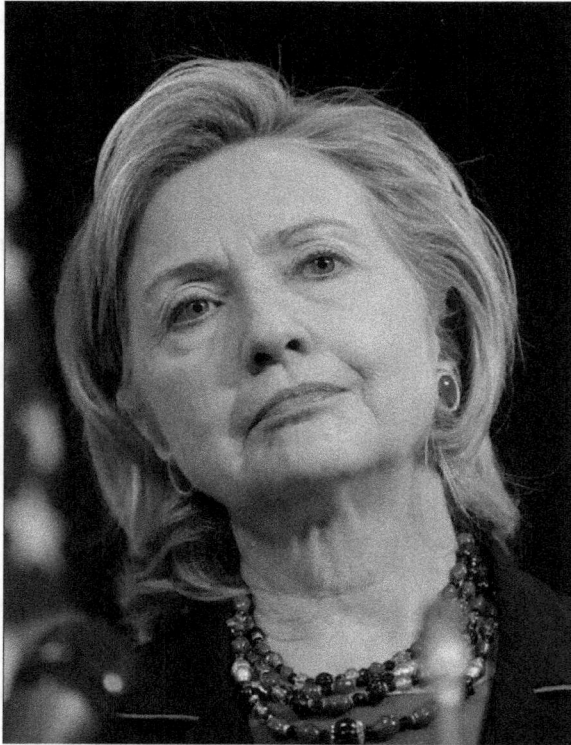

Copyright 2010 The Associated Press/Mandel Ngan

Hillary Rodham Clinton, First Lady – one of many ladies, not the first and definitely not the last!

A back-up for Gennifer Flowers.

An enabler. A door mat.

Mrs. Bill Clinton, Hillary Rottweiler Clinton, Hillary Rob'em Clinton, Hillary Rodman Clinton, Hillary Ryadi Clinton, Hillary Rodham Rodham.

A relentless bitch.

When Bill got caught having sex with intern Monica Lewinski, Hillary blamed it on a vast right wing conspiracy. Did Newt Gingrich hold Bill down and Henry Hyde force Monica's face into Bill's lap?

Paranoid.

Hillary was the Paris Hilton of the 2008 Presidential candidates. She hadn't done anything to be qualified to be President, and neither had Obama.

She claimed she was named after Sir Edmund Hillary who became famous for the first person to reach the summit of Mount Everest on May 29, 1953. She was born in 1947.

When Bill was president, she lived in the Wife House.

Bill Clinton is a good dancer because he had a lot of practice bobbing and weaving, and dodging ashtrays thrown by Hillary.

Hillary's book should have been titled *It Takes a Commune* to raise a child. It takes a Village Idiot to think that.

Hillary's scandals include, but are not limited to:

- Cattlegate, her mysterious ability to turn a $1,000 investment into a $100,000 profit on cattle futures, which experts say is virtually impossible.
- Castle Grande, a real-estate sham used to funnel hundreds of thousands of dollars to the father-in-law of her ex-law partner Web Hubble.

19

- Whitewater, the land deal started at the Rose Law firm where she worked.
- Filegate, 900 FBI files on Republicans.
- Travelgate, fired career staffers then gave the jobs to her cronies.
- Cablegate, as Secretary of State, she authorized her diplomats to steal credit card information and biometric data like fingerprints from foreign diplomats.[15]

During the 2008 Democrat primaries the Hillary Clinton Campaign led a smear campaign against the validity of Obama's Hawaiian birth certificate, claiming it was false and that he was ineligible for the Presidency.[16] Obama allegedly ran up legal bills of nearly 1.7 million dollars on the issue.[17]

Hillary helped start and promotes Media Matters.

As a clandestine strategy, Hillary Clinton's involvement with Progressive John Podesta's Center for American Progress, funded by Billionaire Leftist George Soros puts her in a position to come to power as the country's savior after ratting out all the "bad guys" in the government, that she helped select.[18]

In college she reportedly was a member of SDS, Students for a Democratic Society, a group whose goal is world communism.

In college she wrote her thesis on Saul Alinsky. His first book was *Reveille for Radicals*. He later authored *Rules for Radicals*. Paraphrasing the book's dedication: Let's acknowledge the very first radical ... and he did it so effectively that he won his own kingdom – Lucifer.[19]

Hillary is just a far to the Left as Obama.

Web Hubble could possibly be Chelsea Clinton's biological father, DNA comparisons would prove this.

Barack Hussein Obama, (D), 44th President of the U.S. 2009 - ?

Health Care - Joint Session of Congress

The fourth president with socialistic programs and policies.
Obama is the ultimate "confidence man".

So high were some people's expectations that he was nominated for the Nobel Peace Prize within 12 days after being elected president, even though he hadn't done anything to deserve it. In fact, he was escalating the war in Afghanistan. He should instead be recognized as the biggest con-artist in history.

You can lie to some of your constituents some of the time, you can lie to some of your opponents all of the time, but you can't lie to all of your constituents and all of your opponents all of the time, and get away with it.

The worst thing to happen to America was Bill Clinton being elected President, until Obama.

In 1939, the Secretary of the Treasury under FDR testified "We are

21

spending more money than we have ever spent before and it does not work. … I want to see this country prosperous. I want to see people get a job. We have never made good on our promises. … I say after eight years of this Administration we have just as much unemployment as when we started … and an enormous debt to boot."[20] See any similarities?

Will Rogers said, "When you find yourself in a hole, stop digging." Obama needs to stop spending. It reminds me of a cartoon showing Humpty Dumpty lying cracked on the ground as the King proclaimed: What we need is more horses and more men.

"We contend that for a nation to try to tax itself into prosperity is like a man standing in a bucket and trying to lift himself up by the handle." Winston Churchill

Of likely voters, 55% think Obama is a socialist.[21]

In 2007 he was rated "the most liberal Senator", even to the left of Senator Sanders, an avowed socialist.[22]

Obama is so far to the Left, he is even left-handed.

Obama is an ideologue.

His stated goal is to "fundamentally transform America."

How do you like "change" so far?

Obama has no change, because he has no cents.

Under Obama, we will be the new Socialist States of America.

Has the public learned that actions speak louder than words? Are you happier with an articulate speaker (teleprompter reader) that is destroying the economy through unbridled debt? Or do you prefer a President whose actions kept you safe and free?

Obama's bus tour in mid-August, 2011 to try to convince voters that he will create jobs for Americans, used $1,100,000 buses made in Canada.

America is having Obama trauma.

Obama voters are experiencing buyer's remorse.

Obama Presidency falls under the Lemon law.

America has B.O., Barrack Obama.

Hey Democrats! Obama and Biden, is that the best you've got? Ha Ha Ha!

The audacity of dopes!

Barry.

Join the Velma Hart Fan Club.

Obama's liberal views are in the minority and he is governing against the will of the people.

Obama will be a one term president, but will have done as much harm in the first half of his one term as FDR did in four terms.

Obama said, "The Cambridge police acted stupidly." So has he.

"A government that robs from Peter to pay Paul can always depend on the support of Paul" - George Bernard Shaw

"Government is the great fiction, through which everybody endeavors to live at the expense of everybody else." - Frederic Bastiat, French Economist (1801-1850)

"A government big enough to give you everything you want, is strong enough to take everything you have." - Gerald Ford

After the blowout results from the November 2, 2010 mid-term elections, Obama went into exile traveling to India with an obscene 3,000 person entourage that is estimated to have cost us $2 billion. Who needs 34 warships when he is on dry land? When our country is already so far in debt that we are printing money, why would he spend so much on himself? As *Animal Farm* exposed, some animals are more equal than others. He is thumbing his nose at us in defiance. When England's new conservative Prime Minister came here in July 2010, he flew on a commercial airline in order to save his country money. There is a big difference between conservatives and socialists.

On Inauguration Day, aside from announcing withdrawing the troops from Iraq in 16 months, he should have also proclaimed the economic crisis would be over in 16 months, so he could start repaying the debt then.

On August 29, 2010, Obama declared he's "making decisions for the next generation."

Obama said "as a fellow citizen of the world."

On his trip into exile after the 2010 mid-term elections, while visiting Indonesia, Obama said in the Indonesia language, "It's good to be back home."

Obama's middle name Hussein refers to Husayn, who was the grandson of Muhammad.[23]

In 2008 the Hamas terrorist organization endorsed Obama for President.[24]

Moammar Kadafi, head of Libya, said, "We are…happy if Obama can stay forever as the president of the United States."[25] Hey

Moammar, Obama doesn't exactly feel the same way about you.

Obama had in essence an apology tour, bowing to foreign leaders.

After being snubbed by not being invited to the royal wedding in England, not long thereafter, on May 24, 2011 the Obamas displayed very bad manners by imposing themselves on the royal family with an unwanted visit. Obama started to toast the Queen at a very inappropriate time. Obama had previously insulted their country by returning the gift of a bust of Winston Churchill commemorating 9/11. So America apologizes for his bad behavior and lack of manners.

As a candidate Obama said he would restore our relationships around the world. Being divisive, both here and abroad, he alienated our historic allies England and Israel. He told the French leader that France is America's strongest ally. He betrayed England to appease Russia. He sided with Argentina over the Falkland Island dispute.

At Olympic Games we do not dip our flag to foreign leaders. If Obama was the flag carrier at an Olympics, he would not only dip the American flag, he would probably drag it on the ground and set it on fire.

He has kept his birth certificate secret, causing suspicion that he was not born in Hawaii but in Africa as some claim, thereby making him ineligible to be president. In January 2011, Governor Neil Abercrombie (D) Hawaii announced that he cannot locate a birth certificate for Obama. He produced one, yet to be authenticated, in late April, 2011.

The first multi-racial president. His biological father was from Kenya, Africa. His mother was Caucasian.

Harry Reid (D), said about candidate Obama, he is a "light skinned" African-American "with no Negro dialect, unless he wanted to have one."[26]

Senator Joe Biden (D) said about candidate Obama, "the first mainstream African-American who is articulate and bright and clean and a nice-looking guy."[27] I guess he meant none of the other Black politicians have any of those traits.

Obama along with Louis Farrakhan and Al Sharpton led the Million Man March on Washington in 1995.[28]

In February 2010, Obama, in another redistribution of wealth move, approved a $1.25 billion settlement with Black farmers for an anti-discrimination case claiming loan programs with the Department of Agriculture favored Whites. I can't imagine there are enough Black farmers in the country to have been damaged enough to get anywhere close to that amount of money, unless there were punitive damages awarded. I'd like to know how much the average claimant received versus how much they were injured.

Socialists come in every color.

The first president sympathetic to the Islamic religion.

The first clue could have been at his inauguration if he had said, I Barack Hussein Obama do solemnly swear ... so help me Allah.

He was born to a non-practicing Muslim father. He had a Muslim upbringing by his Indonesian step-father.[29] He lived in and attended first through fourth grades in Indonesia, where he studied the Koran.[30] Obama did not become a Christian until he was 26 years old; when he joined Jeremiah Wright's church where Liberation Theology was preached.

On June 3, 2009, King Abduls of Saudi Arabia gave Obama a gold necklace – bling for the brother.

Obama, when quoting the passage in the Declaration of

Independence, which states "Endowed by their Creator with certain unalienable Rights," he purposefully left out the words "by their Creator".

The difference between how the miners rescue in Chile was handled compared to the Gulf oil leak is telling. Chile's President Pinera said "You have to start working with all your energy and all your resources from the very first moment; you cannot waste a second...from the very first moment we decided to take full responsibility for the rescue effort. Second lesson, never lose your faith and hope, never give up." Pinera showed great leadership. He called out to the world for the best people and methods to solve the problem. During the Gulf Oil Leak crisis Obama did the opposite. For the first two weeks he wasn't engaged, and he turned down international help. Obama blamed BP and expected them to do everything. Obama did not show any leadership qualities.

During the Gulf oil leak crisis:

- Three days after the accident, Holland offered ships and equipment to help with the cleanup efforts. The Obama Administration turned down all offers from 13 countries. Aside from turning them down out of arrogance, he wouldn't waive the Jones Act which protects his union allies.
- British Petroleum's CEO Tony Hayward was criticized on June 19, 2010 for attending a yacht race in England. There were many others in his company that were involved in the clean up, besides he is from England. What about Obama's 7 golf outings, baseball game, music concerts, Broadway play, vacations and campaigning for Barbara Boxer, etc., while the oil was spewing? He is an American, all be it probably a naturalized citizen, shouldn't he be criticized for fiddling while Rome burns?
- JFK had the leadership and 'can do attitude' to conceive of and have carried out a mission of sending a man to the moon and back in a nine year period. Obama's ineptitude

27

shows he doesn't have a clue how to plug a damn hole in the Gulf oil spill in what seemed at the time to be about the same amount of time.

- Obama looted British Petroleum.
- Obama said he is going to hold responsible parties accountable, he should be held accountable for lack of leadership.

The world's most powerful country needs a leader not a blamer.

Miners in China e-mailed about Chile's efforts to free the trapped miners writing, in China they would have been left to die.

Influences in Obama's life: His grandfather and father were anti-Colonialist socialists in Africa, his mother was Far-Left, his maternal grandparents that raised him from age 10 to 17 had attended 'the little red church on the hill' while in Washington state; his mentor in those years was Frank Marshall Davis, a communist; Obama wrote that while at college "I chose my friends carefully. The more politically active Black students. The foreign students. The Chicanos. The Marxist professors and structural feminists"; Reverend Jeremiah Wright's Liberation Theology sermons for 20 years and now Jim Wallis, a Marxist, as his current spiritual guide.

While Obama lived in New York City from 1983 – 1985, he attended a series of Socialist Scholars Conferences. It was there he learned about community organizing, which is a way radicals can advance their cause without being labeled a socialist. The Socialist's ultimate goal is to push the Democrat Party to the left by polarizing the country along class lines. Groups like ACORN would swell the Party with poor and minority voters. Socialism would emerge as the ideology of the have-nots. The idea is to transform America by undercover socialism. The Midwest Academy, which was founded and run by veterans of DSA, Democratic Socialists of America, trained, funded and sponsored Obama.[31]

It seems that all the influences in his life have been from the Far-Left. While a community organizer in Chicago Obama had dealings with Bill Ayres, who was formerly with the radical Weather Underground. Ayres said, "I don't regret setting bombs. I feel we didn't do enough."[32]

A former community organizer/agitator.

The Democratic Socialists of America, the largest socialist organization in the U.S., endorsed Obama in 1996 while he was a state senator, is affiliated with Socialist International, a group with consultative status for the United Nations. While a U.S. senator, Obama introduced a bill, The Global Poverty Act, which would commit the U.S. to spending hundreds of billions of dollars more in foreign aid.[33]

Obamanomics.

In 2001, Obama said on Chicago Public Radio, "I think there was a tendency to lose touch of the political community organizing and activities on the ground that are able to put together the actual coalition of powers through which you bring about redistributive change."

Saul Alinsky authored *Rules for Radicals.* Obama sat alongside Bill Ayres on the board of the Woods Fund, which taught Alinsky tactics of community organizing and is committed to progressive social change. Alinsky viewed revolution as a slow patient process. He taught that true revolutionaries do not flaunt their radicalism; they put on suits and infiltrate the system from within. Alinsky's son wrote in a letter, "Obama learned his lesson well. I am proud to see that my father's model for organizing is being applied successfully beyond local community organizing to affect the Democratic campaign in 2008."[34]

Obama's world view coincides with anti-colonialists which contend that rich nations have taken from the poor, morally believing that there is no limit to taxing the rich in order to give it back to the oppressed. To anti-colonialists doing that is doing good. His actions indicate that he thinks it is bad for America to be a Superpower and that he is going to shape a better America. He is a captive of his father's ideology as an anti-Colonialist tribesman in the 1950's. This explains actions like giving money to Brazil to expand their oil exploration[35] while at the same time he placed a moratorium on U.S. production in the Gulf.

Obama is going against U.S. self interest.

In Obama's January 23, 2010 State of the Union speech he proclaimed the U.S. would produce twice the exports. This statement is right out of the book *1984*, where Big Brother makes claims without doing anything or having any mechanism to achieve them. Just because he said it, doesn't mean it will happen, and under the economic conditions at the time, there was no reasonable expectation that it could happen. The fact that the Media didn't question this is amazing. He also said he was "fighting" against the Banks and the economy.

Obama is implementing a global mass redistribution of wealth. On May 10, 2010, the U.S. Federal Reserve gave the European Economic Union a $1 trillion line of credit. Early in Obama's Presidency, he casually said about Pakistan's problems, he would give them $1 billion more, like it was nothing.

Obama is destabilizing America.

Obama's choice that he announced September 8, 2010 was to not extend the Bush tax cuts on incomes above $250,000. In his class envy philosophy it is more important to punish the "rich" than to increase revenue, save jobs, and help the economy by allowing small business to recover. Most small businesses make that amount of income, so in these lean financial times, he made things even worse. Statistics prove that lower taxes stimulate the economy,[36] as witnessed when President Reagan did it.[37]

In December 2010, the Democrats voted to not end the Bush tax cuts. If they had realized when Obama was elected, that that was best for the economy, like the Republicans knew, the economy and jobs would have rebounded much sooner because there would have been less uncertainty for businesses.

It took Obama two years in office to walk across the street from the White House to talk to the Chamber of Congress. He asked businesses to spend their savings. After he asked for suggestions and assumed regulation might be a factor, approximately 2,000 pages came in. Because of his lack of knowledge and experience with capitalism, he doesn't understand that business doesn't risk money when there is uncertainty. The exact same thing happened when FDR created uncertainty. Obama and Federal Reserve chairman Ben Bernanke haven't learned from history that Keynesian economics doesn't work.

Other Presidents have inherited recessions and pulled the country out of them. George W. Bush and Ronald Regan did, and in a short amount of time.

He said he felt like he was behind enemy lines when he worked in the private sector.

In the TV series America – The Story of Us, that aired April 2010, it was introduced by Obama and told of rebellion. How ironic that the fool couldn't tell that patriots would rebel against him. Big, over-reaching government sparked the Tea Parties to be formed in the tradition of values held by the original American's in their quest for independence, to counteract the 1960's radical values of World Socialism.

When Democrats are elected President, the people chosen have been completely ill-equipped to deal with the serious problems that face the nation. Thank God 9/11 happened when George W. Bush was in office. His assemblage of officials couldn't have been better to handle the 9/11 situation. Can you imagine if 9/11 happened when Clinton's Cabinet was running things? They would have turned it over to the local police departments to deal with it. And now that we have the largest financial problems since the Great Depression, we have Obama and a bunch of anti-capitalists in charge.

Obama is the first President in history to preside over the downgrade in the U.S. credit rating.

A country should only go into debt if it uses the money to grow the economy. Obama is using the money to pay for unemployment, an illegal war with Libya, and entitlements.

On November 8, 2006, House Speaker Nancy Pelosi said, "We will make this the most honest, ethical and open congress in history." Didn't Bill Clinton make that commitment too? Does her assertion jive with "You need to vote on the Bill to know what's in the Bill?" Her name should be pronounced Pelousy.

Obama is a Leftist and has surrounded himself with extreme Leftists that he appropriately titled Czars, to set government policies that are directing the country into a death spiral. These are appointed positions he created, in order to bypass the normal Senate confirmation vetting process. They have no oversight by Congress. Some if not all of Obama's unelected Czar's do not believe in capitalism, and only 8% of his Cabinet has experience in the private sector. This is a very serious situation.

Part of what Cloward and Piven advocated is "inside, outside". Having an outside force of the Far-Left confronting business and Congress, while placing inside the Congress officials that coordinate with them, but do not use hardball tactics.[38]

The founder of the George Soros funded Center for American Progress is John Podesta, he was the head of Obama's transition team staffing the senior levels of the White House, Cabinet members, and the top layer at government agencies.[39] That

32

indicates all the radical Czars were handpicked for appropriate positions of power in the various government agencies. As our country stands at the brink of an abyss, Soros has vigorously and insidiously planned the ruination of America.[40]

The following are some of the appointed Czars, elected officials, and Obama advisors now influencing and running the country.

Andy Stern, a former SDS member and anti-war activist, when President of SEIU, State Employees International Union, said, "We spent a fortune to elect Barrack Obama, $60.7 million to be exact, and we're proud of it."[41]

Van Jones, former Green Jobs Czar, was a former Fellow at John Podesta's Center for American Progress. This African-American Marxist, was arrested in the 1999 Seattle protests against the World Trade Organization. About his time in jail he had this to say: "I met all these young radical people of color ... I mean really radical, communists and anarchists. ... This is what I need to be a part of. I spent the next ten years of my life working with a lot of those people I met in jail, trying to be a revolutionary. By August, I was a communist." He formed a socialist collective, Standing Together to Organize a Revolutionary Movement, or STORM, which held study groups on the theories of Marx and Lenin. The members brought experience in militant street tactics and revolutionary agitation. Changing to tactics outlined by Saul Alinsky, who stressed the need for revolutionaries to mask the extremism of their objectives and to present themselves as moderates until they could gain control over the machinery of political power, he said, "I'm willing to forgo the cheap satisfaction of the radical pose for the deep satisfaction of radical ends."[42] His organizations receive funding from George Soros's Open Society Institute.

Ron Bloom, Car Czar, worked for SEIU, and United Steelworkers Union, he disavows the free market system. He said, "We know that the free market is nonsense. ... We kind of agree with Mao that political power comes largely from the barrel of a gun."[43]

Donald Berwick, the Medicare/Medicaid Czar, He is a radical socialist who supports massive government rationing of medical care. He said, "Health Care is by definition re-distributional. ... must redistribute wealth from the richer among us to the poorer ...". An anti-capitalist, he used the phrase, "in the darkness of private enterprise." "America's health system is 'toxic', 'fragmented', because of its dependence on consumer choice. ... That is for leaders to do."[44]

Carol Browner, Energy and Environment Czar, was involved in John Podesta's Center for American Progress, funded by George Soros and worked on the Socialist International's Commission for a Sustainable World Society, which calls for global governance.[45]

Jim Wallis, spiritual advisor, asserts that Marxism basically is what Jesus was about. He is editor of the intensely anti-American publication Sojourners, which champions communism. He advocates wealth redistribution to promote "Social Justice." When asked about him calling for redistribution of wealth, he said "Absolutely, without any hesitation."[46]

John Holdren, Science and Technology Czar, a former Berkeley Professor, advocates de-developing the USA. In a book he co-authored, he advocated extreme totalitarian measures to control population. He called for a Planetary Regime which would control the global economy with the power of life and death over American citizens. There could be forced abortions and mass sterilization. Single mothers and teen mothers could have their babies seized and given to other couples. There would be enforcement by an armed international police force. He advocated redistribution of all natural resources.[47]

Mark Lloyd, Diversity Czar, was a Senior Fellow at John Podesta's Center for American Progress, and part of the Open Society Institute, both funded by George Soros. As diversity Chief of the

FCC, the Federal Communications Commission, he is an African-American revolutionary out to control the media in order to change public perception. He frequently references his hero, Left-wing activist, Saul Alinsky. He opposes private ownership of media. He advocates that private broadcasters pay an annual licensing fee in an amount equivalent to their total yearly operating costs and have that money redistributed to public broadcasting stations. His efforts, through the Fairness Doctrine, are designed to shift talk-radio to the Left.[48]

Anita Dunn, White House Communications Director, declared in a speech in 2009 that one of her favorite political philosophers is Chinese Communist Chairman Mao Tse-tung.[49]

Todd Stern, Climate Czar, was a Senior Fellow at John Podesta's Center for American Progress, funded by George Soros. He helped negotiate the Kyoto pact. He supports a national cap-and-trade system.[50]

Cass Sunstein, Regulatory Czar, said, "Once we know that people…have some Homer Simpson in them, then there's a lot that can be done to manipulate them."[51]   In 2007 the Supreme Court ruled that Carbon Dioxide and other greenhouse gases are pollutants under the Clean Air Act. The EPA ruled that Carbon Dioxide and 5 other gases harm humans and need to be regulated. The Regulation Czar will regulate businesses that emit them, which include power plants, factories, cars, etc. The EPA issued 600 pages of intrusive regulations. Cass Sunstein has an enormous amount of power to affect the economy and people's lives.

Craig Becker, Labor Relations Czar, was appointed by Obama on March 27, 2010 during the congressional recess. Disregarding the fact that all 41 Republican Senators asked Obama not to appoint the extremely partisan former SEIU, State Employees International Union, and AFL/CIO labor attorney, he did so right after the Health Care Bill was signed.[52]

Robert Creamer, married to an Illinois Congresswoman, was at a White House party in December 2009. He is a convicted felon for bank fraud. While in Federal prison, he wrote the 2006 book *Stand up Straight: How Progressives Can Win*, which described how Progressives could win in 2009 and is a blueprint for future victories. He recommended making Universal Health Care a right and guaranteed by government, and recommended giving amnesty to illegal immigrants. He was involved with ACORN and worked for Obama's campaign.[53]

Gil Kerlikowske, Drug Czar, assigned a full-time officer to a drug court to commute sentences of drug users who completed medical treatment in lieu of going to jail.[54]

Eric Holder, as Attorney General, should be spending his time enforcing Federal laws to protect the U.S. borders rather than attacking a State Law that is trying to enforce the Federal Law. Holder, an African American, instructed the Department of Justice to drop the case of the Black Panther intimidations at a polling place. He was subpoenaed for perjury in mid-October related to the Fast and Furious arms to Mexican drug dealers case. The D.O.J. is not protecting the public.

Arne Duncan, Department of Education, Green Education, he has implemented programs to turn kids into good environmental citizens.

Elizabeth Warren, Treasury Consumer Financial Protection Bureau a former Harvard Professor and bleeding heart Liberal. Naming her as an advisor to set up the agency, Obama circumvented the confirmation hearings and that vetting process. A polarizing figure, she was selected to punish businesses. Obama's establishing this bureau through the Treasury means that it cannot be defunded.

James Clapper, Director of National Intelligence, is the most incompetent choice possible. He may reflect the countries national intelligence due to inferior public education system, but he definitely should not be involved with protecting our country.

Elena Kagan, Obama's choice for Supreme Court Justice, is just like him, no practical experience or qualifications for the job.

In mid-August, 2011 Hillary Clinton made a statement about President Assad of Syria, substituting America for Syria and Obama for Assad she said, "The people of <u>America</u> deserve a government that respects their dignity, protects their rights, and lives up to their aspirations. <u>Obama</u> is standing in their way."

The Obama and his Administration is like an 'occupation' from a foreign power. He should be referred to as "The Outsider."

How do you like socialism so far?

Because of Obama, government now is an immediate threat.

The enemy within, is Obama

Obama is a threat to our way of life.

It is ironic that the threat to America from Obama and his comrades, is spawning a reawakening of an American Revolution style patriotic determination for liberty and freedom. Even though the Progressives and Leftists have been laying their groundwork for many decades, the sleeping giant is quick to rise and defend itself, just as it did with Japan in 1941.

Obama is like King George III, ruling against the will of the people. Obama, Pelosi and Reid aren't like us. They need to be voted out of office. The Founders counted on the people to do the right thing when politicians become corrupt and go against the interests of the people.

The November 2, 2010 mid-term elections were a repudiation of

Obama's economic policies. And in case you didn't understand the message Barry, STOP SPENDING OUR MONEY!

Michelle Obama, First Lady of President Barak Hussein Obama.

Michelle Antoinette, vacation queen. Taking her entourage to Spain while US citizens were out of work, was like a "let them eat Tofu" moment.

Barrack and Michelle are really lousy dancers, as witnessed during the Inauguration Ball. But maybe they could make it on "Dancing With the Czars".

Food NAZI.

In April 2010, during College Spring Break time when there were many drug war murders, she said it was safe to travel to Mexico. She could act as a travel agent spokesperson: come visit exciting Mexico, experience the thrill of dodging bullets from gang war gunfire, play hide-and-go-seek with kidnappers, play 20 questions to guess who's head is in the suitcase, compose ransom note replies, try to figure out good money drop-off locations, play follow-the-leader through tunnels under the border.... Next week Iraq!

Michelle met Barry Obama while both were employed at the Chicago Law firm Sidley-Austin, where former Weather Underground terrorist Bernadine Dohrn worked. Bernadine Dohrn is married to former Weather Underground terrorist Bill Ayres. The firm is the legal advisor to ACORN.[55]

At the age of 44, during Obama's presidential campaign, she said, "For the first time in my adult lifetime, I am really proud of my country"[56]

She said publicly on May 14, 2008 at a campaign fundraiser, "We are going to have to change our traditions, our history, we're going to have to move into a different place as a nation."[57] Why do the Obama want us to do that? And what do you think they want us to change to?

Michelle revealed how the Obama's think when she said in April 2010, "The truth is, in order to get things like Universal Health Care and a revamped Education system, then someone is going to have to give up a piece of their pie so that someone else can have more."[58]

Michelle's friend, given the position to handle social events, botched things up, which allowed the White House party crashers, Tareq and Michaele Salahi, access to the president.

Barrack Obama Sr., President Barrack Hussein Obama's Father

Obama's father, a tribesman born in Kenya, Africa, was a Muslim, a womanizer and an alcoholic.[59]   According to author Dinesh D'Souza, Obama's father and grandfather, as anti-colonialists, were part of the 1952-1960 Mou Mou Revolt against England. Obama Sr. came to Hawaii as a student in the 1950's. He married Obama's mother, when he was already married and had two kids. She bore Obama when she was 17 years old.[60] She was white and he was black. Obama's father ultimately had four wives and eight kids.[61] Anti-colonialists believe that since the rich have prospered at the expense of others, their wealth doesn't really belong to them. If Obama shares his father's anti-colonialists crusade, that would

40

explain why extracting more from the rich is deemed just.

Obama's father was a socialist advocating up to 100% tax for the people at the top. He believed in confiscating wealth. In Obama's book *Dreams From My Father*, he wrote that it was a lifelong quest to make his values the same as his fathers.[62] Obama's mother has been quoted as saying that other white people are not my people. She sent Obama back to Hawaii to live with her parents from ages 10 to 17 after having lived in Indonesia for four years, author Dinesh D'Souza appeared to infer it was because his step-father was too pro-western for his mother.[63] She apparently didn't want her son to have any influences that weren't Far-Left. Obama's African grandmother, Sarah Obama said of him, "I look at him and see all the same things, he has taken everything from his father. The family is still intact, this son is realizing everything the father wanted – fighting for people, the dreams of the father are still alive in the son."[64]

President Obama gave $61 million of U.S. taxpayer's money to Kenya, where his family is from, for its new Constitution, which legalizes all abortions. Under the Siljander Amendment, the U.S. is not allowed to lobby for or against abortion in other nations.[65]

U.S. Senator John Kerry (D), Democrat Presidential Nominee 2004

What should be written on the side of his plane is "Mr. Loser."

Gross polluter.

What would John Kerry need to do for a carbon offset that would nullify the amount of CO_2 that his 757 jumbo jet produces?

For those concerned about carbon footprints, Kerry should be referred to as Big Foot.

What a presumptive fool to purchase a jumbo jet and write President on its side.

America got two Clinton's when Bill became President. If John Kerry won, we would have Kerry and Kerry, for everything, then against everything. "I voted for it, before I voted against it."

Kerry's forehead looks like the forehead of a Shar Pei dog.

Kerry doesn't use Botox, its embalming fluid!

When John Kerry and John Edwards were running, an appropriate bumper sticker would have been, "Flush the Johns, they're full of sh!t."

Kerry is to his supporters as the affluent is to effluent.

In 1993, he gave $175 to charity. In 1995, he gave zero.[66]

As quoted from Saturday Night Live, "He served 4 months in Vietnam and has been talking about it for 26 years."

Clinton talked about a bridge to the 21st Century; Kerry wants a tunnel back to the 1960's.

Kerry would have created a Vietnam type situation in Iraq. Cut and run. Defeat.

Kerry was in the Naval Reserves and his unit was called up to go to Vietnam, he did not volunteer to go.

In 1970, while still in the Naval Reserves, Kerry's meeting with the North Vietnamese Communists violated a code in the constitution which defines treason as giving support to the enemy in time of war. In 1971, he met in Paris with the Democratic Republic of Vietnam and the Provisional Revolutionary Government. He later accused the U.S. government of sponsoring terrorism.

John Kerry is the modern day Benedict Arnold.

Kerry: a failed candidate for President, a failed Senator, and a failed American.

<u>George W. Bush, (R), 43rd President of the U.S. 2000 - 2008</u>

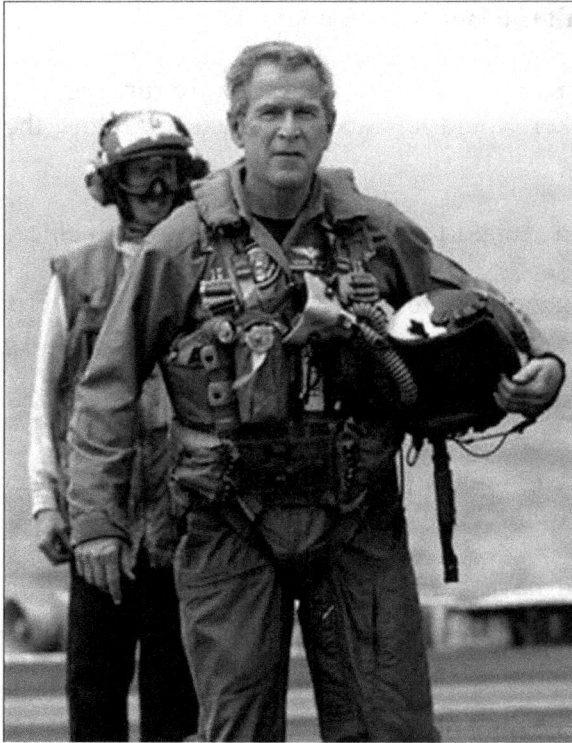

U.S. Navy

Bush was referred to by the media as a "selected" President. He was selected by God.

The mettle of the man is that when presented with 9/11, he confronted and dealt with the situation versus Clinton and Gore who when the World Trade Center was bombed in 1993 basically ignored the real issue.

There are an unknown number of lives that were saved because of President Bush's actions to stop further terrorism.

To paraphrase Bush after 9/11, "Our…freedom…now depends on

us,…this generation…will rally…to this cause, by our efforts, by our courage, we will not tire,…falter,…fail."[67]

The Clinton "War Room" defined Clinton, the Bush "War Room" defined America.

George W. Bush takes action.

Some of the people that asked if Bush was a legitimate President weren't legitimate citizens.

To his credit he attempted to fix Social Security's looming insolvency, but was stymied by the Democrats.

He spent money like a drunken socialist.

The Democrat's Military

F Troop

The Democrats and our national defense, like Gov. Michael Dukakis (D), Democrat Presidential Nominee in 1988 in the tank, is not a good fit.

The poster child of the Democrats' inability to effectively command our National Defense.

The photo of John Kerry, in white naval uniform, displayed in Hanoi reveals his allegiances.

For women in combat, there is the traitor Jane Fonda who gleefully sat on a North Viet Cong anti-aircraft gun during the war. They also could recruit Sara Jane Moore, the Left-wing nut that shot at President Ford in San Francisco in 1975, and "Squeaky" Fromme, who pointed a gun at Ford prior to that.

46

PART 2

THE DOCTRINE OF
POLITICAL CORRECTNESS

Free Speech. The First Amendment states that "Congress shall make no law … abridging the freedom of speech." The courts further expanded it from Congress to apply to everybody: the President, States, etc. The government may not do things that deter from exercising that right. When government doesn't directly prohibit speech, but deters its free exercise, it is called "chilling" the right to speak freely. It is just as unconstitutional, unlawful, and un-American as outright prohibition.[68] So challenge anyone inhibiting you with Political Correctness.

"The very reason for the First Amendment is to make the people of this country free to think, speak, write and worship as they wish, not as the Government commands." - Justice Hugo Black.

In the mid 1960's, not being able to "tell it like it is" started to creep into our society. Some people were offended by the way things really are, so different uses of the language were adopted. For example, job titles were embellished to promote self-esteem, Janitors became Custodians, a dishwasher became a utensil sanitizer, etc. Then it became clear that you couldn't tell the truth in this country. The people left-of-center viewed the world idealistically and pretended things were that way, including how they verbally referred to things. What's worse is they would have a conniption fit if everyone else didn't refer to things the same way they did. This evolved into Political Correctness. Latter, job titles became gender neutral, so a meter-maid was renamed a meter-person. Then they decided to not offend minorities, so Universities were sued for using mascot names such as Seminoles. People are not able to fully express themselves when inhibited by the pressure of political correctness. Many people are fed up with this absurd practice. In order to combat PC, be *Painfully* Correct. Let's call a spade a spade!

Political Correctness is a Liberal, bleeding-heart term used for wide-spread deference to avoid offending the dregs of society, carried out by altering terminology, behavior and policies. In an attempt to elevate the self-esteem of the mongrel component members of the Democrat Party, it targets race, gender, age-bias, sexual affinity, disabilities, occupations and rigid adherence to their political agenda. It is designed to pressure conformity to the common usage of their accepted description of identity groups and advocating for their causes. It punishes dissent by stigmatizing and labeling non-conformers as public heretics. Avoidance of this social stigma compels observance of the new norm. With its imposed orthodoxy, it is an utterly intolerant method of directing behavior and thought.

Making a conscious decision to use inoffensive, inclusive and neutral vocabulary ascribes significance to the speaker's ideas and actions. The vocabulary used reveals what and how a person thinks. Abortion can be referred to as either "pro-life" or "pro-choice". The Left and the media continually use vocabulary that direct the conversation to advance their own political agenda. They refer to opponents as "anti" something like anti-abortion and reserve the prefix "pro" for their leanings. Word-choice represents perceptions and attitudes of both speakers and listeners. The kind of language we use influences the way we view the world, and can actually lead to cultural change.[69] If Politically Correct vocabulary becomes entrenched in our society, which is being promoted through the schools and the media, then the language manipulated by the Left will determine how we perceive the world.

48

It has been Politically Correct for society to be completely secular and especially anti-Christian. However, it has been Politically Correct to not offend Muslims in any way since 9/11/01.

Political Correctness is now expanding into infringing on personal lifestyle choices. Some cities and States are imposing laws that regulate or ban: trans-fat cooking oils, salt, sodas, etc. Also, there are proposals to ban large TV's, McDonald Happy Meals, and even pets. There are cities where there are smoking bans even in your own home. They are taking your choices away from you Homer.

After Ruhm Emanuel, Obama's Chief-of-Staff, made an offensive comment accurately describing Liberals, a Bill in October 2010, erased the word "retarded" from all Federal language and replaced it with "intellectual disability". Liberals do have an intellectual disability for fiscal responsibility.

As was emphasized with the Left's objection to Arizona's Immigration law, it is not politically correct to ask probable illegal aliens for identification even though their presence here is overburdening our schools, hospitals, jails, and assistance programs.

One of the more recent arenas of banned vocabulary came after the attempted assassination of Congresswoman Giffords in January, 2011. Politicians and the media, I suppose, will now refrain from using all words linked to violence like: target, crosshairs, bulls-eye, bullet points, scope out, in our gun sights, take a shot at it, she's a pistol, sticking to his guns, armed to the teeth, slings and arrows, take a stab at it, tug-of-war, battle royal, the Bill was dead on arrival, deathblow, blood on their hands, a hung jury, war room, battlefield, explosive, a ticking time-bomb, bang, bombard, combat, our aim, duel it out, annihilate, bloodshed, warfare, attack, kill, take up arms, wage war, assault, barrage, blitzkrieg, carnage, crusade, a hit piece, onslaught, feud, flak, left to die, oh shoot!, etc.

The union thugs holding "kill the bill" signs that took over the Wisconsin capitol building apparently didn't get the memo.

In January 2011, Congressman Steve Cohen compared the Tea Party to being like NAZI's. Now Jews want the word Nazi banned as an epithet because they claim it diminishes the memory of the Holocaust. It is curious that Cohen, the person that triggered this, is Jewish as well as is Jerry Seinfeld, the one that started the modern day attachment, by using the term Soup NAZI.

It is not Politically Correct now for Superman to be an American citizen. Like Obama, he values the United Nations as a higher authority than the United States.

It seems it is now Politically Correct to scrub every verb, adverb, adjective, and noun that could possibly be used in a sentence that might in some way offend someone.

Politically Correctness uses the tactic of causing the speaker to fear being called: a racist, a sexist, a homophobe, a tea bagger, a bigot, insensitive, etc.

PC uses the strategy that when a lie is told often enough, people will start to believe it, so that, the truth is not believed when it is spoken.

It is a sad state of affairs when you can't tell the truth in your own country. We thought that was confined to Communist countries.

Liberal commentator Juan Williams was fired by NPR, National Public Radio, on 10/21/10 for telling the truth, thus demonstrating that people can't express how they feel without consequences from the Left's PC Thought Police. Juan, who had worked there for 10 years, said without a doubt, someone put heat on NPR to fire him. Coincidently, George Soros, billionaire socialist, had recently given NPR $1.8 million. The shill that fired Juan was his boss

Shiller. Juan said Political Correctness could "lead to some kind of paralysis, where you don't address reality." Government shouldn't be giving taxpayer dollars to businesses that practice censorship.

If anyone disagrees with what is deemed Politically Correct, they will be put in their place and reprimanded.

There can be no deviation from Political Correctness.

YOU MUST SAY AND THINK WHAT IS POLITICALLY CORRECT, COMRAD.

PC is a conspiracy against free speech. - Pat Caddell, Democrat pollster.

PC stifles free expression, it stifles free thought.

PC suppresses free speech.

PC = intolerance.

PC is intolerant of a difference of opinion, insistent that everyone think alike.

The Left espouses diversity, but not a diversity of opinion.

The definition of Diversity to a Liberal is different types of people all saying the same thing, which means agreeing with their Leftist agenda.

The Left are the most intolerant people imaginable. They insist on imposing their will on others.

Fear is a tool; it is a tool to get you to comply or to do nothing. Terrorists silence people through terror. - Glenn Beck

Silence the opposition.

PC is a strategy to get everyone to acquiesce to their Leftist agenda through intimidation and coercion.

PC Liberals are offended by the truth.

The PC propaganda is so pervasive, it is espoused by teachers, the media, politicians, some clergy, etc.

Political correctness tries to change the truth.

PC = to not say anything that will offend anybody.

Shut down free speech.

PC limits free speech.

PC = loss of freedom.

Bullying.

The Politically Correct vilify those who are not.

A constraint of free speech is an attack on liberty.

An assault on free speech.

Deprivation of American freedom.

PC = censorship.

Censorship to control thought.

PC fosters self-censorship.

In December 1999, when baseball player John Rocker was *Painfully* Correct with his description of how things are, he was required to undergo psychological analysis like in *Clockwork Orange*. They insist on everyone saying and thinking what is Politically Correct.

Behavior modification.

Ideological conformity.

PC extremists.

PC in its extreme form results in eras like the Reign of Terror during the French Revolution, 1793–1794, with beheadings of its enemies. Also, Mao's Cultural Revolution from 1966-1976 where revisionists rewrite history books, re-educate the people, and deface plaques that conflict with their message and that didn't fit their beliefs; they inflicted permanent revolution and purges; and carried Mao's Red Book as validation of their actions. In *The Last Emperor*, the movie shows how awful life was during the Cultural Revolution in China. The chilling line in *Dr. Zhivago* that was basically saying, this is how you must think and speak, comrade, is political correctness in a nutshell.

Shariah Law is extreme Political Correctness.

PC = Intimidation.

The Thought Police, which are devoid of a sense of humor, will denounce you.

An aspect of Political Correctness includes the death of humor.

Thought Police.

Cultural behavior Nazi.

PC is the new NAZI behavioral adherence doctrine.

Word choice must conform to political orthodoxies.

Only ideologically-acceptable views can be expressed.

Many excuse and promote PC.

Because of Liberals everything is upside down, i.e., Privacy Laws take the criminal's side and prevents law abiding citizens from learning of a criminal's record. In California Home Health Care, the elderly and disabled are vulnerable in their homes, they are legally not allowed to know if their helper is a convicted felon. The helpers can by law be murderers, arsonists, rapists, etc. This is outrageous. Liberals have no common sense. Because they are losers, they put the other dregs of society at the front of the line for protections at the detriment of people with traditional values.

A politically correct morality.

Political Correctness replaces common sense and good values that had prevailed in our once great nation.

Conservatives have a hunger for the truth; they don't like to be lied to. Clinton apologists apparently did, that's why they reveled in political correctness.

__PAINFULLY__ Correct vs. Politically Correct

Truth vs. lies.

2+2=4

Everyone is sick and tired of Political Correctness! You have my permission to lambaste its practitioners. Enough is enough!

If you are mad as hell, don't take it anymore! Speak you mind.

Get a spine, say what you feel and think. You are frustrated, so let them have it!

It is time to vent!

Being *Painfully* Correct is a release. If you have repressed your feelings because you are surrounded by Political Correctness or by a PC crowd, free yourself, express your emotions. You have a right of free speech and they legally are violating your rights through intimidation.

The U.S. Constitution avows that our rights come from God, God is the truth, and we have the right to speak the truth.

Being *Painfully* Correct is using brutally truthful language and behavior that is unrestrained by concerns or fear of offending or expressing bias towards special interest groups or individuals. There is no sensitivity as to word choice in describing what you see, feel and think. There is no repression of vocabulary or thought. There is no need to choose the delicate semantics of tolerance. By courageously speaking freely, regardless of the consequences, one can laugh off stereotypical labels of racist, sexist or homophobe. There is the compulsion to discredit and then correct the Left's flawed political agenda concepts at every opportunity. Persistent obstinate conformers to political correctness deserve to be ridiculed. When you see, for example, an outrageously flagrant drag queen, don't try to think about how to politely or tactfully choose politically correct words to describe him, just blurt out the obvious. You look ridiculous! At the very least you should say to anyone within ear-shot, hey, the clown's got serious problems. Traditional labels that are currently socially unacceptable are usually true and accurate and are often quite humorous. It's time to break the bonds of obedient conformity!

You are hereby granted permission to castigate Liberals for being Politically Correct.

In order to avoid offending a small percentage of the population, the politically correct instead offend the vast majority. The TSA, Transportation Security Agency, run by that bitch Napolitano, won't profile likely suspects; they instead violate everyone's dignity with gropings and X-ray body scans at airports. The PC mindset is reactionary, to look for items used by terrorist after the fact, instead of profiling likely terrorists. The TSA, that will become unionized, will always be searching for an obsolete bomb conveyance method or device, because the terrorist will keep using new delivery methods. Enough is enough! The crowds should chant "we want profiling, we want profiling, we want ..."

In January 2011, it was announced that SPOT, Screening Passengers by Observation Techniques, has been initiated at airports. SPOT should stand for Start Profiling Obvious Terrorists.

Rebel against Political Correctness.

Do not submit to intimidation.

Don't be pressured to not tell the truth.

Have the courage to stand up against Political Correctness.

"Our lives begin to end the day we become silent about things that matter." - Martin Luther King Jr.

No longer silent.

Speak out and be seen speaking out.

Take a stand!

Stand up for what you believe in. Make a difference.

Speak your mind.

Speak without fear. – Glenn Beck

Spread the Truth!

Stick to your beliefs.

Be empowered by the truth.

Freedom is the soul of the Nation.

America is a beacon of light for many.

The truth can set us free.

We have the desire for life to get better, we don't resign ourselves to accept repression.

Be willing to endure criticism, even persecution. The truth will eventually triumph. Employ perseverance.

From adversity comes strength.

Our forefathers sacrificed all for our freedoms, so don't surrender without a fight.

Be fiercely independent, combat Political Correctness.

Be a rugged individualist, fight back.

Americans are survivors, we will survive Political Correctness.

Americans do not fail, have confidence.

An informed electorate can usurp the plans of the Left.

The plain truth.

Straight talk.

Painfully Correct = unapologetic.

No apologies.

No fear.

The unshakable truth.

Knowledge is power.

As Americans, we reinvented ourselves; don't allow subversives to coerce us into conforming to their standards.

The spirit of America is the best of the human spirit.

Americans have a yearning to breathe freedom.

Freedom is in our bloodstream, it is the fabric of America.

Sustain liberties.

Americans do not take no for an answer.

Tell it like it is.

Stop the bullsh!t.

Use civil disobedience, if need be, to combat absurd Politically Correct dictates.

The Politically Correct do not want anyone to say or do anything that offends anyone. Well nearly everything they say and do offends me: people saying and doing what is Politically Correct is offensive; a person hand-signing at a speech; people playing hacky sack; people constantly using the terms organic, sustainable, and diversity; people that separate their garbage into different colored containers; people prefacing their actions by saying they are "trying to save the planet"; hearing reporters say Latino names with a Spanish pronunciation; phone recordings with messages also in Spanish and needing to press a number to hear the message in English; ballots and other government literature written in other languages; vegetarians; people insisting Global Warming is an irrefutable fact; people talking about carbon footprints; people advocating tearing down dams; environmentalists; hearing or reading biased media reports; people referring to themselves as victims; people with earrings, piercings, tattoos, colored hair, tie–dyed t-shirts, men with ponytails; people that display peace signs; non-Arab Americans that wear Muslim garb; people that drive a Prius, that bumper stickers for Obama, Kerry, and Unions; the ACLU only defending Leftist causes; referring to a known guilty criminal like Jarred Loughner as an alleged suspect; protection of all religions except Christianity; people calling others deniers or birthers; hearing people speaking Spanish that obviously can't speak English and are apparently living here; married women who do not go by their husband's last name; married women who have hyphenated last names; use of the term anti-abortion instead of pro-life; and any anti-American language or actions.

Some people in the Left throw pies in the face of speakers they disagree with. I'd like to become a common practice for people to throw a cream-pie in the face of hand-signers at speeches, so they look like mimes performing their stupid gyrations.

Remember when airline stewardesses were young, thin, attractive, and female? Let's go back to the way things should be.

Painfully Correct versus Politically Correct, the difference is stark.

Declare war on Political Correctness and eradicate it like we are eradicating Terrorists.

Make being *Painfully* Correct a threat to tyranny.

Let's destroy Political Correctness.

Do not be afraid of being called a name.

Political Correctness is analogous to Prohibition in that there are far more people against it than there are for it. Don't be afraid to speak against it, you will find a lot of support in doing so.

Say what you mean and mean what you say.

In 1964, Republican Presidential candidate Barry Goldwater's campaign slogan was "In your heart you know he's right."

In 2007, John Tanner, top Justice Department Official said, "Our society is such that minorities don't become elderly the way White people do. They die first."

Iran's President Ahmadinejad doesn't sugar coat his sentiments for Israel.

The best defense is a good offense.

Convert peoples thinking. Don't succumb to pressure to repeat the party line if you don't believe it.

Use humor while being *Painfully* Correct. Add a word or words that negate their intent and shows how foolish they are. When someone says something is organic, ask them what isn't organic.

Why do people still listen to these pathetic, moron Liberal losers? They are a joke, just ignore them.

Make PC irrelevant.

PART 3

THE DIFFERENCE BETWEEN LIBERALISM AND CONSERVATISM

Liberalism focuses almost entirely on the human condition, on society and culture. Liberals believe that human nature is perfectible. The Liberal mind looks at things as they think it ought to be, instead of the way things really are. They are so caught up in their idealistic vision that they are unable to understand the realities that are necessary to make things function, like financial responsibility. Liberals believe they know the way to make things better and, in their inherent arrogance, expect everyone to buy into their ideas. They want things done their new, better way and not the arcane way things have been done. They take the position that the traditional ways are no longer acceptable. As a result, they start rejecting authority and become anti-establishment. From their superiority-trip mind set, they believe they need to impose their will on the ignorant masses that just don't get it. If left unchecked, this ultimately leads to authoritarian rule. The Far Left does not value individual freedom. The collective fulfillment of their utopian dream is all important. They adopt the concept of relativism, the ends justify the means. Conduct becomes relative in order to reach their goals. In their fuzzy view of life, nothing is always right or always wrong, there is no black and white. Actions and ethics become situational. Their rationalization is, it depends on the nuances of the gray areas. They blame society, the establishment, and institutional norms as an impediment to achieving their objectives. They use big government to impose their will on everyone. They do not place any importance on fiscal responsibility because their goals usually are financially unsustainable. They have an utter lack of understanding of how the free market system works. They therefore become anti-capitalistic and anti-American. They believe that anyone right-of-center is a racist, uneducated, and militaristic. Because Liberals believe they alone are the intellectuals and correct, they present themselves as elitists. Due to the frustration that things just aren't happening the way they envision, they are perpetually angry people.

Liberals' values started changing in the mid-1960's and are now the opposite of Classical Liberalism. They have increasingly become Progressives, which has dark beliefs and goals. A Classical Liberalism tenet is pluralism, which welcomes a plethora of ideas, opinions and beliefs and allows differing views to exist and thrive.[70] Another tenet is toleration, which respects and upholds the right of others to profess distinctly divergent viewpoints.[71] Liberals today have adopted Political Correctness, I refer to them as "PC Liberals", which demonizes and is intolerant of any difference of opinion, just look to college professors as a good example of a PC Liberal. The Democrat Party that had been slowly co-opted by Liberals has more recently been hijacked by Progressives. Most Democrats are not that far to the Left and should realize that the radicals running their Party are violating many of their fundamental principles. The mid-term elections on November 2, 2010 was a turning point. It was a good start, but more Democrats need to wake up and understand the consequences of their support of the Obama Administration by continuing to vote for Democrats simply out of past loyalty to party affiliation. There needs to be a new wave of Reagan Democrat converts. Your country's future, your children's future, your financial wellbeing, your lifestyle, and your liberties and freedom depend on it.

Classical Liberalism, which wants limited government and individual freedom, spawned Adam Smith, who wrote the *Wealth of Nations* in 1776. His concepts transformed the field of economics and established the free market as a self-correcting mechanism. During the Great Depression, John Maynard Keynes introduced Keynesian economic theory that required government intervention to stimulate the economy through massive deficit spending and public work programs.[72] Keynesian economics did not work. There was a double dip depression during the 1930's and what brought the country out of the Great Depression were the products and jobs needed to supply our participation in World War II. The laissez-faire approach advocated by Secretary of the Treasury Andrew Mellon under Presidents Harding and Coolidge, which brought us out of the Depression of 1920 worked so effectively it produced the Roaring Twenties. After the near Recession of 1946 had been averted by again implementing the Mellon/Harding/Coolidge approach, Keynesian economics had been discredited. Unfortunately, the neo-socialist Obama Administration regressed back to the Left's icon, FDR as a way to expand Big Government. So instead of implementing sound economic practices of the self-correcting free market system and cutting spending and lowering taxes to stimulate the economy, Obama has increased our debt to the extent that the country may be bankrupt soon and never recover.

Doing the same thing over and over and expecting different results is a definition of insanity. - attributed to Albert Einstein. That is analogous to the idealist's expectations that communism will work somewhere, anywhere. Communism was practiced to the fullest extent in Russia for 74 years and failed; it has morphed into a hybrid communist "State Capitalism" system in China since their revolution in 1949; Cuba has been stagnant since its Revolution in 1959; all of Eastern Europe has rejected communism; Europe today is going broke from socialism and as a result is moving to the right politically; and the State of California that is controlled by liberals has had massive deficits for years. It is illogical to all of a sudden expect socialism to work in America. Hey, the experiment is over. Socialism doesn't work. We're going back to capitalism and self government. Got it?

There are two polar opposite types that comprise Authoritarian Rule, the ones that desire to control others and the ones that want to be taken care of. In the latter group, I am not including people that are forcibly being controlled beyond their will. There are people who did not grow up in a disciplined household that yearn for it. Some of these types actually enjoy being in jail, where they are told what to do about every aspect of their lives, what to wear, what to eat, where to be, and when to go to bed. These people do not want the responsibility of self-government. They want to be taken care of through entitlements. They want free Health Care, free housing, food stamps, etc. They just want to be fat, dumb and happy.

A recruiting tool for Liberals is the attractiveness of fueling Class Envy. Liberals promote viewpoints and design situations that pit race against race, and instigate class warfare, for their benefit. Class envy and jealousy make some feel like justified victims. Some feel comfortable in the role of a victim; it is any easy excuse for them being such lazy, good for nothing losers.

Liberals have a wished for fantasy of the world as it should be, but whose values should determine what the world should be?[73]

Liberals favor: Big Government, socialism, redistribution of wealth, punitive tax rates for the rich, government regulations, a Welfare State, universal health care, entitlements, strong unions, pensions, unemployment insurance, bureaucracies, public schools as a means of indoctrination, revisionism, a biased media, separation of church and state, human rights, abortion, civil rights, social justice, same-sex marriage, case law, outrageously large trial lawyer settlements, World Court, no punishment for criminals, anti-death penalty, legalizing drug use, excessive civil disobedience, anti-establishment attire, appearance, lifestyles, and behavior, multiculturalism, open borders, environmentalism, and globalization.

Conservatives - Most people throughout history have been conservative by nature, in their lifestyle by necessity, and hold traditional values due to their culture. Historically most of the population has been rural workers striving to own land in order to produce enough to have a better life, in modern times people want to own their own home. The lineage of landowners hold property rights and the work ethic it took to be able to attain that position very strongly. Conservatives forged from their condition are pragmatic and therefore see things as they really are. They enjoy reality. They derive a sense of fulfillment from hard work. They embody individual responsibility. They thrive on stability, continuity and heritage. They are comfortable with the tried and true methods of keeping order in the universe. They consider new ideas in terms of how well they will work within established frameworks. They weigh the cause and effect to make decisions. They recognize the need for laws to maintain an orderly society. They hold dear, as a core value, the inalienable right to individual freedom and liberty. They embody rugged individualism. They are patriotic, self-reliant Americans. They do not need government and do not want Government intrusion. They only have an appetite for limited government. They recognize that the U.S. Constitution is the greatest document ever conceived for protecting freedom and liberty and it is worth dying for to keep it in tact. They support a strong military. They demonstrate an unwavering loyalty to defend America. They are strong believers in the Second Amendment. They understand the workings of Adam Smith's *Invisible Hand*, and know the Free Market System and laissez-faire capitalism is the best path to prosperity. They adhere to prudence in government spending and debt. They are opposed to socialism and communism. They oppose excessive business regulations and most environmental regulations. They oppose being taxed. They try to preserve traditional values and traditional morality. They believe in traditional family values and are pro-life. They have respect for authority. They are for the death penalty. They practice religious values.

It is like there are two different groups occupying the same country, Liberals and Conservatives. Different values, different goals.

Conservatives want elevation of the individual versus elevation of the collective.

"The government is best which governs least." - Thomas Paine.

PART 4

THE PURPOSE
OF THIS BOOK

The purpose of this book is to defeat evil. I want everyone in the world to have freedom and liberty. You would think that everyone would want that, but ones in the Devil's claw want to control and oppress others. It is incomprehensible to me that some would make that choice, but unfortunately it is true.

The U.S. Constitution states that our rights come from God. The Devil is trying to deny us those rights by making some believe that rights come from government, that rights are from a man-made authoritarian power. All humans, according to Gnostics, have divine origins, the Devil tries to obscure that fact. He tempts people with worldly pleasures and false promises. The Devil can successfully obscure the truth. God created souls that are free! Government has no power over your spirit or soul. You can choose to allow government worldly powers to control you, or instead, set yourself free! Do not succumb to forces denying your rights. Assert that, light triumph over darkness. Live as children of light.

The U.S. Constitution, as written by the Founding Fathers, is a magnificent document written with divine intervention that limits the power of government. It therefore limits the ability of evil doers to control your life and rob you of your freedom and liberty.

When you see photographs of the other planets, and see how barren they are, you realize we have been given paradise. When you see pictures taken by the likes of National Geographic of gorgeous pristine areas teaming with life, you realize Earth is the Garden of Eden. Superficially it appears that Environmentalists are doing the right thing to protect the planet, but the Devil has twisted their logic causing them to demote humans to the least important creatures. We could be living with nature in a responsible way like the Americans Indians. Libertarians and conservatives would concur that we should live within our means. The Devil has perverted the Environmentalists good intentions to instead control humans. God wants us to enjoy the Earth and be free, life is magnificent. We could be living in paradise, but the Devil has screwed it up. His influence of evil has caused all the misery, deceit, lies, immorality, injustice, prejudice, adversity, suffering, malevolence, abuse, callousness, persecution, murders, pestilence, harm, violence, greed, destruction, corruption, wrong, sacrilege, perversion, cruelty, bribery, wickedness, affliction, betrayal, malice, mayhem, revenge, jealousy, vanity, envy, brutality, intolerance, ruthlessness, exploitation, theft, torment, cheating, plight, depravity, and viciousness in the world. Instead of enjoying life, liberty and the pursuit of happiness, Liberal's through laws and regulations, have turned everyday life into a complicated quagmire.

THE FURTHER YOU ARE TO THE LEFT, THE FURTHER YOU ARE FROM GOD. Communists are atheists. Atheism is a breeding ground for the Devil. Mothers aborting their offspring is a clear example of the Devil's work. The Left is doing the Devil's bidding. Those that would oppress others through Totalitarian Rule are caught in the Devil's clutches. The perpetrators' callous disregard for human life inflicts torture, slavery, and tyranny. There are different degrees of influence the Devil has on people. Again, the further to the Left, the greater the Devil's influence.

The best way to fight Evil is to expose it.[74]

68

Divulging the Left's agenda:

The immediate problem is that, as crazy as it sounds to reasonable people, there is a carefully orchestrated effort by some Leftist groups, most notably Progressives, to destroy America from within and replace it with a very Left wing government. Their plans have been in the works for many decades and they relentlessly keep putting the pieces together in order to achieve that end. The attack is from every imaginable front. Life in America is about to change unless you and I do something about it.

I can't comprehend why free people in the United States of America want to willingly be enslaved by Socialism. The craziness is that it is a domestic movement, it is all from within our own country.

The Cloward and Piven Strategy from the 1960's is to collapse the economy by overwhelming the system with the poor through Welfare. To overload government bureaucracy with impossible demands, bringing about the fall of capitalism. Current programs that facilitate that plan are Health Care, which is one-sixth of the economy, the Financial Reform Bill, the proposed Cap and Trade scheme, unfunded pensions, foreign aid, deficit spending, monetizing our debt, and the all the stimulus spending.

Obama getting us involved in Libya, in yet another war, is a way to further drain our resources and spread our troops thin.

Obama is doing his best to "fundamentally transform America." He is rapidly implementing policies and regulations that are directing us toward a less prosperous, less free nation.

The Financial Reform Bill, passed in July, 2010, contains over 2,300 pages. By design it is implemented through the Treasury so it cannot be held up or altered by Republicans in Congress. There are 400 Boards and Commissions yet to be set up and their policies written. This is a huge uncertainty for business.

In order to greatly expand the number of recipients on food stamps, in April 2010, Obama changed the income limitations so that earning 200% of the poverty level would qualify. By October 2010, a record 43 million people are now on food stamps.[75] Obama also extended unemployment insurance for up to 99 weeks and in the Lame Duck session they extended it an additional 13 months for eligible unemployed workers to be able to collect benefits.

On November 3, 2010 the Federal Reserve announced they will again monetize our debt through Quantitative Easing, which means they will be buying their own debt, which means they will be creating money out of thin air. They will buy back $600 billion of Treasury bonds between November, 2010 and June, 2011. This is inflationary and is expected to devalue the dollar by 20% within a couple of years. Printing money without anything to back it up is insanity. When Germany did this after WWI it took a wheelbarrow full of money to buy a loaf of bread. Keynesian Ben Bernanke of the Federal Reserve had said earlier on that he would not do this. The Federal Reserves' mandate is to maintain a strong dollar, they are doing the opposite. The value of the dollar in 1913 when the Federal Reserve was established is only worth 4.5 cents today.[76]

Our debt has become so massive that our financial stability is in question. A major rating company has warned that the U.S. credit rating may be lowered. Efforts are under way for the U.S. dollar to no longer be the world's reserve currency. If that happens, the Federal Reserve will no longer be able to print money to spend our way out of the problem. There will be hyper-inflation and our economy will be destroyed.

The EPA, Environmental Protection Agency, is used as a means to achieve the Left's goals because almost every aspect of our lives is touched by the EPA and other Federal Regulations. Regulations have the force of law, breaking them can result in fines and jail time. Federal Agencies create about 10 regulations for every law passed by Congress.[77]

If Virginia loses its case contesting the Federal government's ability to force Virginia's citizens to purchase Health Care coverage, it is the end of checks and balances; the States rights and independence from the Federal Government, it's about liberty.

The conditions for a power grab are: a struggling economy, high unemployment, high dependence on government, uncertainty and fear. – Glenn Beck

A component of the Left's strategy is to "Turn a National fiscal crisis in a socialist direction."[78]

Obama's friend Bill Ayers was in the Weather Underground. Its goal, as stated in their 1969 Manifesto, is to create a dictatorship within a new democracy that develops into socialism. And they want an end to capitalism in the USA.

On July 2, 2008, Obama said "We cannot continue to rely on our military in order to achieve the national security objectives that we've set. We've got to have a civilian National Security Force that's just as powerful, just as strong, just as well funded." It would be a political Reserve Corps funded with one half trillion dollars.[79] That sounds like preparations for a dictators' army.

Remember, Hitler was democratically elected too.

The Obama Administration is making Congress irrelevant by use of unelected Czars who are not vetted,[80] by implementing regulations by executive order, and by having the EPA use laws that are already on the books.

If successful, the proposal to abolish the Electoral College will put an end to the USA being a republic. Our Founding Fathers and the Left know that democracies do not last. The U.S. government is

71

set up as a representative Republic, and that structure should not be replaced.

If the government can control the media, it can control the content of information. In the Soviet Union, the state owned Pravda was used to disseminate propaganda.

Obama said "information becomes a distraction, a diversion. It's putting new pressure on our country and on our democracy."

Leftists are trying to stop conservative free speech on the internet. The Obama Administration first lobbied the FCC to impose Net Neutrality. After a court decision shot down the FCC's ability to regulate the internet and Congress not wanting to approve it, the FCC declared it a utility, so it can go around the court and regulate it. The FCC implemented its regulation during the Lame Duck session in December, 2010. A new proposed Bill would make the implementation not subject to judicial review. That amounts to a government takeover of the internet.

Net Neutrality regulations were put in place to silence the opposition. Obama's allocation of $7.2 billion for grant and loan programs through the Stimulus Bill is designed to diminish the 'digital divide' by accelerating broadband access to underserved rural areas.[81] This money is likely just a first installment. What the Left wants is to eventually be able to reach everyone in order to spread their propaganda through government controlled networks, just like 'Big Brother' did in the book and movie *1984*. Robert McChesney, co-founder of the public policy group 'Free Press' and professor at the University of Illinois, in his article *U.S. Media Reform Movement: Going Forward*, paraphrased Marx. McChesney states that the goal is to make media policy a political issue and to reform the media system, asserting that whoever controls the media will control the political environment and ultimately all of society.[82]

The internet super highway needs to be transmitting correct information, namely the unbiased truth, not a jaundice politically slanted perception of it.

Al Sharpton echoed a way for the Left to eliminate conservative media, he contends: on publicly regulated airwaves the FCC has a responsibility to set standards; the public cannot be offended based on their race or gender. The Politically Correct thresholds will eliminate right-of-center viewpoints. The FCC Commissioner wants Broadcast stations to pass a public values test in order to keep their license.[83] It is not free speech if the government dictates values.

Writing and enforcing regulations has been described as a fourth branch of government. The super-agency, the Office of Information and Regulatory Affairs, OIRA, under Obama, is promoting Net Neutrality. The Administrator is Cass Sunstein. The President directs agencies to follow certain principles in rulemaking. Reframing the cost-benefit analysis to take account of "the role of distributional considerations, fairness, and concern for the interests of future generations."[84] The scope of what those words can cover is staggering. As a side note, Unions get preferential treatment through related regulations.

The Cybersecurity Act of 2009 would give Obama the authority to "declare a cyber security emergency and order the limitation or shutdown of Internet traffic to and from any compromised Federal Government or United States critical infrastructure information system or network, " for an indefinite amount of time.[85]

Obama, starting in July, 2010, is seeking the FBI to have the power, without a court order, to seize from businesses Electronic Communication Transactional Recordings. This requires businesses to release their employee's e-mails to the government. This has profound implications for First Amendment speech rights.[86]

Obama, starting in September, 2010, is seeking a law to ease online snooping by the government without a search warrant. There is technology that allows them to see what you are doing on Skype, Blackberry and Twitter. This is government surveillance by cyber-snooping the internet.[87]

The U.S. Department of Justice declared that Americans have no right to implied privacy of location; meaning government can track and record your web searches, cell calls, etc. They can subpoena Google files and read your e-mails.

Without privacy, we are not a free people.

The 9th Circuit Court ruled the government can trespass on your property to place a GPS tracking device on your car without a warrant and track your movements. This invades "unreasonable searches and seizures." This upsets years of legal precedent regarding protections under the Fourth Amendment.[88]

Obama is diminishing America's nuclear capabilities and cutting back on NASA's missions.

In April, 2010 Obama changed our nuclear strategy. He placed unprecedented limits on when they can be used, weakening the country's ability to defend itself. The NPR, Nuclear Posture Review, restricts their use. The USA won't use nuclear weapons if attacked from chemical or biological weapons. He signed a disarmament agreement with Russia. In December, 2010 Congress approved the START Treaty, which is detrimental to the USA because it cuts our defense capability.

In October 2010, the Obama Administration began allowing Russia's state-owned nuclear-energy company to purchase 51% of a Canadian company which owns uranium mines in Wyoming. The Russian company that has sold uranium to Iran before will then control 20% of America's uranium production.[89]

Using information from the 2010 Census, Obama is employing a tactic used by FDR, which is to shift projects and money to Democrat dominated locations, which is in effect transferring wealth, influence, and power to a political party.[90]

Obama violated a rule of contract law. Instead of bondholders, who are legally in first position, getting their money when General Motors went broke; Obama funded the Union's Retiree Health Care Trust first. The bondholders only received 5 cents on the dollar.

A section concerning private property has been in the Left's playbook and growing in use since Stuart Chase coined the term New Deal. It is not taking over private property or industry in the old socialistic sense, the formula now is "control without ownership." Can you do whatever you want on your own property? No. Property must be zoned for specific uses. If your house is on your property, you likely are in a residentially zoned area. You probably do not have the right to use it for anything else, such as commercial, retail, offices, industrial, agriculture, mining, etc. Developers that have bare ground often discover that bodies of water as small as mud puddles are considered Waters of the United States and are claimed by the Army Corp of Engineers to be within their jurisdiction. The land cannot be developed until studies are performed, permits are issued and mitigation measures are taken. All of this usually takes years and costs thousands of dollars. If you don't comply you cannot build on it. So whose property is it really? If you don't pay your mortgage, the bank takes it; if you don't pay your property tax, the city or county government takes it; if you don't pay your income tax, the State or Federal government can take it. Rights attached to property are like a bundle of sticks, you may own the property, but someone else may own its mineral rights; someone else may own its water rights; someone else may own it air rights; someone else, like a utility company, may have easements across it; or you may live in a neighborhood with CC&R's, Conditions, Covenants and

Restrictions that control what you may or may not do on it. There may be restrictions that prevent you from cutting down a tree on your property if it exceeds a certain diameter. In a socialistic government it isn't necessary to own all property, as long as the government can restrict, regulate and tax it, they effectively control it without ownership.

If government gives rights, it can take them away.

Government continues to eliminate our ability to make choices.

Big Brother, as predicted in the book *1984*, is here. Technology has enabled government to know everything about you, what you look like, where you are and what you are doing nearly all the time. The Patriot Act permits Federal Agents to issue their own search warrants instead of needing to obtain one from a judge.[91] The Act allows them to plant electronic surveillance devices in your home and seize your property.[92] The Act requires financial information be tracked by the government, starting when bank accounts are opened. Social Security numbers identify you in several ways. Credit cards reveal your movement and purchasing habits. Trojan Horse programs can record your every computer keystroke. Cell phone transmissions and land line calls can be intercepted. Satellites in space and drones in the sky can photograph your movements. Skype and your cell phone can be turned on by the government without your knowledge or consent. Google keeps a record of everything you search for on the internet, thereby developing a profile of what your interests are. Google Earth can show pictures of where you live. You willingly provide your photos and reveal your personality on social networks like Facebook. If the government wants to, through data mining and surveillance, they can easily find out everything about you. And that is scary!

The Left has all the pieces of the puzzle in place. The Devil's claw is about to be clenched. The only hope for decent people to retain their liberties, are from actions taken resulting from Americans strong desire to live free.

The Left is the enemy of man's freedom.

Freedom is the last thing the Left wants.

This is a battle against enemies of the Constitution and Socialism's failed policies.

"When governments fear the people, there is liberty. When the people fear the government, there is tyranny." - attributed to Thomas Jefferson.

Do not become enslaved by Totalitarianism.

When the financial downturn occurred by mid-September 2008, God had gotten the entire world's attention, nearly everyone has been affected financially. Because the world has become so materialistic, He chose financial instability as the vehicle to deliver his message. We are at a pivotal point in history. Obama's actions have opened people's eyes to see what Authoritarian Rule might be like. In response, God-loving, independence minded patriots rose up in the form of a Tea Party Movement with the realization that a fight for freedom will require a united effort against the powerful forces of the relentless Progressives who have been establishing their agenda for decades. With perseverance, if successful, we will again bask in liberty, experience freedom, break the chains of all types of slavery and see the light of day. This may be a time of miracles. May God bless the efforts of the Tea Party Movement.

Our liberty is a gift from God.

America is in the fight of its life, not from foreign terrorists, but from the enemy within. Everyone currently or potentially right-of-center needs to do everything they can to fight against those seeking to destroy our way of life and deprive us of our freedom.

"The cause is just." - Samuel Adams 1778

Americans want to be free to pursue their dreams. Limited government leaves people free to pursue their own dreams.

Our children's freedom is at stake!

"All that's necessary for the forces of evil to win in the world is for enough good men to do nothing." - Edmund Burke

"The only way to defeat Evil, is with good. ... Evil doesn't understand the light. ... Stand in the light." - Glenn beck

We need to find the things that unite us. The commonality that brought the 13 colonies together was a thirst for freedom.

Freedom is our heritage, we earned it. We need to defend it.

Freedom is worth protecting, it is worth fighting for. And Americans fight for freedom.

A patriotic revival has manifested itself in the form of the Tea Party. It occurred due to the radical actions by the Obama Administration in subverting our freedoms. An incident can fuel the fires of revolution. That incident is a threat to our economic stability, and a president doing things that are not in the national interest. The citizens are taking back their country.

In Tea Party style fashion, other countries ruled by tyrants are revolting. It started in Tunisia and spread across the region. After Wikileaks exposed corruption, the masses, outraged by injustice, rose up in a grassroots effort to claim freedom. The truth for other countries is spreading through Twitter and other social network systems. For America, the truth is spread through conservative talk radio and the Fox television network. When the revolt started in Egypt, the government shut down cell phones, text messages, the internet, and all social web sites and networks. The tyrants in power need to silence political dissent. It is so scary that Obama is trying hard to be granted a kill switch for the internet. Despite the Left and tyrannical regime's best laid plans, the people by sheer number, can have more power than the few at the top. The unknown is, whether the subsequent form of government will be better or worse than the prior one. But there is hope for freedom and with luck, liberty throughout the world!

Spartacus represents an underdog taking on the powerful, a champion of the multitudes, a man that wants to live on his own terms, dies fighting for freedom and justice, an eternal symbol of resistance against tyranny.

Freedom for all.

Let freedom reign!

Samuel Adams spoke of God's gifts of talents and virtues, bestowed on men, with a divine purpose and law, and that the blessings of providence are to be enjoyed by all.

Twenty-one years prior 1776, George Washington was in a battle, in which Indians specifically targeted him, but were not able to shoot him. Four bullets passed through his coat, and two horses were shot out from under him. He escaped without a wound.[93] The chief prophesized that he would be the founder of a mighty empire.[94] Washington said there were at least 67 instances that the American cause of independence would end if not for direct intervention from God.[95]

Citizens need to be informed as to what is going on within our country.

"Whenever the people are well-informed, they can be trusted with their own government..." - Thomas Jefferson

An enlightened citizenry is indispensible for the proper functioning of a republic. Self-government is not possible unless the citizens are educated sufficiently to enable them to exercise oversight. It is therefore imperative that the nation see to it that a suitable education be provided for all its citizens.[96]

"I know no safe depositary of the ultimate powers of the society but the people themselves..." - Thomas Jefferson

Thomas Jefferson adopted something that Spain had learned and required. "In the constitution of Spain ... no person ... should ever acquire the rights of citizenship until he could read and write." The people "cannot approve what they do not understand. Peace is best preserved by giving ... information to the people. Educate and inform the whole mass of the people. Enable them to see that it is in their interest to preserve peace and order, and they will preserve them. They are the only sure reliance for the preservation of our liberty." - Thomas Jefferson

"When people get the facts they will correct the mistakes." – attributed to Thomas Jefferson

"Dare to read, think, speak. Knowledge will prevent us from being slaves." - John Adams

Americans are lovers of liberty.

It is the spirit of America that everyone should have access to knowledge and to maintain liberty.

Guard the Republic.[97]

Defend freedom.

Freedom is like air, when you have it, it is taken for granted, when you don't have it, you can't live without it.

Ronald Reagan exposed: The U.S. Constitution is the last best hope for freedom and liberty, and it is under attack. Loose it here, and the world will surely decline into tyranny. "Government does nothing as well or as economically as the private sector. Whether we believe in our capacity for self-government or whether we abandon the American Revolution and confess that a little intellectual elite in a far-distant capital can plan our lives for us better than we can plan them ourselves. We will preserve for our children this, the last best hope of man on earth, or we will sentence them to take the first step into a thousand years of darkness."[98]

Do not take your freedom and liberty for granted, you may lose it.

PART 5

BASIC PRINCIPLES OF THE FOUNDING OF THE UNITED STATES OF AMERICA

The American experiment was to see if self government works. Can ordinary people govern themselves? In the past, people were ruled by Kings, the Church or dictators.

Prior to the Constitution, the Articles of Confederation described the form of government used, which reportedly didn't work because it was too close to anarchy. By 1785 Thomas Jefferson and James Madison worked on a different style of government. They decided on a Representative Republic not a democracy. They felt democracy was worse than a monarchy or anarchy. The Constitution, which was ratified at the Constitutional Convention in 1787, outlines the best form of government as chosen and agreed upon by our founding fathers.

The Founders of the Constitution were against any centralized power. They wanted balance, so they designed checks that had enough power to be effective. Government's powers are enumerated powers, meaning they are limited to those that are specifically spelled out. They knew that pure Democracies never work. However, there are even flaws with Republics, which are the special interests. So the Constitution was designed to diminish the influence of special interests. They structured a system whereby the people would be self-governed. They wanted to slow things down, so there would be time to have second thoughts, so judgments would be more reasonable. Original intent of the Constitution means the people have spoken, and only the people can change it through the Amendment process that is constitutionally prescribed. If the Supreme Court can change that, we would no longer have a free government; we would no longer have checks and balances; government would become an oligarchy or be ruled by despotism.[99]

Federalism means the Federal government has limited powers. There are 16 enumerated powers granted to the Federal government by the States. The States formed the Federal government, retaining for themselves that which they did not delegate. The powers not delegated are retained either by the States or the citizens.

The enumerated powers granted to Congress by the Constitution are in Article 1, Section 8, these include: the power to levy and collect taxes and pay the Debts; provide for the common Defense and general Welfare; to borrow money on the credit of the United States; regulate Commerce; establish a uniform Rule of Naturalization, and uniform Laws on Bankruptcies; coin Money, regulate the Value thereof, and fix the Standards of Weights and Measures; provide Punishment of counterfeiting the Securities and Coin; establish Post offices and post roads; promote Science and useful Arts by securing for limited times to Inventors and Authors the exclusive Right to their writings and discoveries; create Federal Courts inferior to the Supreme Court; punish Felonies committed on the high Seas; declare war; raise and support Armies; provide and maintain a Navy; make rules for the regulation of the land and naval Forces; provide for calling forth the Militia to execute the Laws of the Union, suppress Insurrections and repel Invasions; provide for organizing, arming, and disciplining the militia; exercise exclusive Legislation over the District of Columbia, for the erection of needful buildings; and to make all Laws necessary for carrying into execution the foregoing powers. That's it, those are the only things Congress has a right to do. Would you say that they have exceeded their scope a little?

The Government has the power to coin money, but not to print paper money.

When the Constitutional Convention of 1787 ended, and the question was asked, what have we got? Benjamin Franklin replied, "A Republic, if you can keep it."

We are a Republic. We choose representatives that vote on laws. If the public doesn't like how they perform, we can vote them out of office.

Our Colonial roots reflect an innate resentment towards government.

We are a government by the people. "The power under the Constitution will always be in the people." – George Washington

Article 5 of the Constitution allows the people to evolve the Constitution through Amendments. There have been 27 Amendments. Of those, there have been perversions to the original intent and structure of our government. In 1913 under President Woodrow Wilson, Progressives passed the 17th Amendment. Prior to this Amendment, U.S. Senators were appointed by their State Legislatures. Members of the House of Representatives were directly elected by the people, but the Senate would derive its power from the States. The idea was to have the Senators be the representatives of the States' interests. Because of this change, lobbyists only need to go to the Senators for national causes, not for their State causes. As a result, we have unfunded mandates. The Founders didn't intend for the federal government to have much power. In 1821, Thomas Jefferson warned: "When all government … shall be drawn to Washington as the center of all power, it will render powerless the checks provided of one government on another, and will become as venal and oppressive as the government from which we separated."[100]

Declaration of Independence

Distributed to the public on July 4, 1776 the Declaration of Independence states: "We hold these truths to be self-evident, that all men are created equal, that they are endowed by their Creator with certain unalienable Rights, that among these are Life, Liberty and the pursuit of Happiness. That to secure these rights, Governments are instituted among Men, deriving their just powers from the consent of the governed..." The last entry reads, "And for the support of this Declaration, with a firm reliance on the protection of divine Providence, we pledge to each other our Lives, our Fortunes and sacred Honor."

David Barton of Wallbuilders puts it this way: There are five philosophical points in the Declaration of Independence 1.) there is a Creator, 2.) he gives certain unalienable rights, 3.) he has a moral law which governs people, 4.) the government exists to protect the rights he bestows, 5.) below God given rights, we are ruled by the consent of the governed. The purpose of the Bill of Rights goes back to the Declaration of Independence, to make sure we have the right to practice what the Creator indicated for us to do.[101]

The Bill of Rights, ratified in 1791, are the first ten Amendments to the Constitution, they do not restrict the citizens, they restrict the government.

The Founders believed each individual is important, and this importance did not come from a grant from the State, this importance came from the source of his life.[102] Man was made in the likeness of God, he has a destiny to achieve. Man also has a purpose and has the inherent freedom to achieve it. So, the Bill of Rights doesn't limit citizens, it limits government. If God is removed, then government issues rights or takes them away.[103]

Natural Rights pre-exist government, they come from God. The Constitution is a hedge against encroachment by the government.

The Constitution doesn't grant rights, it states these rights exist and government won't interfere with them. The government's powers derive from our consent. The Constitution is a defensive document; it acknowledges that there is going to be relentless pressure to reduce those rights.[104] Some rights are immune from majority rule. The Constitution is a defense against the tyranny of the majority. The Constitution protects us from ourselves. The government is not immune from its own laws. Inalienable rights means they cannot be separated from us by government. The Constitution enumerates rights of the people that the government is not permitted to trample on. The purpose of government is to protect liberty, not to run our lives. The First Amendment was expressly written to enable the press to keep the government transparent. The Fourth Amendment is our right to privacy.

Freedom lets you chose what do with your life.

PART 6

ECON 101

The Democrats view financial matters as static, meaning everything always remains the same, and so if one item is changed it has no affect on the other components. But the economy is dynamic, meaning one change usually changes everything else. For example, Obama claims that if the Bush tax cuts are kept for those making over $250,000 per year, the money will be lost and will need to be replaced by borrowing money. First of all, the Government only has money that entities have given it, it doesn't have its own money to lose. A tax cut just means the government is taking less of your money. To put things in perspective, when the Democrats use the phrase "for the wealthiest Americans", substitute "for small business owners." Small businesses employ the majority of the workers. Tax cuts free-up capital which allows small business owners to invest in equipment. So, if they aren't taxed as much, they have more money to offer their employees raises or even to hire more employees. As a result, productivity increases and the economy grows; more people make higher incomes so more revenue is collected from income taxes. Therefore, there is actually a net increase in revenue from tax cuts. Reagan lowered the top tax bracket from 70% to 28%[105] and the government collected more revenue than it ever had before, and that's a fact.[106]

Democrats operate under the mistaken belief that the wealth of the country is finite, that it is a zero sum game, so in order to give money to some they must take from others. The reality is, if more money is generated, there is more money earned by more people, so there is more to go around. The Main Stream Media perpetuates the myth that the economy acts like a zero sum game.

The Democrats want to kill the goose that lays the golden eggs. Their policies are short sighted and fed by a strong desire to punish the rich instead of trying to raise the most revenue and strengthen the economy.

Liberals are detached from economic reality. They do not understand the basic laws of economics. As a result, the government taxes what is efficient in the economy and subsidizes what is inefficient.

When a corporation is taxed it either: raises the price of the product it produces, cuts its dividend to its shareholders, or lays off workers. The corporation passes the cost along to the consumer, or the shareholders have less to circulate through the economy or its workers suffer. So, the middle class is ultimately affected.

Business doesn't like uncertainty, expending money is a risk, if they don't know the tax rates or the policies Congress will impose they will not expand by hiring or purchasing new equipment.

On February 8, 2011 Obama announced wanting to raise business payroll taxes by increasing the level of worker's wages subject to Federal unemployment tax paid by employers from $7,000 to $14,000 thus giving the States more money to pay for their unemployment insurance benefits.[107] This will make matters worse on many levels.

The top 1% of taxpayers pays over 40% of the total income taxes.[108] Redistribution of wealth is built into the system by it being structured as a progressive tax rate.

The top 3% of the marginal income tax bracket earners accounts for 25% of all Consumer spending,[109] so if they have less money to spend, sales are down which cascades, slowing the economy and causing employees to be fired.

The top 10% of earners pay 70% of the total income taxes.[110]

Small Businesses provide 50% of all private sector jobs.[111]

BEFORE 1913 THERE WAS NO INCOME TAX, except during the Civil War and briefly in 1894 during that depression. There was no income tax until Progressives were elected. The Progressives used it as a way to fund Big Government.

The tax rate is on a progressive scale, meaning as ones income raises so does their tax rate, causing them to pay a greater percentage of their earnings through income taxes. This is based on the notion of an ability to pay and is inherently unfair. A fair way would be a flat tax so everyone pays the same percentage of their income. The current method penalizes success. High income earners are the most productive. It is foolish to penalize them and limit their ability to expand, invest and provide jobs. The Progressive tax rate concept is just that, a Progressive idea from 1909, later enacted by President Woodrow Wilson in 1913. Income tax, capital gains tax, excise taxes and Inheritance taxes are used as a social equalizer, redistributing wealth from the rich to the poor. The tax structure was motivated by class envy. The income tax structure that was instituted by Progressives is backwards; it is a disincentive to being productive and rewards the unproductive through welfare and entitlement receipts. Taxes subtract from economic activity.

When Liberals use the word "fairness" relating to taxes, they mean the wealthy should pay far more than their equal share.

When taxes are increased, philanthropy and charitable donations decline, so the poor suffer as a result.

In 1913 the income tax rate was 7% and supposed to stay low, by 1918 it was 77%.[112] It has been as high as 94%.[113]

The government acts as if all the money in the country belongs to them and they let us keep a little of it. They consider any money that they don't collect, like from a tax cut, a loss.

Inheritance Tax or Death Tax, which the IRS calls Estate Tax, is a Progressive method to redistribute wealth. This socialistic policy taxes a person's net worth upon their death. It is a double tax because people have already paid income tax on it as they earned it. 2010, because of the Bush tax cuts, was the first time that there weren't any estate taxes since their inception in 1916. The tax rate has been as high as 77%.[114] The rate had been at 55%, above an exempted amount, since 1984 until the Bush tax cuts slowly reduced them, so over half of what a person had saved up all their lives goes to the government instead of to their family or charity. The compromised amount starting in 2011 will be 35% for amounts over $5 million. Karl Marx advocated for a 100% inheritance tax, the U.S. has been as close as 77% of the way there. This tax is devastating for small family owned businesses and farms and should be repealed.

UNTIL 1929 THERE WEREN'T ANY ENTITLEMENTS.

The problem with the economy and why things are so screwed up in this country is because both Houses of Congress making the laws and regulations have been controlled by Democrats for 55 out of the last 77 years! Republicans have only controlled both Houses for 14 of those 77 years.

From 1787 to 1920 the Federal Government accounted for 3% of GDP, Gross Domestic Product, now it is over 25%.[115]

Anyone can make money in the USA and if they work hard enough, can even become rich. It is the land of opportunity. There aren't obstacles preventing people from getting ahead. On the contrary, there are many government programs to help people do better financially. People aren't locked into the station in life that they were born into, as is the case in most places in the world. Most billionaires are self-made. The most visible example is Oprah Winfrey. People can make money by: hard work, investments, inventing something, being a professional athlete, being a professional musician, winning the lotto, a court settlement, inheritance, etc.

Obama encourages people, especially youth, to work for the government. But government employees do not produce anything that generates revenue, they just provide services and therefore that is not helping the country's economic problems. It is actually worse because the taxpayers pay their salaries and pensions. Plus, the government takes money out of the private sector in order to fund its employees and projects, leaving less for people and businesses to invest. Citizens should instead be encouraged to work in the private sector generating products and income that in turn is taxed thus stimulating the economy and providing tax revenue to fund necessary government services. Obama does not understand economics because he has never run a business.

The Left complains about outsourcing jobs, but government regulations and high union labor costs force companies to do business in other countries where things are less expensive and easier to accomplish. Liberal policies are the source of the problem.

Union pensions are unsustainable and will cause the country to go broke. Instead of the way pensions are structured now, they need to be defined contribution plans like 401K's.

Keynesian Ben Bernanke, Federal Reserve Chairman, in early April, 2010 said, "To avoid large and unsustainable budget deficits, the nation will ultimately have to choose among higher taxes, modifications to entitlement programs, such as Social

93

Security and Medicare, less spending on everything else from education to Defense, or some combination of the above … But unless we as a Nation demonstrate a strong commitment to fiscal responsibility, in the longer run we will have neither financial stability nor economic growth."

The international oil price is pegged to the U.S. dollar, so as the Federal Reserve prints money, causing inflation, the price of oil goes up. These Liberal Keynesian policies take money out of your pocket every time you put gas in your car. Do you Liberals like having less money to spend on other things, like drugs? Do you fiscally responsible people realize that voting in elected officials that appoint people like Ben Bernanke directly affects you financially?

Keynesian Ben Bernanke, Federal Reserve Chairman, on June 22, 2011 said "We don't have a precise read on why this slower pace of growth is persisting…".[116] Well Ben, it's because Keynesian economics doesn't work. You are having us repeat the mess of the Great Depression.

There are similarities between what the U.S. is doing now and what Germany's Weimar Republic was doing from 1919 – 1933. They had a lot of debt from World War I and didn't manufacture anything. They started printing money, but there was nothing to back it up. Their hyperinflation caused $1 trillion paper Marks to be worth $1 U.S. dollar. We are no longer on the gold standard, our money is only backed by trust.[117] We are counting on being 'too big to fail' on the world stage.

On July13, 2011 Ben Bernanke said gold is not money. You can keep your paper bills Ben, I'll take gold any day as having more value.

In 2010 the USA dropped to 9th on the list of countries that have the most economic freedom. Aspects that determine that freedom are:

- Rule of Law; ours decline every time Obama chooses which laws to enforce or ignore. In the General Motors bailout instead of following contract law and giving bond holders priority, he gave it to the Union's pension fund.
- Secure property rights; ours are being eroded.
- Freedom from corruption; our government is getting more and more corrupt from the top down.
- Government spending; ours is taking more in taxes to fund spending.
- Labor freedom, mobility; our government is not business friendly, the length of time to start business projects with burdensome permits and regulations is detrimental.[118]

Government's self defeating economic policies continue.

America used to be a manufacturing giant that dominated the global marketplace. Manufacturing has been on the decline in the U.S. since 1979. We have lost our industrial base; it has foolishly been replaced by the service industry and the financial industry, which is nothing more than manipulations of expectations that inflate paper with nothing of substance to support it. Since 2001 the U.S. lost 42,400 factories and 90,000 manufacturing companies are now at risk of going out of business. The U.S. lost 1/3 of its manufacturing jobs since 2000.[119] Consumption accounts for 70% of GDP and roughly half of that is spent on services.[120] We consume more and produce less. Our trade deficit will continue to grow.

The machine-tool industry is the backbone of an industrial economy; it is the means by which all products are manufactured. It is essential to maintaining the country's national security. It has collapsed in tandem with manufacturing. The U.S. will be increasingly dependent on foreign manufactures even for its key

95

military technology. America's technological supremacy has declined alongside its manufacturing supremacy. The proximity of research, development and manufacturing is very important to leading-edge manufacturers. China is beginning to attract and pull high-end companies with design and R&D capabilities out of the U.S. It is difficult for U.S. companies to compete against Asian countries that pay their workers a fraction of what Unions here have extracted. Most Asian countries do not have OSHA or environmental regulations; the workers do not pay for health care; they provide zero-interest financing; they provide subsidies for energy, land and equipment; grant tax holidays; and some devalue their currency. U.S. manufacturers want our government to shift its economic policies away from consumption to incentives that favor investment in new factories, equipment and jobs. Not only has Obama not done that, he appointed Ron Bloom to be his senior councilor for manufacturing policy.[121] Czar Ron Bloom worked for SEIU, and United Steelworkers Union, he disavows the free market system. He said, "We know that the free market is nonsense. We kind of agree with Mao that political power comes largely from the barrel of a gun."[122] So much for America's economic future under Obama.

Socialism doesn't work! The idealistic hippies while at Woodstock and those living in communes believed they could create a better society. Those attempts failed. The Leftists now, that were teens then, are in Federal, State and Local governments and as a result the geographic locations where they are the majority, like California, are financial disasters.

A communal system doesn't work because of human nature. There is no incentive to work hard if all production is shared. Theft occurs because of greed and self interest. Publicly owned land and buildings that are owned by everyone, are managed by no one. There is no reason to care for commonly owned property. The Pilgrims started off as a commune and nearly starved to death, losing 50% of their group. After the Governor introduced the concept of private property, they flourished. When there is private ownership people take care of their possessions, they become good stewards of the land. When you get to keep what you produce, you are rewarded for your hard work. Prosperity ensues. This was the beginning of capitalism. The profit motive ensures optimizing supply and efficiency.[123] The government does nothing well. Regulations complicate matters and the Bureaucracy just slows everything down. Capitalism is clearly superior to Socialism and Communism.

President Calvin Coolidge, 1923 to 1929, helped get the country out of the Depression of 1920 by effectively using sound conservative fiscal measures advocated by Secretary of the Treasury Andrew Mellon. This led to the Roaring 20's, a time of great prosperity. Instead of abiding by those successful policies as a guideline to solving today's economic mess, Obama is following the failed socialistic method that FDR used. The Left, including Obama and FDR, believe big government spending will stimulate the economy. They keep drastically changing the rules which creates uncertainty for businesses. Entrepreneurs refuse to invest, and sit on their cash when there is uncertainty. As a result, unemployment continues to rise. That approach caused a double dipped depression during FDR's reign. What brought us out of the Great Depression was manufacturing jobs needed for World War II and the conscription of 12 million men into the military. Coolidge cut spending and taxes. He had government get out of the way of business and allowed to it thrive. History serves as proof that Progressive policies do not work. Progressives control the education system and through revisionism, they distort or do not report particular historical events; they glorify FDR's actions and necessarily hide Coolidge's accomplishments and policies. The economy will only improve after spending and taxes are cut and the market place has certainty in its future.[124]

There was fear of a Depression in 1946 when the economy was transitioning from a wartime economy back to a peacetime economy. The debt had been 120% of GDP form 1943 - 1945.

Government spending fell as war contracts were canceled and approximately 10 million soldiers came back into civilian life. Instead of following the failed Keynesian policies used by FDR, the laissez-faire approach of Mellon/Harding/Coolidge was employed. Labor markets adjusted quickly once they were unfettered by government. The self-correcting and healing forces of the market are effective when they are allowed to work. Most economists today acknowledge that FDR's interventionist policies extended the length and depth of the Great Depression. Business investment boomed as government spending receded.[125] This is a classic illustration of how the reverse is true, that government spending crowds out private sector spending. So, the 1946 Depression was averted using proven conservative policies, yet Obama and the Democrats insist on adhering to failed socialistic policies. Relating this to today, Japan's stimulus efforts in the 1990's led to reduced economic growth and long-term unemployment. The Federal Reserve printing money reduces investor confidence which leads to falling investment. Health Care legislation and possible Cap and Trade will enormously increase labor costs so employers do not want to hire more workers. The continual extension of unemployment benefits just makes it longer before unemployment rates will decrease. Deficits have lowered optimism about the future. Consumer confidence is at a 27 year low. So, just as Hoover has been accused of doing everything wrong when the Great Depression started, Obama will be associated with blindly repeating FDR's failed policies. All Obama has done is put us unimaginably deep in debt, prolonged a recovery, strengthened the Unions, and vastly expanded government.

The definition of a "headwind" in the economy is Obama, Bernanke, and the Democrat party blindly following Keynesian Economics, which means uncertainty for businesses and no job for you. Can't you see for yourself that Keynesian Economics does not work? You are being duped. What the liberal professors have been teaching is a lie.

PART 7

LET'S BE *PAINFULLY* CORRECT …

The Environmental Movement

In the mid 1980's the Environmental Movement was hijacked by the political Left who became radical environmentalists. They used Green language to cloak their anti-capitalist agenda. The movement is now comprised of anti-American peace nicks, Leftists and neo-Marxists. In Europe the Movement is full of communists.

To its followers, Environmentalism is their religion. Gaya, mother earth. Earth is the most important thing and man is the least important. Environmental Laws protect everything else more than man. They are anti-human. Destroy an eagle's egg and go to jail, but it is okay to abort a child.[126] Prince Philip of England said if he was reincarnated he would want to come back as a killer virus to reduce the human population to a sane level,[127] which is an insane statement. Environmentalists are trying to desecrate religion because its followers are their biggest opponents. Many scientists do not believe in God. Some Environmentalists reworded the Pledge of Allegiance to, "I pledge allegiance to the earth and all the life it supports, one planet in our care, irreplaceable, with sustenance and respect for all."[128]

The first Earth Day, April 22, 1970, coincided with Vladimir Lenin's birthday.

Environmental equality is a term meaning the redistribution of wealth from developed countries to undeveloped countries. The Environmental ideological goal is control.

A Crusade.

Sacrifice for a higher purpose, to save the planet.

Eco-Justice.

We are living under the new EnviroNAZI Regime.

The Leftist in the Movement don't want cars because they pollute, but what bothers them even more is the fact that people have the freedom to go wherever they want whenever they want. Their penchant is to limit your freedom by having everyone use public transportation.

The environmentally conscious.

They are all concerned about that ecology thing.

Spain has lost two regular jobs for every one green job it creates. Their unemployment rate is over 20.9%.[129] Their public-sector debt is 65.2% of GDP and forecast to reach 67.3 by year-end 2011.[130]

The members of the Movement are producing environmental larvae.

The bottom line is, they don't want any humans on the planet, because they pollute.

EPA, Environmental Protection Agency

Established in 1970 by Executive Order from Richard Nixon.

ESA, Endangered Species Act was enacted in 1973. The law doesn't consider affects to humans. In a California case involving Delta Smelt, Judge Wanger is trying to set president that the collateral damage to humans should be taken into consideration. Shutting off the Delta Pumps in order to protect the non-indigenous minnow, is depriving 23 million people of a reliable water supply and putting 400,000 acres of farmland out of production. This is eco-terrorism.

The EPA Endangered and Threatened Species lists includes the following creatures: Blunt nosed leopard lizard, Orangefoot Pimpleback Pearlymussel, Spring Creek Bladderpod, West Indian Whistling-duck, Middle-toothed Land Snail, Fabulous Green Sphinx Moth, Portuguese Dogfish, Pygmy Siltsnail, Red-cockaded Woodpecker, Shortnose Sucker, Cowfish, Dogbill Cat, Alabama red-belly Turtle, Smalltooth Sawfish, Southern Hog-nosed Snake, Big-eared Bat, Appalachian Monkeyface Pearlmussel, Dark Pigtoe clam, Conehead Katydid, Devil's Hole Pupfish, Caribbean Coot, Hairy Rattleweed, Thin-footed Bush Cricket, Hogfish, Point-headed Grasshopper, Red-legged frog, Fairy shrimp, and Kangaroo rat.

The *Painfully* Correct Endangered list: Conservatives, religions other than Islam, common sense, your money, a healthy fetus, the Ten Commandments, our rights under the U.S. Constitution, tobacco, guns, an unbiased education, and morals.

The EPA is the jobs killing arm of the Left.

Obama used the EPA to bypass the traditional procedure for Congress to debate and vote on Carbon emissions regulations. On December, 9 2009 the EPA decreed emissions to be dangerous, so began regulating them. The EPA is presumed to be set up to act within the laws that are already in place without further authorization from Congress.

Since the EPA ruled that Carbon Dioxide is a poisonous gas, that makes it illegal for humans and animals to exhale. I think the EPA officials ought to lead by example and be the first to stop exhaling. But don't hold your breath.

Environmentalists

Environmental, emphasis on the mental.

Naive idealists.

Isn't it ironic that the people that drive electric cars are the ones most against the dams needed to power the electric cars?

A female named Toni in England had herself sterilized after having an abortion to "save the planet".[131] It takes balls to do that! I wish they would all do it.

They assert that "environmental issues do not have boundaries", like city limits. Well Environmental nonsense knows no bounds.

Darwin's adaptations within a species should include "Asphalt Fairy Shrimp".

Litigious environmentalists.

Environmentalists are paranoid about genetically engineered food.

Obama, like other environmentalists, have child like beliefs that solar and wind power and other Green technology will immediately replace oil and coal use. It is seriously dangerous for the president to set policy for the country's energy needs based on a naïve understanding of reality. Solar and wind currently account for just .7% of our energy. Obama has effectively shut down offshore oil drilling in the Gulf.

Do you know the difference between a dead dog lying in the road and a dead Environmentalist lying in the road? There are skid marks before the dog.

Environmental Militant, James Lee, on September 1, 2010, influenced by Al Gore's movie, occupied the Discovery Channel building with guns and explosives. While holding three hostages he was shot and killed by police. His written demands included human sterilization, dismantling the US economy, and finding solutions for Global Warming. It will be warm where he's going. He was concerned about the environment and overpopulation. That's one less environmentalist anyway. His thinking exposes the raw beliefs held by environmentalists: "the planet does not need ... environmentally harmful humans."[132]

Environmentalists believe conservation is the answer to everything. California hasn't been able to build a dam in decades due to environmentalist opposition. The water storage system was designed to supply water to a fraction of today's population, yet when there are a few years of drought, their answer is to conserve. Well, you have to have something before you can conserve it. There needs to be an adequate storage capacity for the current population. California's population is now 37.3 million people!

Eco-friendly

They believe in renewable energy and being socially responsible. What about Eco-terrorism!

Eco-insanity.

The Green Movement

Greenies.

The Green Revolution is a brilliant marketing technique designed to convince consumers to pay more for their products simply by repackaging them and labeling them as Green Products. And a lot of dunces are falling for it. There is a sucker born every minute. Capitalism lives on!

Watermelon = green on the outside and red on the inside, meaning communist.

Green radicals.

Green endeavors are not economically sound, or private enterprise would do it on their own. Our current politicians have government take money from productive people that are creating jobs to subsidize green projects that can't make a profit. This effectively stifles the economy. European countries found for every green job they create they lose two to five private sector jobs.

Solyndra, the solar panel company, squandered the $535 million loan that it was given by the Obama Administration. Alternative energy schemes were put on the fast track without due diligence. This company's principal investor was a major Obama campaign contributor. Obama blatantly practices Crony capitalism for favored industries and political donors. It is outrageous that another $16 billion was given to solar companies shortly after the Solyndra scandal. The Obama Administration refused to release certain documents to a congressional committee. Obama put investors ahead of the taxpayers for getting repaid in case of default. Solyndra's CEO plead the 5th.

Van Jones, a self-described communist, who was Obama's Green Jobs Czar and is the founder of Green For All, advocates a clandestine economic revolution, moving America towards a Green Economy. He said, "From 1964 to 1968 complete revolution was on the table for this country. And, I think this Green Movement has to pursue those same steps and stages. ... We want to move ... to something eco-capitalism."[133] He reportedly said that a revolutionary proposes a more just order.

104

Jones' vision is to use "green" as a deceptive maneuver to destroy the existing American system: "We are going to push it and push it until it becomes the engine for transforming the whole society." "The green economy will start off as a small subset" of a "complete revolution" against "grey capitalism" and toward a "redistribution of all wealth." As Green Czar he was set to distribute $30 billion of our tax dollars. His environmental concerns seem to be a facade for massive spending, over burdening the system and being a catalyst for revolution. He has called for an end to prisons and the freeing of all inmates. He wants to "build a pipeline from the prison economy to the green economy," including hiring parolees to insulate homes and offices. His approach to creating green jobs and attaining green-justice.[134]

Mexico has a political party named the Environmentalist Green Party. California and other states have a Green Party.

Global Warming

Global Hoax.

Alleged Global Warming.

The seriousness of the charge requires investigation.

Deniers.

Be a denier of the Big Lie.

I am proud to be a Global-Warming denier!

People that believe that Global Warming will destroy the Earth are incredibly gullible.

To put this in perspective, in 1973 Science Digest proclaimed, "the world's climatologists are agreed" that we must "prepare for the next ice age." In 1975 science magazine reported, "the approach of a full-blown 10,000-year ice age."[135]

The Global Warming premise that the Earth is susceptible to catastrophe if its temperature rises slightly, is dead wrong. The Earth is not fragile. The Earth is just the opposite; it has the ability to self correct all problems. The most devastating event was when the meteor slammed into the Earth and caused the extinction of the dinosaurs. There have been massive volcanic eruptions that have spewed ash over vast reaches. During the first Gulf War, Sadam Huessein set numerous oil wells on fire that took a long time to extinguish and were expected to have lasting detrimental effects. The enormous quantity of oil from the Gulf oil leak that seemed so catastrophic at the time, rapidly dissipated. All these catastrophes have been ameliorated.

According to Sean Hannity's Fox TV special in the Fall of 2010 titled the *Green Swindle*, Maurice Strong, a United Nations bureaucrat, conceived the strategy that if governments are convinced that Global Warming has to stop immediately, then the governments can control every aspect of people's lives. He wants a United Nations run world government. He tried to get nations to give up their sovereignty, and proposed a global tax on the use of oceans, the atmosphere, and outer space. His supporters use fear of Environmental Armageddon to illicit compliance.

Climategate was exposed in November 2009, when a hacker released emails from the University of East Anglia's Climate Research Unit divulging a plot by Michael Mann and Phil Jones to hide the truth about the earth's true temperature record by severely manipulating the data concerning the Global Warming Theory.[136] They buried information that showed temperatures during the Medieval Warm Period, from approximately 800 AD – 1,300 AD, were warmer than today.[137] As a reward they received $2.4 million in Stimulus money and $20 million from Europe and the

United Nations. They conspired to suppress research that challenged the Theory and even conspired to get an editor fired that wrote about scientists challenging their data. It has been dubbed the biggest scientific hoax in world history. The scandal revealed that corruption of climate science is a worldwide problem and has caused grave damage to the integrity of climate science.[138] Evidence of deceit by climate scientists that deliberately falsified data to obtain additional research funding is criminal fraud. There was a criminal intent to defraud the public of massive amounts of money with a cap and trade scheme as part of a Global Warming movement. NOAA, the National Oceanic and Atmospheric Administration, conspired in the manipulation of global temperature records along with NASA,[139] which failed to comply with the Freedom of Information Act for over three years.[140] The Mainstream Media buried the Climategate story in order to advance an ideological Leftist agenda. As part of the worldwide Climategate cover-up, newspapers like USA Today refused to report on it, The New York Times claimed it was not meant for the public to see, for two weeks after the story broke ABC, CBS and NBC did not mention it,[141] it was censored by liberal Wikipedia, and Google did not provide links to it. Google interferes with searches for material deemed not politically correct. Al Gore is on Google's advisory board. All this is motivated by money and power. Obama announced he was doubling down on his commitment to the worldwide environmental agenda, pushing forward with a cap and trade scheme using taxpayer dollars. Left-leaning scientists contribute to the alarmist propaganda to create hysteria, warning of a pending eco-catastrophe.

Eco-alarmist.

Man's biggest contribution to Global Warming is manipulating the data of Global Warming.[142]

Outraged that not everyone is buying their assertion, and determined to silence skeptics, they refer to the "denier's" position as 'climate blasphemy'. One zealot even declared, "it's completely immoral, even to question "the U.N.'s scientific "consensus." The Weather Channel's climatologist advocates that broadcast meteorologists be stripped of their scientific certification if they express skepticism about predictions of manmade catastrophic global warming. In 2006, the eco-magazine *Grist* called for Nuremberg style trials for Global Warming skeptics. In 2007, Robert Kennedy Jr. said of skeptics, "this is treason, and we need to start treating them as traitors." In 2008, the Guardian reported that NASA's James Hansen called for trials of climate skeptics for high crimes against humanity. In 2008, David Suzuki called for government leaders skeptical of Global Warming to be thrown in jail. In June 2009, the liberal blog site TPM said, at what point do we jail or execute Global Warming deniers? There are calls for capital punishment for 'global warming deniers.' These environmental fanatics are similar to bible literalists that believe without question the orthodoxy of manmade climate change and want to persecute heretics. [143]

There was a magazine ad, in October 2010, of a young girl standing on a melting ice mound with a hangmen noose around her neck and her hands behind her. Sick minds.

Cap & Trade

A job killer.

The government caps the amount of carbon, CO^2, that companies and industries can produce and allows them to trade credits. It is as bogus a scheme as mitigation. It is a way for those in control to profit, while not reducing pollution. This is Market Socialism. It rations energy use.

The Green Left understands that the direct route to government control of almost everything is to stigmatize, as a planetary menace, something involved in everything – carbon. [144]

The Left wants to limit your carbon footprint with boot-jack control.

Follow the money. This carbon trading scheme prompted the creation of the Chicago Climate Exchange, CCX, which helps prepare businesses and markets for potential regulations at the international or federal level by reducing greenhouse gas emissions through a rules-based exchange platform. The founder and the father of carbon trading, Richard Sandor, obtained grants from the leftist Joyce Foundation, of which Barack Obama was a board member. CCX was bought by Climate Exchange PLC, of which Al Gore is part owner through his stake in Generation Investment Management. Climate Exchange PLC was bought in 2010 by Intercontinental Exchange for $600 million. Sly Al knows there is a lot of green in Green!

The market value of all Carbon Trading permits is estimated to be $7 trillion by 2050.[145]

Publicly, Obama had said that he wants the USA to reduce emissions to 1990 levels by 2020, and reduce them an additional 80% by 2050. That means he wants America's fossil fuels energy use to be what it was in 1910. Got a horse? It would cost the gasoline, electricity and natural gas industries $2 trillion, which pass the costs on to the rate payers, meaning consumers, meaning YOU! Obama said, "under my plan of a Cap and Trade system, electricity rates would necessarily skyrocket."[146]

The point is to punish the use of fossil fuels so clean energy would become more attractive. This might sound like a good approach, if you have no grasp of finance. But you the consumer will share in paying the $2 trillion.

The Waxman-Markey Bill is an opportunity to expand government.

Kyoto – The objective was to reduce carbon emissions, redistribute wealth, and force developed nations to de-industrialize. It was designed to harm only the USA by exempting 155 other countries including the biggest polluters, China and India. In 1997, Congress was opposed to the U.S. signing the Kyoto Accord. Al Gore, with blatant disregard for the Senate, agreed to an International Treaty obligating the USA to reduce its emissions by at least 5% below its 1990 levels. It would cripple the U.S. economy. Electric rates would have increased at least 50%, gasoline would have increased $1 per gallon, and natural gas price would have increased 30 – 50 %. In 1998, Clinton signed the Kyoto Protocol but the Senate wouldn't ratify it. In 2009, Gore and Obama went to the U.N. Climate Change Conference in Copenhagen. The goal was to force industrialized nations to pay developing nations .5% of their GDP as a means to redistribute wealth.

Hillary Clinton, on September 22, 2010, said she wants $50 million for cook stoves to be sent to Africa and "wants Global Standards for cook stoves." This is a scheme to send the stoves to Africa and have them subsidized by big banks in exchange for carbon credits. She also wants to boost access to large scale carbon financing, which is a means to redistribute wealth. She additionally wants to have the standards adopted all over the world, in a move toward Global governance.

Half of the USA's energy comes from coal, and there is a seemingly endless supply here. But Obama and the environmentalist will do all they can to not allow it to be used.

Carbon Offset

Yet another guilt inspired scam whereby someone, like say John Kerry, that travels around in his 757 jumbo jet then buys something else that doesn't pollute as much, like a Hummer, so he feels like he's sacrificed for the planet.

If the polluters that offset their carbon footprint by buying credits were alive during the Civil War, they would have been the type that would have paid for someone else to go to war to fight in their place. They don't make the tough choices; they just pay for their guilt.

What carbon offsets are the celebrities making for the cocaine and other drugs they consume that are imported from Columbia and other distant drug producing locations?

Green Peace

Do-gooder pirates.

Organic

The term and the distinction is Bull Shit! What isn't organic?

Liberals are just paranoid of pesticides.

Environmentalists have organic rocks in their heads.

Bio-Diversity

Environmentalists are bio-tech phobes. Rice with modified genes adds vitamin A to rice, which would save the lives of millions of kids in the world, but the environmentalists in Europe won't allow its distribution.

Sustainable

Sustainable is the most over used, nauseating word of this era.

What is unsustainable is: socialism, the taxed run out of money; unfunded union pension plans; printing and creating money not backed by anything of value; deficit spending; and entitlements.

111

Vegetarians

In an advertisement to sell Free-Range chickens to eat, name them i.e., Herbie. That should cut down on the number being slaughtered.

Tofu freaks.

PETA, People for the Ethical Treatment of Animals

People Ingesting Tasty Animals - Hey, if you can't eat them or wear them, what the hell good are they?

Cass Sunstein stated that livestock and wild animals should have legal rights and should be empowered to file lawsuits; that the human consumption of meat is a practice that should be ended permanently.[147]

Everyone wants animals to be treated well. PETA are extremists attacking capitalist from yet another direction.

Government

George Washington said, "Government is not reason … it is force. Like fire, it is a dangerous servant and a fearful master."

"Government is a powerful and dangerous tool and so it must be wielded carefully and only when moral, constitutional, necessary and proper."[148]

Intrusive Big Government.

The Democrats like and want Big Government.

Big Government proponents have an insatiable appetite and desire to spend money.

112

Government officials do not regard themselves as public servants; they regard themselves as our masters.[149]

"Government's view of the economy could be summed up in a few short phrases: If it moves, tax it. If it keeps moving, regulate it. And if it stops moving, subsidize it." - Ronald Regan

The only thing government produces is misery and dependence.- Glenn beck

Government is used by the Left to redistribute wealth. It takes from some citizens to give to their constituents.

When government delivers a service, costs goes up and quality goes down.[150]

The government employs 17% of the workforce or 22.5 million people.[151]

Liberals want to govern and restrict the producers in society.

The U.S. Constitution is an obstacle to Liberals because it limits the power of Government.

Big Government usually ends up with an abuse of power, i.e., Waco, Texas - Janet Reno; constitutional rights - freedom of religion; and requiring citizens to purchase health care insurance and penalizing them if they don't.

"A society of sheep must in time beget a government of wolves." – attributed to Bertrand de Jouvenel 1903-1987

Global Governance

The government report, *Global Trends 2025, a Transformed World*, has the same world view as Obama's. They expect us to give up sovereignty for Global Governance.

Transnationalism means our Constitution is subordinate to International Law.

The Left promotes a global legal system.

Entitlements

"In general, the art of government consists of taking as much money as possible from one class of the citizens to give to another." - Voltaire (1764)

Reward for voting to keep Democrats in office.

Nanny State.

The federal government spent 19% of GDP, Gross Domestic Product in 1970, in 2011 it will spend 25% of GDP.[152]

Politicians essentially bought votes with promises of entitlement programs. The commitments they made cost more than the economy can afford or deliver.

Regarding Medicare and other give-away programs, the entitlement mentality of the recipients demand they continue to receive the benefits even though the country can't afford it.

The takers are unaffiliated applicants for public-sector funding.

The Left believes in the collective; government will do everything for you. When the Democrats control government you can be a degenerate, not produce anything, collect welfare, get food stamps, and live in government housing; the only thing they ask of you is to keep them in power so they can keep you dependant on them.

This is the new form of slavery; both types rob dignity and deprive hope.

The Democrat Party is the new plantation master on the Uncle Sam Plantation.[153] With hand extended, 'Massa, gives me whats you can.' Government housing projects are the slave quarters.

Dependency is too easy.

The national safety net has become a hammock[154] for the lazy.

Ben Franklin said, "I think the best way of doing good for the poor, is not making them easy in poverty, but leading or driving them out of it. … I observed in different countries, that the more public provisions were made for the poor, the less they provided for themselves, and of course became poorer. … There is no country in the world where so many provisions are established for them; … There is no country in the world in which the poor are more idle, dissolute, drunken and insolvent."[155]

President John F. Kennedy said, "Ask not what your country can do for you, but what you can do for your country."

The government really controls all of our live. The government enslaves both the dependants of the give-away programs and the taxpayers that are obligated to pay for it through taxes.

Health Care System

There has been a Liberal conspiracy for years to make the Health Care System be so expensive and screwed up that the country accepts socialized medicine, Universal Health Care.

The newly enacted Health Care system is designed to be so unprofitable for private insurance companies that they will drop out of that business, which is Obama and the Left's intent, so that by default we have the "single payer" system that they really want.

An Obama campaign promise was to have bi-partisanship and transparency by having CSPAN film everything. The Health Care

115

meeting on Sunday 12/6/09 was unprecedented, the President met in Congress with Democrats only and no CSPAN.

The Bill was not bipartisan; to merge both Bills, the House and Senate bypassed normal committees.

The Bribe Bill. Obama had to use expensive bribes to get Democrat legislators to vote for it.

On December 16, 2009 Obama said, "If we don't pass it, here's the guarantee ... the Federal Government will go bankrupt."

Obama forced this unpopular Bill on the country. The majority of the people do not want it. It is a flagrant disregard of the citizen's wishes.

One of the 16 enumerated powers given to the Federal government is the Commerce Clauses. Its original intent is to keep commerce regular between the states. The government has abused its use by expanding its meaning to include regulating everything. Obama is claiming it can force citizens to buy Health Care insurance. There was a Virginia court case in December 2010, about the Federal government forcing citizens to buy something they may not want or need, and taxing them if they don't buy it. The Fed's claim Health Care is a "good" and its acquisition is a commercial activity, thus regulable by Congress and they can regulate any human behavior they want and can tax anyone for anything they want. The State of Virginia has regulated the delivery of health care for 200 years and the Fed's can't take that power away. The ruling was that it is unconstitutional, the Federal government over stepped it bounds, that it can't make you buy something if you don't want it.[156]

The Union's shake-down of the Health Care Bill, came when they demanded they would not pay for their Cadillac coverage by threatening to not vote for Democrats.

Universal Health Care by definition is redistributive.

The Left's tactics of trying to sell the majority of the population on Health Care, etc. are to achieve socialistic ends.

Obama circumvented the vetting process and appointed Don Berwick as Head of Medicare and Medicaid. Berwick loves England's Health Care system of rationed care, where government officials make cold and calculated decisions on who lives or dies for the greater good of society.

Obama is going through a back door to implement shared end-of-life decisions, to make sure grandma is shovel-ready.

After the Death Panels were expressly removed from the Health Care legislation, they were reinstated during the Lame Duck session in December, 2010 by instituting a policy whereby Government pays doctors to have end-of-life discussions with their elderly patients.[157]

Obama is granting waivers, exempting selected unions, businesses, and swing States. In a nation that until now, had always followed the rule of law, Obama is violating that rule. If the laws don't apply to everyone, there is despotism.

There was Cash For Clunkers, this is Health Dare for Suckers.

"If you think health care is expensive now, wait until you see what it costs when it's free." - P.J. O'Rourke

"Universal opposition to Universal Health Care." - Glenn Beck

Mediscare.

Welfare

Since LBJ enacted Welfare in 1964 during his "war on poverty", it has cost nearly $16 trillion and is projected to cost another $10.3 trillion over the next ten years.[158] And not only are there still poor people, but there is a Welfare class that has been on welfare for generations. It has become a way of life, by design. There is a marriage penalty built into the benefits calculation rewarding single mothers. As a result, the number of children born out-of-wedlock has grown from 7% to over 40% during the life of the program. The out-of-wedlock birth rate among African-Americans is 72%, but then that is also their culture.

Bailouts

For their Wall Street buddies.

In Capitalism it is survival of the fittest, you let the ineffective fail.

In Socialism the government pumps taxpayer's money into inefficient businesses and prolongs the agony.

Education

Thomas Jefferson, going back to 1779 and thinking people would do what is best for the country, wrote of providing a suitable education for all its citizenry, enabling them to exercise oversight of self-government. By 1821, similar to today, he realized, "We are now trusting to those who are against us in position and principle, to fashion to their own form the minds and affections of our youth. ... This canker is eating on the vitals of our existence, and if not arrested at once, will be beyond remedy."[159]

The public schools' goal and that of most colleges is to indoctrinate instead of educate.

118

Teachers and professors use the class room as a political platform.

Students are pressured to repeat the teacher's liberal views or risk getting a bad grade is coercion.

The Liberals' agenda is to dumb down the voting population. Democrats want to keep their constituents dumb and dependant. They prey on the minorities.

Schools 41 States want to stop teaching cursive writing. The students won't be able to read signatures.

Education, or the lack there of, has been used throughout history to control people. The lack of education was used to keep some particular groups of people down. Some examples are: in the Middle-ages only monks were educated; for a couple of hundred years the English made it illegal for the Irish in Ireland to be educated; slaves in America were intentionally not educated; in NAZI Germany they burned unapproved books; and in Communist Russia and China it was illegal to read certain books. Today in America the government controls the education system. Teachers unions operate it and disseminate chosen biased information.

The citizens need to know their county's history to feel part of its National Identity. That is why the teachers aren't teaching the kids pertinent aspects of our history.

Steve Jobs, in his biography said, until the teachers unions were broken, there was almost no hope for education reform.

Because of the caliber of the unionized teachers, the U.S. public school system is the worst system in the industrialized world, even though it spends the most on it. The system is intended to dumb down the public so they, for example, are unaware of the Founding Fathers reasons for aspects of the Constitution. When people are educated, they become equals, because knowledge is power. For

119

the betterment of the country, there needs to be a separation of school and State. Our schools function as indoctrination centers.

The NEA, National Education Association, includes as recommended reading for students and teachers, Saul Alinsky's *Rules for Radicals*. The dedication in this book is to Lucifer.

Just as College Affirmative Action gives points for being a minority, it seems like teachers applying for a position are given points for being anti-American. Pro-American is like being Pro-Life to them.

The school books are sanitized of inflammatory language to not offend anyone. School books couch events according to political agendas. They present material the way they wish things ought to be.

In the mmm mmm mmm nursery rhyme song about Barack Hussein Obama very young school children were taught, it includes the stanza "equal work means equal pay". That sure sounds like something done in communist countries. Why here? Because the Left is targeting our kids!

The term "For the children" is the Left's justification for having fiscally irresponsible programs.

Vouchers would provide more diversity of ideas; it would broaden the scope of possibilities instead of a standardized single view. The three foundations of the ancient Greeks were education, athletics, and spiritualism. We are missing spiritualism in schools.

Since public education is so dominant, there is little completion as to a private alternative, there is no incentive for teachers to teach well.

The unfortunate kids that suffered through (wholistic) spelling, now need phonetic awareness.

Big Education. Some universities have billions of dollars in endowments and pay no taxes. Yet, as tuitions keep increasing faster than the rate of inflation, they do not use the endowment money to keep tuitions low, why? Tuitions have increased more than 900% since 1978. There is approximately $800 billion in outstanding student debt and the federal government is on the hook for most of it.[160] Could they be following the Cloward and Piven overburden the system to collapse the economy strategy?

A Liberal Arts education just teaches the students to be good little Liberals. Students should earn a degree in a subject that will enable them to pursue a profitable career.

School sports in America are based on age, not ability. Which team an individual is placed in should be based on their skill level and their athletic ability. A cookie cutter approach, lumping everyone together that is the same age isn't always fair for the individual nor the team. Children develop at different rates. Some are more athletic than others. Requiring an exceptionally gifted child to be on a team simply because they are the same age is limiting their potential. This follows the "lowest common denominator" approach, versus the "let the best excel" method. Europe allows skiers, for example, to progress based on their ability. To compete internationally, the U.S. should adopt a policy for athletes to be able to advance at their own rate.

Jared Lee Loughner, who attempted to assassinate Congresswoman Gabrielle Giffords in January 2011, attended a high school that is part of the Small Schools Workshop which was founded by Weatherman terrorist Bill Ayres. In 1995, when Obama was chairman of the Chicago Annenberg Challenge, CAC, it gave grants to the Workshop. Ayres was instrumental in recruiting Obama to serve as the chairman. Ayres also recruited Mike Klonsky to head the Workshop. Klonsky, identified as a Maoist,

121

traveled to Beijing, where he held friendly meetings with the Chinese leadership. This could explain why Loughner read the Communist Manifesto.[161] The CAC's agenda called for infusing students and their parents with a radical political commitment in favor of activism.[162]

The owner of Facebook, Mark Zuckerberg, gave $100 million to a New Jersey school district in September 2010. He would have gotten a lot more bang for his buck if he contributed the money to fiscally conservative political candidates that would improve the education system for the entire country. He will come to realize it isn't the amount of money per pupil that educates, it is good teachers and effective curriculum. There's a Zucker born every minute.

Courts

There is no justice in the U.S. Justice System.

If you are unhappy with the legal system and you voted for a Democrat, you are part of the problem. The Democrats appoint liberal judges.

The Democrats going against the will of the majority of the voters sue and the Liberal judges they appointed overturn elections: Florida 2000 presidential election; California Propositions: 8 Marriage Protection Act, 187 denied public services to undocumented immigrants, 208 political finance reform, and 227 English Language in Public Schools; Wisconsin's collective bargaining law invalidated are but a few examples. Vote anyway you want; the Democrats will just keep doing what they want as if you don't exist. They are insistent on getting their way because they think they know better than you. Seem a little like *Animal Farm*?

Obama, through his Attorney General, Eric Holder, doesn't

enforce laws he doesn't agree with, like the Defense of Marriage Act. Obama is deteriorating the Rule of Law.

Democrats don't want criminals to be jailed or punished in any way.

Criminals have more rights than their victims. A criminal's right to a fair trial can come to override the injustice to his victim.

Obama's Health Care program won't spend the money to prolong grandma's life, but the Liberals have taxpayers pay for incarcerating murderers on death row for 30 years.

By using the practice of case law instead of abiding by strict adherence to the Constitution, the Courts effectively rewrite the Constitution case by case. The law continually gets further and further from original intent.

Rent Control Laws, like those in San Francisco, prevent the owner from evicting a tenant even if the owner wants to use the property for themselves. The law is structured so that the evil rich owner must provide lodging for the poor helpless tenant no matter what.

The Democrats are Borking (filibuster and block) Republican nominees for judgeships. Federal Judges are appointed for life.

Trail Lawyers

You can sue some of the people some of the time, and sue some of the people all of the time, but you can't sue all of the people all of the time, yet!

The legal system allows anyone to sue anybody for anything, regardless of how ridiculous, outrageous or frivolous the claim may be. The sued party must then defend itself, consuming valuable time, man-hours and hard earned money.

The O.J. Dream Team = Slime Team, accomplices to murder.

There was a lawsuit involving a shooting at a McDonald's and the lawyer sued the gun company and McDonald's because both were "too easy to get to." So, with that same reasoning, if someone drowns, why not sue God because there is so much water and it is just "too easy to get to."

ACLU

American Criminal Larceny Umbrella.

On September 30, 2011 Obama had two U.S. citizens murdered in Yemen, which is a violation of the Constitution and International law. There was no due process, no Miranda Rights read, no evidence, no trial, and no ACLU objections.

I wish these Leftist pigs would do time for every crime committed by the scum they got exonerated.

Civil Rights

The Left uses race as a weapon, claiming Civil Rights infringements in order to shut opponents up and get their way without dissent.

Constitutional Rights

The Democrat Leftists have been and are eroding our Rights and Liberties:

- The First Amendment – You've got a right to say it, even if what you say isn't right.
- The Second Amendment. The Democrats do not believe in law abiding citizens owning guns.

"Faced with a hostile Congress to even slight restrictions to the Second Amendment, the Obama Administration is exploring potential changes to gun laws that can be secured strictly through Executive action…"[163]

Cass Sunstein, Regulation Czar, said, "We ought to ban hunting, if there isn't a purpose other than sport or fun. That should be against the law."[164]

"The strongest reason for the people to retain the right to keep and bear arms is, as a last resort, to protect themselves against tyranny in government." - attributed to Thomas Jefferson.

The Fourth Amendment is based on one of the precepts in the Magna Carta from 1215, that a man's home is his castle and the authorities can't enter without having a search warrant.[165]

Search and seizure – In September 2003, the Minnesota Supreme Court ruled that game wardens can search boats without the consent of the owner and without probable cause. The court put the protection of natural resources ahead of the Fourth Amendment protection against unreasonable search and seizure.

The Patriot Act violates the Fourth Amendment protections. Sometimes people give up their rights for added security.

The Kelo vs. New London, Connecticut case the Supreme Court ruled on in 2005 expanded the concept of eminent domain from the limitation of "public use" to the much broader "public purpose."[166] This enables towns to take private property from homeowners and small businesses to give the property to large corporations in order to increase tax revenues. The justification used was that the project was a public use to further economic development under the Takings Clause of the Fifth Amendment.[167] In this situation the developer couldn't get financing, leaving the home site a vacant lot.

Eminent Domain should more appropriately be referred to as Enema Domain.

The Democrats want to severely restrict individual property rights. The Liberals don't believe in individuals having property rights.

Thomas Jefferson envisioned the States would act as sentinels of the liberty of the people; they would protect the people from unconstitutional overreaches by the Federal government. The 10th Amendment states: "The powers not delegated to the United States by the Constitution, nor prohibited by it to the States, are reserved to the States respectively, or to the people." States have the right to nullify Federal Law. The Federal government can't tell citizens they are required to buy a product against their will. The people have the power, so applause to Missouri State Senator Jane Cunningham for placing on the ballot, and winning with a 71% vote, to exempt its citizens from Health Care. Some are proposing a call for an Amendment Convention. If States are recognized as having the sovereignty they are afforded in the Constitution, then it could be an end to unfunded mandates by the Federal government because the States wouldn't go along with it.

The Fourteenth Amendment provides for not denying any person the equal protection of the laws.

The Supremacy Clause of the Constitution means the Constitution and laws in pursuance thereof is the supreme law of the land.

The International Court of Justice

Based in The Hague, Belgium.

Globalism. A way for small insignificant countries to punish America and other countries that are more important than themselves.

The United Nations

A second attempt at the League of Nations, Woodrow Wilson's baby. It is the Progressives' dream to have a one world government.

An effort to bring about global governance.

There are calls for the U.N. to have "effective governance of the High Seas."

The U.N.'s charter was signed in 1945. This international organization of 192 Member States is committed to maintaining international peace and security, promoting social progress, and human rights. It works on issues of the environment, gender equality, and the advancement of women.[168]

A U.N. resolution led to the partition of Palestine in 1947.

An irrelevant organization.

A joke.

Useless.

They did nothing to effectively solve the genocides in Rwanda, Sudan and Darfur.

They do not condemn Communist China's occupation and cultural destruction of Tibet.

When Northern Ireland had British troops and Ulstermen battling the native people for many years, they did not consider that a problem.

The United Nations is a corrupt organization, i.e., its Oil-for-Food scandal in Iraq; and the Ammo dump – giving news to CBS and the New York Times in order to influence U.S. elections and help John Kerry; and hundreds of U.N. Peacekeeping Forces have been investigated around the world for sexual exploitation.

The U.N. places Member States as heads of committees that are widely known for abuses of that issue, like placing China on the Human Rights Council. It is a complete joke.

Since the 1960's the Third World nations members have been anti-American. We foolishly pay the largest percentage of the annual budget. We also give the same countries foreign aid that vote against us in the U.N. Some, like Obama, use the U.N.'s supposed authority to erode the sovereignty of the United States.

The U.S. was being assessed 25% of the UN's annual budget. In 2011 the U.S. was assessed 22% of the UN's annual budget.[169]

World Bank

According to the World Bank website, it is part of World Bank Group, WBG formed in 1945. WBG is a group of five international development institutions owned by member governments that focuses on developing countries. It is part of the United Nations. It makes loans to poor countries at preferential rates and gives grants to the poorest countries. World Bank's mission is to fight poverty. It advances the vision of inclusive and sustainable globalization. It has more than 10,000 employees in over 100 countries worldwide.[170] Until 1967 it had been fiscally conservative. Since then the size and number of loans has greatly increased. Loans expanded from infrastructure needs to social services. Environmental groups and Leftist interests were included in lending decisions. Projects now include green concerns. There is now the Clean Technology Fund and the Clean Air Initiative. There is an increasing emphasis on climate change. Member countries pledged tens of billions of dollars in aid for 80 of the poorest countries. It has committed a couple of billions of dollars to fight AIDS. The Leftists interests criticize it for using free market policies, having a limited focus on global governance and having a limited recognition of rights to food and land. I guess getting hundreds of millions of dollars for free isn't good enough if they have to employ capitalist principles.

IMF, International Monetary Fund

The IMF began operations in 1947. It is a global entity charged with overseeing the international monetary system. There are 187 member nations. The USA contributes by far the most at 17%, China 8%, and France 3.8% of funding. In 2009 it lent $60 billion to emerging market countries.[171] It gives highly leveraged loans to poor countries to facilitate development. The organization now wants to take the voting power away from the developed nations and give it to the emerging nations. Yet another redistribution of wealth vehicle on a global scale. They just want to bleed us dry.

Our tax dollars, that partially fund the IMF, are spent to bail out Greece and other failed socialistic countries.

In April 2010, the IMF proposed a tax on all financial institutions, a 'financial activities tax.'

Dominique Strauss-Kahn, head of the IMF until the Spring of 2011, allegedly attempted to rape a minority that was a New York hotel housekeeper. She may have been setting him up to blackmail him for money. It's odd he didn't spot that, since he had successfully been raping the U.S. of money to give to minorities for years.

WTO, World Trade Organization

It began in 1995, replacing GATT (the General Agreement on Tariffs and Trade), which started in 1948. The WTO is a forum for governments to negotiate trade agreements. The purpose is to help trade flow freely by ensuring having transparent international trade policies. Since 2001 its goal is to improve the welfare of the peoples of the member countries.[172]

Taxes

The Infernal Revenue Service.

The Eternal Revenue Service.

In the past, Kings gave away their power in return for money. Today, government keeps taking your power and your money.

Some on the Left refer to taxes as contributions, but many on the Left don't contribute.

The tax code structure punishes success. Democrats are more interested in punishing success than raising revenue as evidenced by their votes to not extend the Bush tax cuts.

The Democrats want to tax the rich and give it to people that won't work.

The Government doesn't earn money, it simply prints it.

The Government does not earn money, it passes enforceable tax laws that citizens are coerced to abide by, to bring in revenue. Unfortunately, Government has grown so large, its bureaucracies are so inefficient, its regulations so burdensome and the progressive tax structure designed for the redistribution of wealth so punitive, it has gone far beyond the original purpose to defend the Country and regulate Commerce.

There are Leftists that are proposing having a Global Tax.

The USA has overspent and is broke, but instead of reducing spending and living within our means, we are printing more money to spend. We are borrowing from producer nations like China, in the sense that they are buying our Treasury Notes, which is our debt. The USA, for the most part, is no longer a manufacturing country, we are just consumers. So, we are spending but not producing anything to make money to cover our debts. That is a recipe for bankruptcy. China's "President" said the U.S. dollar dominated currency system is a product of the past.[173] China is forging a post-American globalization.[174]

Regulations

The Financial Regulation Bill enacted in the summer of 2010, can shut down a business that is a perceived threat to the government. The SEC, Securities and Exchange Commission, is now exempt from the Freedom of Information Act, so the public cannot find out what is going on. This is setting up for some really scary abuses of power and government seizure of control.

Unions

Union's have priced their workers out of a job. Union members, wake up!

A good parasite doesn't kill its host.

When the high wage and benefits exceed a sustainable level, the business either goes broke or moves to a location where the cost to operate is less.

A union is an organization of calculating, anti-business people who coerce workers into threatening employers to pay unrealistic wages and benefits. Businesses are then forced to raise prices. This goes on everywhere and is inflationary. So, when the new pay raise no longer has the same buying power, the union strikes again to demands even higher wages. If the price of the product is no longer competitive, the business closes or goes out of the country where labor is cheap. The union has just duped the worker into pricing himself out of a job. The anti-capitalists have damaged the economy and the country that much more.

Unions are Labor Cartels whose function is to reduce the amount of labor in an industry in order to drive up wages for those that still have a job.[175]

Unions pressure the legislators they were able to get elected to have policies of compulsory unionism.

Unions wrap themselves in the American flag. They have always been and still are comprised of Communists, Socialists, Democrats and Organized Crime. The leadership is anything but for America, even though most of the members are. The members want job security. The Union bosses use their members as pawns in order to achieve their political agenda. The Unions' goal is self explanatory "Workers of the world unite".

Unions are going global, for political power not for the benefit of their members.

SEIU, State Employees International Union, President Andy Stern in 2007 said, "People are making investments in politics, and they expect a return on their investments. There's not ideology involved in corporations. They're looking for returns on their investments. ... Let's just publicly finance these elections ... unless we want people investing in politics ... we're going to have a distorted political system. I'm totally involved in distorting the political system, you know, with contributions. That's what we've become in America, so we have to do that."[176]

In the November 2, 2010 mid-term elections, the four biggest Unions were spent over $200 million to get Democrats elected.

132

Unions should be taxed. Why aren't they?

Half of the top ten biggest donors to politicians are unions. They get Democrats elected; then the elected officials negotiate the public sector compensation and benefits favorably as a payback. The taxpayers suffer. Also, union workers are paid by seniority not by effort, productivity or efficiency. So, they can get by with doing the least amount possible.[177]

California, like France, is run by Public Sector Unions. When Schwarzenegger began as Governor, he had five fiscally responsible propositions to cap spending that he put on the ballot in order to go around the unions. The unions, teachers, SEIU, State Employees International Union, prison guards, etc., have so much influence and money to spend on ads, they defeated all five propositions even though passage would have been better for the State. That was the point when it became obvious that the unions have way too much power.

During the horrific fires in California in October of 2003, that burned over 740,000 acres, destroyed over 4,500 homes, and claimed 22 lives, Governor Davis, being loyal to Unions, did not ask for the help from the military that has a large presence in the area. Areas that supported him in the Recall Election were sent help first. Politics is more important to Democrats than citizen's lives and safety.

Unions were originally created to stop abuses, now it is the opposite. The Unions are doing the harm, like making it impossible to fire bad teachers.

In mid-August, Congress passed a $26 billion gift to teachers and Health Care workers, both are unionized.

Unions are bankrupting the country through unfunded pensions and benefits.

Obama gave Wisconsin a whopping 10% of the Stimulus money. Of that $700 million, $600 million went to public service unions.

The Stimulus was to stimulate the union's coffers.

Obama's American's Jobs Act, is just more money for unions.

Look out for the Union label.

12% of workers are in Unions.

When you see a bum with an "out of work" sign, try to guess what union he belonged to.

Chandler, owner and editor of the LA Times, referred to Union workers as bums.

NAFTA in Spanish means, kiss your job good-bye.

The 10/2/10 One Nation Rally

Obama sent out an encouraging e-mail to the endorsing organizations through his Organizing For America.

Union members were required to attend.

It was funded by the Tides Foundation. Details about Tides are in Part 8.

Some of the 400 organizations endorsing the event:

- Communist Party USA
- Democratic Socialists of America
- International Socialist Organization
- Progressive Democrats of America
- SEIU, AFL-CIO, UAW, Teamsters, United Steel Workers

- National Council of La Raza
- National Education Association, American Federation of Teachers
- NAACP
- Solidarity
- Apollo Alliance
- Peace and Freedom Party
- Sierra Club, National Wildlife Federation,
- NYC Environmental Justice Alliance
- Green For All, (Van Jones's group)
- Organizing For America, (Obama's group)
- Sojourners, (Obama's Marxist preacher Jim Wallace's group)
- Code Pink, (ties to Hamas)
- Campus Progress, (a George Soros group)
- Jeremiah Wright's church

Glenn Beck's 8/28/10 Rally was one nation under God, the 10/2/10 Rally is One Nation with the Devil.

One attendee spoke of violence against the capitalist class, a civil war between the classes.[178]

This supposedly Eco-friendly crowd left behind tons of garbage, Glenn Beck's Rally left none.

The Media

The Main Stream Media's principles aren't in the main stream.

The Lame Stream Media.

The Old Stream Media.[179]

The Media Industrial Complex.[180]

Vicious attacks from the Main Stream Media.

Liberals are in the minority, but because they control the major media outlets they use propaganda to make their ideas seem like it is what the majority of Americans believe, but it is not. A Gallop Poll in October, 2009 revealed people in the U.S. consider themselves: 20% Liberal, 40% conservative, and 36% moderate.[181]

The Liberal Politicians have an incestuous relationship with the Media. The Mainstream Media is a mouthpiece for the Democrat Party. They are complicit.

The Mainstream Media is a "pit of hatred" like what they predicted Glenn Beck's 8/28/10 Restoring Honor Rally to be, but wasn't.

The Mainstream Media are the hate mongers for falsely characterizing and portraying the Tea Party Movement as hate mongers.

The Mainstream Media and the Democrat Party's tactic is to falsely label everyone on the Right a racist and a hate monger, when in reality the Left is full of hate and some Blacks are clearly racists.

I can't stand hearing reporters pronouncing Latin names with a Spanish accent. Why don't they do that for every ethnic group? Say Gov. Arnold Schwarzenegger with a strong Austrian accent.

The New York Times published damaging information from Wikileaks, but regarding Climategate, the inconvenient truth is they wrote, "The documents appear to have been acquired illegally and contain all manner of private information and statements that were never intended for the public eye, so they won't be posted here."[182] What hypocrites!

Weinergate, treatment of the tweet photo of New York Democrat Representative Anthony Weiner's wiener demonstrates the bias in the liberal media. The Democrats preference was to keep Weiner under wraps, but the truth about Weiner should have come out straight up. If you've ever heard him speak, you realize that Weiner is really a prick.

The Mainstream Media perpetuates the Left's stereotypical depiction of the Tea Party as violent, which they are not. As in the incident when Congresswoman Gabrielle Giffords and others were shot, the media immediately assumed the assailant was a Tea Party member. It turned out that the mentally deranged Jared Lee Loughner did not listen to talk radio and was not on the Right politically. He, on the contrary, was the opposite of a conservative. He reportedly burned the American flag, read the Communist Manifesto, was an atheist, and worshiped the Devil. According to Caitie Parker, a classmate, "He was left wing, quite liberal." The Media falsely accuses the Right of being violent because that is the image the Left wants the general public to associate them as. The fact is, most of the violent nuts are from the Left, like the guy that flew a plane into the IRS building in Texas in February, 2010 and the Florida school board shooting in the winter of 2010. Many on the Left are paranoids like Loughner. Shortly after Obama called for civility, a Left wing activist, James Eric Fuller, made a public death threat to a Tea Party spokesman. Republican Wisconsin legislators had death threats made against them during the union protests in February, 2011. One message from a female union teacher read, "We have all planned to assult (sic) you by arriving at your house and putting a nice little bullet in your head."[183] It would be nice if the country could live up to the expectations of 9 year-old Christina Green that was killed the day Congresswoman Giffords was shot.

The Mainstream Media never reported the assassination attempt on Missouri Governor, Jay Nixon, on September 14, 2010, because the African American college student assailant was a self-described Leftist radical who was into environmental extremism, anti-capitalism, was Christophobic and a fan of Che Guevara.[184]

For you Liberals that thought Baghdad Bob, Iraq's Minister of Information, was such a joke, now you know how the rest of us think when we watch the Nightly News by the original three broadcast companies. The difference is, we know we are being lied to after hearing the truth from Rush Limbaugh earlier in the day and then listening to slants and spin, and recognizing the omissions from their reports, especially by the then Clinton defenders.

Iraq's Minister of Misinformation, Baghdad Bob, didn't lie any more than any Clinton defender.

When you hear something outrageous on the American news, point out to others that it sounds like the Iraqi News Network or the Iraqi Information Ministry News Network.

The suicide bomber that killed 35 and wounded 180 in a Moscow airport in January, 2011 was an Islamist from the southern Caucuses. The Media rarely tells you that the Chechen Rebels are Muslims.

The Main Stream Media came up with the concept of Red States and Blue States to graphically show political races on a map. They purposefully used red for Republicans so that color would not be used to associate Democrats with Communists, as red is throughout the world. Since Republicans have been assigned that color, you can think of it in connection with red-blooded Americans. You can think of the Left as so far from God's warmth they are freezing blue.

The Left uses Aesopian Language, double talk, as a deceptive device. They say one thing and mean another. To them the word "democracy" means the domination by the communist state.[185]

The Left no longer has a monopoly on the media.

This book is part of the 'new media' that educates the public and encourages self-education about the Constitution and how the Left works.

In WWII, the slogan "loose lips sink ships", made everyone cautious not to give away our troop's location to the enemy. CNN broadcasting from Baghdad during the Gulf War was used by Iraq to redirect their weapons to be more accurate. After 9/11, the Liberal media pointed out every conceivable weakness in the U.S. for Terrorists to attack. This is aiding and abetting the enemy.

The San Francisco <u>Comical</u> (Chronicle).

CNN = Clinton News Network.

CBS News = Communist Broadcast System

NBC News' Tom Brokejaw.

Walter Cronkadile

Chris Mathews' Slime ball

Keith Oberdork

Farce the Nation

NPR=National Propaganda Radio, National Progressive Radio, National Political correctness Radio

ABC News' Dan Rather-than-what; Dan Blather, the Un-American Broadcast System.

Eason Jordan of CNN revealed in an interview that he knew of Iraq's torture chambers and tactics since the first Gulf War.[186]

139

What kind of an uncompassionate slim-ball would keep that to himself?

Newsweek ran a false story of a Qur'an being flushed down a toilet by an interrogator at Guantanamo; at least 15 people were killed as a result. They later retracted the story; oh gee sorry we caused people to die because of our bull sh!t story. Newsweek should be flushed down the toilet, after first using its pages appropriately.

Activists

Malcontents.

People with a hair up their ass.

The Anti-War Movement

Peace monger.

Isn't it interesting that the Conscientious Objectors that avoided the Draft in the Vietnam era by refusing to use a gun and instead worked at a Post Office are the ones that later went "Postal" and shot all their co-workers.

The anti-war protesters were completely ineffective in preventing the war in Iraq. They only identified themselves as being anti-American.

Protesters for the former Kosovo were as much as advancing through song, "All we are saying, is give war a chance."

The anti-war protesters are overly concerned about prisoners at Abu Ghraib having the guards put panties on their heads. The terrorist's prisoners no longer have heads to put panties on. Which is worse?

Gun Control

The Second Amendment is the teeth to ensure the exercise of First Amendment rights.

The election Obama caused more gun and ammunition sales than at any other time in recent memory.

The American Flag

The Left never regards the American flag with reverence; they use it to burn and spit on.

The Pledge of Allegiance

The Left does not pledge its allegiance to America, it pledges its allegiance to America's destruction.

Jimmy Carter appointed Liberal Judge Lawrence Karlton who ruled that in California a mandatory Pledge of Allegiance is unconstitutional in public schools. Students can opt out because God is mentioned.

Right Wing

In the Liberal's mind, the following right wing values are bad:

- traditional values
- belief in God
- adhere to the U.S. Constitution
- exercise their Second Amendment rights

Liberals label citizens with traditional, mainstream, patriotic, American values as right wing nuts.

The Leftists would consider George Washington a right wing extremist.

141

McCarthyism

The label the Left associates people with, when the Left's un-American activities and affiliations are discovered.

Religion

"Religious Right" vs. "Immoral Left"

The separation of church and state myth: The phrase separation of church and state does not exist in the U.S. Constitution. The purposeful distortion takes its roots from something Thomas Jefferson wrote in a letter. The establishment clause in the First Amendment reads "Congress shall make no law respecting an establishment of religion, or prohibiting the free exercise thereof." The Founders experience with England was a State sanctioned religion that required tithe, which was the same as taxing people. They knew that a State run religion was a way to control people's behavior and did not allow individuals the freedom to practice a different faith.

The U.S. Constitution guarantees "Freedom of Religion". Liberals are forcing Christians to conform to pro-abortion, in order to be appointed to a Judgeship. Aren't they prohibiting the free exercise of religion? They apply a religious test on the confirmation of judges.

Social Justice is being preached in churches today by liberal leaning clergy. The Left has infiltrated religion just as they have in schools, the media, the judicial system, charitable foundations and politics.

The Left fears religion like Dracula fears a cross.

"God is on your side, if you are on his side." - Glenn Beck

142

The Middle East is the epicenter of religious zealots and religious fanaticism.

Be leery of religions that believe they are the only ones that are allowed in Heaven.

There are intolerant: Christians, Jews, Muslims, Atheists, Agnostics, etc.

Jews

The Torah states the Messiah will be borne by a Jewish female. With so many Jews having abortions, how many times has the Messiah tried to come into the world only to be aborted? Guilt!

The Jewish religion instructs women to bear as many children as possible. So why are most Jews pro-abortion?

Liberal Jews speak of diversity, being inclusive, and are all for humanitarianism, but that is only while here on Earth, because they believe they are the only ones allowed into Heaven. I guess they feel sorry for the poor slobs that are forbidden entry. But if heaven is comprised of only Jews, I'm not sure I would describe such a place as heaven. New York, Miami, and Israel are certainly not my vision of heaven.

My three favorite Jews: Jesus, Barry Goldwater and Charlton Hesston.

In 2000, Pope John Paul II initiated a very inclusive event, having Jews in a Vatican Holocaust Remembrance.   He inducted conductor Levine into the highest Catholic Order.   Around the same time, when the Pope was in Israel, the TV news showed a clip of an old Jewish lady saying the Pope is the enemy.

The Jews didn't learn from the Holocaust to not persecute, because that is what they are doing to the Palestinians.

143

Sodom and Gomorrah was in Israel wasn't it?

Why is it okay to be anti-Christian but not be anti-Semitic?

Jews have a huge influence in this country, it might be said that they control it. They seem to control the: banks, jewelry industry, media, and film industry. They are very prevalent in the legal system, the financial system, medicine and politics. Most are Jews first, so America is somewhere down the list. If quotas based on population proportions were implemented like they try to do for Blacks, there would need to be a major redistribution of occupations.

Let's see if the Jews in the Far-Left will continue to vote for Obama after he advocated having Israel return to their pre-1967 borders.

There is a new Green Product, recycled toilet paper; Jews have been doing that for years.

U.N. Resolution 181 called for Israel's existence in 1949. Before that the area was Palestine.

Jews chose Barabbas and the Golden Calf.

Christians:

Regarding the Left-leaning advertisements asking, "What would Jesus drive?" Let's see, a Jew with 12 disciples; how about a stretch Yugo.

Andrea Mitchell said the rains at Ted Kennedy's funeral were God crying. They were probably tears of laughter over Teddy's hypocritical letter to the Pope.

B.C. = Before Christ, A.D. = After Dat.

144

A skydiver during Rapture will see all sorts of people going up past him.

On August 13, 2010, in reference to Obama's support of a mosque being built at Ground Zero, the White House spokesman said, "As President it's his responsibility to stand up for the Constitutional principal of religious freedom and equal treatment for all Americans." So, why not also support Nativity scenes?

Since Baptist do not believe Catholics can go to heaven because they are baptized when babies not when they are adults, St. Peter at the Pearly Gates would say to the Pope, you led a good life and your beliefs in Jesus are really close, but you didn't get the baptism thing exactly right, I'm sorry but I just can't let you in.

The Catholic Church's values haven't changed; the criticism of Pope Benedict shows what a detrimental affect Leftist Ideology has had on many people.

When King Henry VIII 1509-1547 burned Catholic monks at the stake, they then became Friars.

What is with this fish symbol on the back of cars, I believe in fish?

When Earth is visited by space aliens, the first question should be, have you come across planets inhabited only by Mormons?

To defeat ignorance, tyranny, and fanaticism, are the three eternal enemies of the free mind of the Free Mason. Seek light to become an enlightened citizen is their mantra.

Rachel Scott, a 17 year-old student at Columbine High School in Littleton, CO., in April 1999, had already been struck by several bullets when her assailant asked her if she believed in God. Her profession of faith resulted in her execution-style slaying. She is a modern day Christian martyr. Information on www.rachelschallenge.org.

145

Liberation Theology: Obama was not a Christian until at the age of 26, after catching flak for not attending a church while trying to build coalitions of Black churches as a community organizer.[187] Obama went to Reverend Jeremiah Wright's church and heard Wright's sermon 'The Audacity of Hope', after which he continued to attend that church for 20 years.

Liberation Theology is a perversion of Christianity. There is also Liberation Philosophy, both of which are political theologies based on Marxism and racism from the 1960's. Obama speaks of "collective salvation," which is a tenet of Liberation Theology, as opposed to individual salvation, which is a Christian belief. Liberation Theology asserts that liberation of the oppressed from unjust economic, political or social conditions must come in the form of reparations from Whites. Salvation for Whites is realized from minorities achieving economic and political parody via redistribution of wealth and Whites confessing and repenting for being racists. Pope Benedict XVI wrote, "Whenever politics tries to be redemptive … where it wishes to do the work of God, it becomes, not divine, but demonic."[188]

Muslims:

Their wildest wish come true would be an Israeli Civil War.

The reason the Islamists want to kill Westerners so much is because of the immoral behavior and beliefs of the Liberals.

Rewards murder with 72 virgins. Actually the word virgin was misinterpreted, it really rewards with 72 raisins. Imagine the surprise and disappointment when he realizes he will spend eternity with a bunch of raisins instead of 72 virgins.

The Islamist's equivalent to the Ten Commandments I guess includes, thou shalt kill, thou shalt revere suicide bombers, and thou shalt not covet they neighbors wife wearing a spandex burka.

146

The Qur'an says women should dress modestly and that they should <u>not</u> cover their faces. So, the whole Burka Barbie idea isn't going to be true to Islam, darn.

Liberals consider it acceptable "art" to have a crucifix in urine and to have a painting of the Virgin Mary smeared with elephant dung, but a cartoon of Mohammed justifies death? Where's the tolerance?

How people dealt with the Tsunami in Indonesia in 2004, a Muslim country, is very telling. America is the most generous country on Earth and earned an A+ in its efforts to help. Indonesia deserves a D-. They were ungrateful and wanted our troops out of there as soon as possible.

Islam started when Mohamed had a revelation in 610 AD. They still want to live like it was in the 600's.

A Caliphate is a theocracy empire. This would be many Islamic countries unifying under one new world order. The last Caliphate ended with the Ottoman Empire in 1923. The Islamic Brotherhood was formed in Egypt in the 1928; they want to restore the Caliph and impose Islam on the entire world through Shariah Law.

Shariah Law is a political program that for approximately 1,000 years the Muslim authorities believe must be imposed on the entire world, to be ruled by a theocracy, a Caliph, via Jihad, waged by violence or by stealth ways.[189]

Anjen Choudary with Islam4UK said, "We do believe as Muslims, the East and West will be one day governed by the Shariah.

Indeed we believe that one day the flag of Islam will fly over the White House."[190]

There are many branches of the Muslim Brotherhood in America under various names, like the Muslim American Society.

147

The Muslim Brotherhood's stated goal in the U.S.: "The Brotherhood must understand that their work in America is a kind of grand Jihad in eliminating and destroying the Western civilization from within and sabotaging its miserable home by their hands and the hands of the believers so that it is eliminated and God's religion is made victorious above all other religions."[191]

Mosques in America have been infiltrated by radicals. Political Islam is converting moderate Muslims to become home grown terrorists. The radicalization of Muslims is growing.

Pew Research questioning males, 18 to 33years old coming out of mosques in America, reported 25% agree with suicide bombings.

There are Islamic schools in the USA that are owned and run by Saudi Arabia, like the Islamic Saudi Academy; that are breeding grounds for potential terrorists.

There are 826,000 foreigners in the U.S. on student visas, 35,000 are from Saudi Arabia.[192]

Wikileaks in November, 2010 revealed that Saudi Arabian donors remain the chief financiers of Sunni militant groups like al-Qaeda.[193] The Saudis are two faced liars. They are religious fanatics.

"Jihad, aided and abetted by some Muslim nations, is the biggest threat on the planet."-Bill O'Reilly

There are approximately two million Muslims in the USA.

The G8 gave $40 billion, partially from your tax dollars, to the Arab Spring movement.[194] Glenn Beck rightly predicts that Islamists will use the goal of the liberation of Palestine as an excuse to destroy Israel, capitalism, and the U.S.

148

Islamists are against any free speech. They consider any criticism of Islamic terror to be blasphemy and in need of being outlawed. Politically Correct attitudes just appease their extreme and abhorrent practices. Critics are charged with offending a religion or ethnicity. Islam is to be inoculated from inspection, criticism and condemnation.[195]

It is not Politically Correct to profile Muslims, so everyone must endure intrusive screenings at airports.

Communism goes against human nature and must force people to abide by it edicts, so it eventually can be overcome. Islam is a religion. Religion is at its follower's core. Believers will fight to the death to defend their religion, so it is impossible to persuade them to change. Militant Islamists want to impose Shariah Law on the rest of the world. Americans love and will defend freedom and liberty to the death. This truly will be a battle of good versus Evil.[196]

Islam and its values are completely incompatible with America's values of women's rights, freedom of religion, anti-murder, etc. We should learn from history, Islam conquered parts of Europe, Africa, and the Middle East. Even though it will be hard and unpleasant now, it will be much more difficult in the future to break the bonds of slavery from Authoritarian Rule. Islam (and Unions) should be ousted from America now.

Eastern Religions:

Reincarnation is analogous to the concept of Purgatory. Catholics believe your soul is a part of you at conception and when you die, if you have sins to work off, your soul goes to Purgatory, once you have done your penance you get to go to heaven. Reincarnation is very similar. Your soul is a part of you at conception and when you die, if you have not attained nirvana, or call it perfection, your soul, in another body, comes back to live on Earth again until you learn to be a good enough person that you attain nirvana, which is

149

essentially like going to heaven. Reincarnation sets a standard to achieve, that your soul doesn't go to heaven until you are a perfect person. Christians believe in God's forgiveness. So, a murderer can live the worst life imaginable, but just before he dies, if he has an authentic change of heart, he can ask for forgiveness, be granted salvation, and be allowed to spend eternity in heaven. That is like social promotion, where Tyron can't read but is graduated from High School illiterate. If that is the case, heaven is the same as Earth, filled with imperfect souls. Eastern religions believe only souls that have attained perfection earn and deserve nirvana. So, if a murderer did truly learn that that single immoral act was wrong, he would still come back to learn to correct all the other sins of his life.

Atheists:

My favorite tombstone - Here lies an Atheist, all dressed up and nowhere to go.

It is okay to make fun of Atheists because they can't come back to haunt you.

If what you believe in is what happens to you after death, at least when we get to heaven we will be rid of those damn Atheists!

Evil people on their deathbed are encouraged to "go toward the red light".

There are those that attack God, family, America, etc. around the clock.

Unfortunately, the degree to which the Liberals have gotten their way in the courts, with all the secular laws passed, the State Religion is essentially Atheism.

The further you are to the Left, the further you are from God. Communists are atheists.

The Chinese Communist atheists, continuing under Chairman Hu, have intentionally ruined the Tibetan way of life. Tibet, the secluded and once forbidden area to foreigners, now has a railroad for swarms of tourist to disrupt their lifestyle. Its people are on a welfare system for the intent to cause them to lose their culture and discontinue the traditional ways of providing for themselves. The Communists persecute and oppress the Tibetans. The Communist forced the Tibetan spiritual leader to leave the country in 1959. As a result of Chinese occupation, approximately one million Tibetans have died and six thousand monasteries have been destroyed. The atheists have tried their best to destroy the most spiritual place on Earth.[197]

Since 84% of Americans believe in God, why let a small portion of the population determine things?   Hey atheists, you're in the minority, so shut the f#*k up!

In General:

Life on Earth is a class room, God presents challenges, how you deal with them is the test.

Strive to attain these qualities in order to become a better person: honesty, integrity, fairness, compassion, virtue, courage, hard work, perseverance, humility, valor, empathy, sincerity, generosity, charity, patience, mercy, gratitude, chastity (just kidding), practice moderation, be just, be trustworthy, be industrious, be determined, be optimistic, be loving, do no evil, and have faith.

In general, do unto others as you would have them do unto you.

Evolution

Liberals believe in Evolution, but don't believe in competition or practicing survival of the fittest in sports or in life. Some Conservatives believe in Creation and know that the economy is always changing, that a change in tax policy is not a static event. These two outlooks are counterintuitive.

The way creation versus evolution is presented is black and white. It seems more likely that God created the universe many billions of years ago and set in place the laws of physics, meaning properties of gravity, etc. plus the mechanism of evolution. The world and everything in it is constantly changing, there is nothing in our experience to indicate that anything stays the same. It is a huge stretch to not believe evolution is in effect. It is a very empty universe to not believe God created it and everything in it.

A species causing its own extinction – Dodo sapiens.

The Ten Commandments

Liberals don't want tax dollars spent on the Ten Commandments in schools, but do want to spend tax dollars on so called art that defiles Christian symbols, like a crucifix in urine.

Since the Ten Commandments have seemingly been expunged from society, here they are:

1. I, the Lord, am your God. Thou shall not have other gods before me.
2. Thou shall not make for yourself an idol.
3. Thou shall not take the name of the Lord, your God, in vain.
4. Remember to keep holy the Sabbath day.
5. Honor your father and your mother.
6. Thou shall not murder.

7. Thou shall not commit adultery.
8. Thou shall not steal.
9. Thou shall not bear false witness against your neighbor.
10. Thou shall not covet your neighbor's house. Thou shall not covet your neighbor's wife, nor his male or female slave, nor his ox or ass, nor anything else that belongs to him.

Multiculturalism

Multiculturalism = anti-assimilation.

Identity politics.

It excludes by overemphasizing rather than de-emphasizing the categories that keep us from seeing each other as just humans. - Norah Vincent

Apparently al-Qaeda and the Taliban have not bought into this whole multicultural thing. And the Israelis just aren't getting along with their neighbors.

Being a "melting pot" was something America had always prided itself on. It united us and made us strong. Bowing to the gods of Political Correctness converted that into its antithesis. Multiculturalism is divisive because it excludes those outside their group. Multiculturalism establishes barriers, where a melting pot eliminates barriers and makes us one.

David Cameron, Prime Minister of England, said, "Under the doctrine of state multiculturalism, we've encouraged different cultures to live separate lives apart from each other and apart from the main stream. We've failed to provide a vision of society to which they feel they want to belong. We've even tolerated these segregated communities behaving in ways that run completely counter to our values."[198] What he has wrong is, they reject our vision of society. The Islamists ultimately want us to conform to their Shariah Law.

Who gives a sh!t about the Turd world anyway?

Diversity

To be inclusive.

There needs to be diversity of thought, especially in our schools.

Screw diversity, we need uniformity, things in common, like the English language.

Eugenics counteracts Diversity.

Victims

Victim - anyone not taking responsibility for their actions.
           - Slackers
           - Lackeys

Gays

Confused.

Mixed-up.

Deranged.

A disorder.

Whose with Aids are Plague rats.

Fudge packers.

Pickle smokers.

Pickle packers.

154

Skippers and prancers.

Happy Americans.

Pooftas.

Homos.

Queers.

An abnormal sexual preference.

Sexual orientation from disoriented people.

Socially misaligned.

Let's face it, you're not normal.

The only gay I respect is the Enola Gay.

Some things should be obvious, but for those that need it spelled out: Thou shalt not butt f#*k thy fellow man!

On June 26, 2003, a U.S. Supreme Court ruling reversed a Texas Law banning sodomy. A ramification is that in the USA now, there are group's rights instead of individual rights. Until 1960, every state had an anti-sodomy law, now there are none. Texas argued that sodomy has nothing to do with marriage, conception or parenting, cautioning this could lead to allowing same-sex marriage.[199] Texas was right.

TV. The incrementalism tactic employed by the Left, introduced gays into TV shows as far back as in the late 1970's in the show

"Three's Company." The rate of exposure had increased to the point that by the Fall of 2003 there were has so many gays in shows, kids should not have been allowed to watch TV. The analogy is with the number of Blacks on TV. In the 1960's, the number of Blacks in TV shows kept increasing to make it seem that they were much more prevalent in society than they really were at the time. The strategy worked to some degree. Whites became so used to seeing Blacks in all situations and places on TV; they were no longer shocked to see them in real life in places where they traditionally had never been. Well guess what, the Liberal TV moguls are trying to desensitize the public to gays being acceptable everywhere also.

Aids is a communicable disease, so those infected should be quarantined. You wouldn't want to intercept a sneeze would you?

Some gays going through TSA screening at airports probably fantasize about having an enhanced cavity search.

Ellen DeGeneres – Ellen Degenerate.

Ms is used for a female that you don't know if they are a Mrs. or a Miss. Mstr. Should be used for a male that you aren't sure if they are gay or straight.

Now that there are gay marriages, do they say 'does Party A take Party B ...?' If they are gay Leftists they could say 'does comrade A take comrade B ...?'

A new definition of a "byline" could be, mixing genders indiscriminately within the same sentence.

Feminists

Feminists are dysfunctional in a normal heterosexual relationship, so they are frustrated beyond belief.

Feminists don't just get PMS they have PMZ; all the time!

156

Feminists are hormonally homicidal.

Feminist's definition of a father: the biological sperm donor.

The modern one parent family produces neglected mongrels.

There should be a law proposed that when a male says "stop" to a female that is bitching at him and she does not, it then becomes grounds for a "mental anguish" suit.

True Feminists can be whatever they want, including being a straight, Republican, pro-life, stay-at-home mom.

NOW, National Organization of Women, have proven themselves to be just a front for promoting a liberal agenda. They are an organization that is supposed to stand up for women's rights, yet they never said anything about all the women Bill Clinton abused, harassed and raped, nor did they help Christine O'Donnell the Tea Party candidate in Delaware. When Meg Whitman was called a whore by her opponent's staff while running for Governor of California, NOW criticized her, and she is a self-made success just like what the NOW organization encourages women to be. They do not have any credibility. Rush Limbaugh refers to them as NAGs, National Association of Gals.

The NAGs complained about the 2010 Super Bowl Ad, with quarterback Tebow's mother talking about not having an abortion as doctors recommended, then him gently grabbing her, as violence against women. But no complaints about a hard tackle taking 80 year-old Betty White down into the mud. These people are pathetic in how blatantly biased they are.

African-Americans

Involuntary African-Americans - Descendants of former slaves.

157

Voluntary African-Americans - Caribbean Blacks who are successful workers and do not believe in Welfare.

Emancipated African-Americans - Abraham Lincoln waking up with the worst hang over of his life said, I freed who!

It is not necessary to say you are African-American, it's obvious.

You never hear anyone say they are European-American.

You never hear the term Israeli-American.

It will be nice when some groups consider themselves Americans instead of a hyphenated American.

I have a dream people will be able to judge not by the color of one's skin, but by the content of their character. – MLK Jr.

What will be the next term they will refer to themselves as: Ebonies, Darker Americans, Mixed Americans? Whites feel they have to tip-toe around how to refer to them because the preferred term keeps changing.

Ebonics, people with an attitude that can't spell.

Whites are ebonicly challenged.

Some Blacks are delusional thinking their ancestors in Africa were like royalty, i.e., the movie with Eddy Murphy *Coming to America,* and choosing the name Queen Latifah.

I understand there is a Black swim team sponsored by the KKK.

Representative Sheila Jackson Lee (D) whose district includes the Johnson Space Center, while on the Subcommittee that oversees space policy, asked a NASA official if the Mars rover was going to where the astronauts left the flag.[200] Can you say clueless?

Democrats don't consider African-Americans that are Republicans as true to their race.

As a monolithic block, 80% of Blacks have voted for Democrats since 1964.

Approximately 65% of the Black middle-class work for the Federal government.[201]

Concerning Leftist Blacks, the term African-American sounds suspiciously close to anti-American.

The socially engineered.

Progressive Margaret Sanger, who founded Planned Parenthood in 1916, started the Negro Project in 1939, which tried to wipe them out through birth control and eugenics. She referred to them as an unfit group and wanted to design a better population.[202] "We do not want word to go out that we want to eliminate the Negro population."[203]

The heart and soul of parenting is the capacity for sacrifice. Black males obviously lack that capacity.

Most African-Americans have slave owner ancestors. What the hate the most, they are.

Kwanza was started in 1966 by an American college professor.

Bill Gates is a fool to give billions of dollars to Africa to stop Aids. Their culture is such that they start having consensual sex at age nine. Their culture would have to change in order to prevent the spread of Aids, and that isn't likely to happen. It would be just as affective to tell them to stop f#*king.

Hispanics

Mexicans.

Mexicans are Montezuma's Revenge. The Conquistadores' descendants intermarrying with Native Americans forever became Mexicans. That was his lasting curse on them.

Macho, in English, means stupid.

La Raza means The Race, by its very name it identifies them as The Racists.

Hispanics are being influenced to vote for Democrats even though traditional Hispanic values are aligned with conservative values. The vast majority of Hispanics are religious, pro-life, have strong family ties, and are anti-gay. Why help get politicians elected that will enact laws that go against your values?

Immigration

Immigration Reform - A voting source.

Undocumented Democrat voters.

Use Emergency Rooms and schools as deportation centers, identify illegal aliens, and then immediately deport them.

Illegal Aliens – neuter them, then deport them. So if they return they can't produce more children that burden our economy.

Businesses should put advertisements on the border fence because so many illegals go past it.

It is not Politically Correct to secure our borders. Does that make any sense?

160

Profiling = common sense.

Racial Profiling, it works for a reason. It's obvious.

Bank of America, run by Liberals in San Francisco, earned the reputation as Bank of Amigo.

Regarding our border with Mexico, can you say sieve?
Locate the border state's National Guards near the border with Mexico, erect sniper towers, place warning signs at the US border, then shoot anyone crossing illegally. That should work.

We have Rights in this country. One Right that is not offered in some other countries is the Right to leave. If you really aren't happy here, I sincerely hope you exercise that Right.

In 2009, Leftist Lloyd Carter said, "What parent raises their child to become a farm worker? These kids, they're the least educated people in America or in the south west corner of the (San Joaquin) Valley. They turn to lives of crime. They go on welfare. They get into drug trafficking and join gangs." All true, but in his PC world, he isn't suppose to speak the truth out load.

There should be impenetrable borders to keep out both drugs and illegal aliens. There was 700 miles of border fence authorized to be built in 2006,[204] but Democrats don't want to implement it. The costly virtual fence doesn't work.

Arizona's Immigration law, signed by Gov. Jan Brewer, is just enforcing what the Federal government refuses to do. It is amazing and telling that the Obama Administration is suing Arizona to prevent the laws enforcement. Former Supreme Court

Justice Sandra Day O'Conner was brought in as a judge to defeat the case that was herd on 11/1/10.

A 2010 study showed that illegal immigrants use $100 billion more in federal, local and state services than they pay in federal taxes.[205] Some of the costs are from Medicaid, food assistance, school aid, and imprisonment. States suffer greatly from emergency room visits, impacted schools, crime, etc.

Illegal immigrants cause economic terrorism.

According to a fact checker of the L.A. Times, purported statistics in L.A. County:

- A sizable percentage of warrants for murder are for illegal aliens.
- A considerable percentage of people on the Most Wanted List are illegal aliens.
- Over 27% of all births are to illegal alien Mexicans on Medi-Cal, whose births were paid for by taxpayers.
- Some of the occupants of HUD properties are illegal aliens.
- An estimated 50% of all gang members are most likely illegal aliens.

The following are unsubstantiated percentages:

- 11% of the inmates in California detention centers are Mexican nationals here illegally.
- 29% of inmates in federal prisons are illegal aliens.
- 29% of illegal aliens are on welfare.

Over 70% of the U.S. population growth and over 90% of growth for California, Florida and New York is from immigration.[206]

When Meg Whitman was running for governor of California in 2010, she was accused of hiring an illegal immigrant. The employee lied about her legal status and provided forged documents. If an employer would still question a prospective employee, they could face harassment charges. The illegal's attorney's position is that the employer is still guilty even though they hired through an employment contractor. The box that Liberals are creating leads to the solution employers are forced into, and that is to not hire Hispanic potential employees for fear of not knowing their real legal status and to avoid the risk of being accused of hiring an illegal. So, if all Caucasians will not hire any Hispanics, maybe they will eventually go back home to Mexico, which would be great. So thank the Liberals for that outcome.

What a difference between the USA and Iran's illegal immigration policy. Iran held three American hikers for over one year in solitary confinement for inadvertently crossing over an unmarked border. In the U.S. there have been an estimated 20 million Mexicans and other illegals that stream across our fenced border. They get free medical care, their children get a free education, and some even vote.

The USA should have the same policy that Mexico has for illegal immigration, which is the toughest on the continent: it is a felony to be an illegal alien in Mexico, foreigners who fail to obey the rules will be fined, deported and/or imprisoned as felons, those attempting re-entry can be imprisoned for up to 10 years, foreigners who violate the terms of their visa may be sentenced up to 6 years, a Mexican who marries a foreigner with the sole objective of helping the foreigner live in the country is subject to up to 5 years in prison, a penalty of up to 2 years in prison and a fine imposed on foreigners who enter illegally, visitors who enter under false pretenses or who violate the terms of entry are imprisoned or deported, those who aid in illegal immigration will be sent to prison, Mexican authorities keep track of every single person in the country, each tourist and immigrant is assigned a unique tracking number, foreigners with fake papers may be imprisoned, those working without a permit can be imprisoned, and immigrants must not be destined to be burdens on society. In an era when some on our Supreme Court and politicians on the Left seek to bring American law in line with foreign norms, we

163

should propose that the North American Free Trade Agreement, NAFTA member nations standardize their immigration laws to match Mexico's law.[207]

Racial Profiling

Duh!

Political Correctness is putting our National Security at risk by not profiling obvious Middle Easterners at vulnerable locations.

Voter Registration

The country is a reflection of what the majority of the voters vote for.

Democrats keep expanding the voter pool including more groups that will vote for them. The strategy is that people dependant on Entitlements are almost guaranteed to vote for Democrats. If the requirements to be eligible to be a qualified voter were still as the Founding Fathers framed it, Democrats would never win any election. Originally eligibility to vote was up to each State's rules; but generally a voter needed to be a propertied, free male citizen, at least 21 years-old.

- The Literacy Test that was a requirement to voting was abandoned after the Civil Rights Act of 1964. The politicians think so little of Blacks that they enacted the Voting Rights Act of 1965, which ended the use of the literacy test in the Deep South. The non-permanent provisions of the Bill have been extended four times, the latest was in 2006.[208] So they still don't think enough Blacks are literate. Hey, I don't care what color your skin is, if you can't read the ballot you shouldn't be allowed to vote.

- The 1970 Voting Rights Act banned literacy tests in 20 other states.
- In 1971, during the Vietnam War, the 26th Amendment lowered the age requirement from 21 to 18. The justification was that if 18 year-old soldiers can die for their country, they should be able to vote in their country. Fair enough, so make an exception that combat soldiers can vote at 18, but everyone else must be at least 21. The real reason was that with all the political unrest in the 1960's they assumed all of the youth would vote for Democrats. Young people are still in school or just out of school, where they have been indoctrinated by Left-leaning teachers. Young people are idealistic and haven't had the practical experience of paying taxes to fund what they vote for. Plus they are easily deceived by propagandists.
- In 1975, the Voting Rights Act was amended to include language assistance to minorities.
- In 1977, President Jimmy Carter granted amnesty for millions of undocumented illegal aliens.
- In 1994, the National Voter Registration Act, the Motor Voter law, made it easier for illegal aliens to vote and for fraudulent voting to occur. The Act allows people to register to vote simultaneously with an application for a driver's license. Registration rolls grew by 20%. The lax standards make it harder to verify the identity of voters. As a result, registration rolls throughout the nation are enormously inaccurate. In some counties the voting roll numbers are bigger than the voting-age population.
- It has been proposed that felons now be legally able to vote.
- Our soldiers' absentee ballots are often purposefully not mailed to them in time, because the majority of which vote for Republicans.
- ACORN - In 2000, the Democrats promoted Operation Big Vote to register more African-American voters and get them to the polling booth. There are many thousands of

bogus registration cards. It casts doubt on the integrity and outcome of elections.[209]

- In California it was proposed that 14 year-olds vote having a fractional share of a vote. There are many different minority groups that have a high percentage of youths that predominately vote Democrat.

- In 2009, the SEIU, State Employees International Union, Executive V.P. said, "two things that matter for the Progressive Community ... number two, we reform the immigration laws, it puts 12 million people on the path to citizenship, and eventually voters."[210]

- Portland, Maine has a proposal to give "legal residents," that aren't citizens, the right to vote, San Francisco and Chicago are considering similar legislation.[211]

- Bill Ayres is promoting, "Every resident in a country with an American military base within its borders ought to have the right to vote in an American Presidential election ... Imagine, hundreds and hundreds of millions of people voting for the American President from countries as diverse as Cuba."[212]

- The D.R.E.A.M. Act, Development Relief and Education for Alien Minors, proposal made in November 2010, would grant illegals under 35 years-old, regardless of their criminal record, legal status, provided they for two years either attend college, join the military or work in certain government agencies. The Act does not require any type of degree be earned. And after they gain legal status they can have close family relatives attain legal status also. There is no cap on the number of illegals allowed to do this.[213] The requirement to have been here before the age of 16 years old will be falsely claimed. Once an application is filed, no matter how fraudulent, the federal government is prohibited from deporting the applicant. They are not required to earn a degree. This unfunded mandate is mass amnesty and is expected to cost $6.2 billion per year.[214] In June, 2011 the California Supreme Court let stand the ruling allowing

California's D.R.E.A.M. Act to happen. On October 8, 2011 Gov. Jerry Brown signed it into law. It will go into effect in 2013. There are an estimated 25,000 illegals that graduate from California High Schools annually. If the applicant claims a hardship, they do not even have to put in the two years. The other absurd aspect of this is that after a degree is earned, they can't legally be hired to work. There should be no benefits available for illegals. Benefits will act as a magnet to attract more to enter illegally.

Illegal voting cancels out legitimate votes. There have been votes recorded from illegal aliens, felons, in dead people's names, and people voting twice. The Motor Voter law was supposed to ensure voter integrity. In November 2009, the Obama Administration announced that they would not enforce the requirement that States clean up their voter rolls. There are 16 States in violation of the National Voting Rights Act. One county has 113% of the voting age population registered to vote. There are more people registered to vote than there are people eligible to vote. Attorney General, Eric Holder, dropped the case against Missouri for voter fraud. He is not going to pursue any of the cases demanding States clean up voter rolls. This corruption violates the rule of law[215] and is another example of how Democrats get laws passed by promising to do something good, but plan to do something dastardly in the future.

The most undesirable in society are invariably Democrats.

Obama, referring to comprehensive immigration reform, said on October 25, 2010, "If Latinos sit out the election instead of saying, we're gonna punish our enemies and reward our friends who stand with us on issues that are important to us. If they don't see that kind of upsurge in voting in this election, then I think it's gonna be harder, and that's why I think it's so important that people focus on voting on November second." [216]

Voter fraud by the Democrats is rampant. In Clark Co. Nevada, where Harry Reid's son is a County Commissioner, members of the SEIU are the voter machine technicians assigned to "fixing" them. Some machines were set to record a vote for Harry Reid, when the button for the Republican was selected. The SEIU, State Employees International Union, expects to contribute $44 million to the Democrat Party.[217] Free food and cards were given out for Reid voters. It is illegal to give anything of value in exchange for voting.[218]

The requirement of owning property in order to vote still makes the most sense. If you have to pay for it, you will carefully consider what you vote for. When over 50% of the voting public doesn't pay taxes, they will vote for proposals that redistribute wealth to themselves and the country will ultimately go broke. We are almost to that point now, which is by design.

When the country was formed, an adult was considered to be anyone over 21 years of age. People today are so much more irresponsible than that era. A person 21 then is equivalent to someone today of about 30, call it age indexing. A wiser voter would be someone 25 years old that has finished their education and has worked and paid taxes for a few years. The 18 to 24 year-olds are much more idealistic and do not have any practical experience from which to base a good decision. I advocate starting an effort to change the voting age to 25 years old based on age indexing from 21 in 1776 until today. The exception would be those serving in the military could vote at age 18.

ACORN

Founded in 1970, ACORN has increasingly been involved in illegal and unethical voter registration fraud. Before the recent split up, there were 400,000 members, in 850 chapters in over 100 cities. They have separated into different groups using different names, but it is essentially the same and now harder to identify.

168

For example, in February 2010, in California they became the Alliance of Californians for Community Empowerment, ACCE.

Obama has long standing affiliations with ACORN.

George Soros funds them.

Pro-Choice

Abortion.

Anti-Abortion is a negative term for pro-life.

A woman's right to choose, but they don't want you to choose life.

A woman's right to murder.

Who would be for abortion, God or the Devil?

Pro-choice is the Devil's choice.

Murdering the most innocent among us.

God is pro-life, the Devil is pro-abortion, who is influencing you?

Only immoral Liberals would abort their offspring, and those are just the type of people we want a lot less of.

Abortions by Liberals is preventive medicine for the economic health of the country.

The only good Liberal, is an aborted Liberal.

Liberals, keep aborting your offspring, please!

Abortion = Liberal excrement.

Liberal larvae - some make it, some don't

Liberal's baby pictures are sonogram images of fetuses before they abort them.

The confusion Liberals have as to when someone becomes a human being, whether it is at conception or birth. Use logic, God knew Jesus would come into the world, so, he had angels tell Mary in advance. Therefore, Jesus became "flesh" at the annunciation or conception, not when he was born.

"The sacrament to Liberalism is an abortion." It is their rite of passage. - Rush Limbaugh.

The law passed during the Clinton years that bars pro-life advocates from protesting within 35 feet of abortion clinics, violates free speech. They are the only citizens with this restriction.

Government appointees have to pass a litmus test given by Democrats about their stand on abortion.

A Morning After pill with a "high rate of effectiveness" means a high kill rate.

In a radio ad in the Fall of 2003, a man smoking was not affecting just himself but the lady next to him and the baby inside her. A *Painfully* Correct observation would be: it's okay, they are in an abortion clinic.

Father = sperm donor

In order for the Health Care Bill to be approved, Obama needed the votes of the pro-life Democrats. To appease Representative Bart Stupak, Obama issued an executive order stating there would be no federally funded abortions through the Bill. We'll see how long that lasts.

Why are Liberals so worried about killing people in a war, but so willing to kill their own offspring?

The Left called soldiers in Vietnam baby killers, people having abortions are the real baby killers.

Easy access to guns doesn't make people kill other people, murderers kill other people; just as easy access to abortion clinics doesn't make people kill their offspring, murderers kill their offspring.

Abortion is murder.

The one child law in Communist China requires forced abortions if a woman with a child becomes pregnant again, and performs a hysterectomy if women become pregnant a second time.[219]

In Illinois, a baby from a failed abortion was left to die in a closet in the hospital. Then Illinois State Senator Obama didn't vote for a measure to prevent it from happening again, he just voted present.

A good lesson from Karma would be if abortion advocates keep coming back as a fetus and experience late-term abortions until they finally get it.

Late-term abortion is a near-life experience.

A Late Term Abortion is cruel and unusual torture. The tool used pierces and breaks the baby's skull and goes into its brain killing it. Criminals being executed, which are usually heinous murderers, are to feel no pain. Can't you see the delight the Devil has when every innocent soul is submitted to that horror?

Human Shields – a good argument for <u>very</u> late-term abortions.

171

In January 2011, Dr. Kermit Gosnell was arrested for illegally performed late-term abortions. He would have mothers deliver babies that were more than six months in the womb and he would cut the babies spinal cord with scissors to kill them. The law allows abortion only up to 12 weeks of pregnancy. Abortion beyond 24 weeks is outlawed because a fetus can survive outside the womb. Gosnell had been performing abortions since 1972.[220] What kind of monster could do that to innocent human beings?

In May 2010, regarding the Gulf oil leak, a Democrat said, "God is a Democrat." Let me give you an example of why the Devil is a Liberal, late term abortions.

Abortion is abhorrent, Late-Term abortion is diabolical, now some want a mother to have the right to legally kill their baby within the first 30 days after birth, infanticide. Can't you see Satan's hand in this?

Peter Singer, a Professor of Bio-Ethics at Princeton University, rejects birth as a dividing line between what he considers persons and non-persons. He believes that no new born should be considered a person until 30 days after birth. He promotes infanticide and believes physicians should kill some disabled babies on the spot. Recently 14 congressional Democrats attacked a Bill written to protect newborns who survive abortion procedures.[221]

In England, Virginia Ironside said, "If a baby's going to be born severally disabled or totally unwanted, surely an abortion is the act of a loving mother. If I were the mother of a suffering child … I would be the first to want to put a pillow over its face."[222] In their minds they believe they are compassionate, because they are blinded by Evil.

A term for when a female aborts a late term fetus, that only minutes later would be born, murder.

172

PART 8

CORRECT ME IF I'M WRONG,
BUT ISN'T IT TRUE THAT ...

Patriots

There is a big difference between having legal status in the USA versus really being a bona fide American. Too many of these alleged citizens are living in our country for the wrong reasons. Ones that refuse to assimilate, refuse to learn how to speak English, and are only loyal to their native land, feel far differently about the country than patriotic Americans. Some come here strictly for jobs and better living conditions.

"Alleged Americans" are technically citizens, but are loyal to another country, ideology, or theology: another country, i.e., Mexico; another ideology, i.e., communism; another theology, i.e., Islam. All ethnicities, ideologies, and religions are welcome here, but citizenship means you put America first. Technically, being a citizen does not necessarily mean you are a loyal patriotic American. Some gain citizenship just to be part of a sleeper cell and are here for the sole purpose to inflict terrorism. Some come here from Mexico to have an "anchor baby" so their entire family eventually comes and establishes residency in order to benefit from all the give-away programs in America. These Alleged Americans should be stripped of citizenship and deported.

Obama is an Alleged American.

The Times Square bomber became a citizen just to inflict terror. Do you think of him as truly an American? He may technically be a citizen, but it doesn't mean he should be one. But because he has citizenship, he should be hung for Treason.

Alleged Americans – go back to your own country!

U.S. Citizens fighting for the Taliban against America, like John Walker of Marin Co., are domestic born terrorists. That is treason.

Naturalization Oath paraphrased: I declare, on oath, that I absolutely and entirely renounce all allegiance and fidelity to any state or sovereignty, of which I have been a citizen; that I will support and defend the Constitution and laws of the United States of America against all enemies, foreign and domestic; that I will bear allegiance to the same; that I will bear arms on behalf of the United States when required by the law; and that I take this obligation freely without any mental reservation or purpose of evasion; so help me God.

Independents

This is a growing group of disillusioned Americans that want a change to the status quo. They took a chance on Obama, but are even more disappointed now that he is President. This group is no longer just comprised of moderates, there are many libertarians, conservatives and other types.

A Conservative is a Libertarian with common sense about social issues.

I applaud Libertarians for being fiscally responsible but they don't like war, what's up with that?

Moderates

A fish.

Lack intestinal fortitude.

A Democrat that doesn't have the cojones to admit it.

Democrats

Left of normal.

Demo Rats, Dumbycrats, The Democrazys, Cut and Run Democrats, Demo Jackasses, Dumb Jackasses, the Party of Jackasses.

A dependant.

Democrats keep the little guy little.

Small minds, big government.

A victim.

The Democrat party is a refuge for miserable people.

Too many Democrats suffer from Liberalitis.

Democrats kill the innocent through abortion and free the guilty, through clemency.

The Democrats are always talking about doing things for "the children," they must mean the ones they choose not to abort.

Most Democrats lack any economic sense.

A vote for a Democrat is a Dolt Vote. You would have to be a dolt to do it.

Divisive partisans.

Rhetoric vs. action. Symbolism vs. substance. Intensions vs. results.

The United Snakes of America: Senator Byrd, Representative Jim Wright, Tom Daschle, David Bonior, Harry Reid, Nancy Pelosi, etc.

An example that Democrats just want power by staying in office is, when they didn't want fellow Leftists to vote their ideological conscience for Ralph Nader.

The Democrats beliefs:
Big Government, regulations, tax the rich, dumb down education, no individual ownership of guns, don't punish criminals, very limited property rights, entitlements, strong Unions and anti-capitalism.

Democrats give the Poor, empty promises. They have been identifying the same problems for many decades, but never fix them. They just need the issues for a campaign slogan to get votes in order to stay in power.

Democrats are being extremely irresponsible for refusing to solve the looming insolvency of entitlement programs like Medicare and Social Security.

The Democrats hate big business, some to the point of being anti-capitalists.

Democrats denigrate Big Oil, Big Tobacco, Big Insurance, etc.

What about Big Labor, Big Education, Big Government and the Big Idiots that run it?

The Left uses moderate Democrats to do their bidding. The left has co-opted the Democrat Party. They are behind the scenes coercing moderate Democrats to advance their Leftist agenda.

Maxine Waters (D)-California, in 2008, threatened to nationalize the Oil Industry during a Committee Hearing saying, "This Liberal will be about socializing ... uh, um ... basically, taking over, and the government running all of your companies."

The Democrats are hung up on race.

The Democrats suffer from Class Envy and they promote Class Envy. They blame the rich for their failures and want to destroy the system out of frustration.

Democrats never saw a war they did oppose or want to lose.

The Democrat's mascot donkey has chicken feathers instead of hair.

Defeatists.

During both World Wars, Democrats were in power in the USA. The Europeans needed our help sooner. Wilson did not send troops until the last year of the war. FDR did not send troops until after Pearl Harbor was bombed.

In 1996, the Democrat's Bridge to the 21st Century, was to drag out old Frank Lautenberg and the very Liberal 1984 Presidential candidate looser Walter Mondale. It showed just how shallow the pool of leaders was in the Party.

The Democrats don't want criminals to go to jail, at the same time they don't want law-abiding citizens to own guns to defend themselves. They apparently want society to be traumatized by crime.

The Anti-Reform Party.

General Harry Reid, a phony American.

Senator Harry Reid (D) got Obama to abandon the $10 billion Yucca Mountain Nuclear waste site, a total waste of money.

Going against the will of the voters in the 2010 mid-term elections, the Democrats tried to get everything they wanted via a $1.3 trillion Omnibus bill in the 2010 Lame Duck Session. This nearly 2,000 page bill was written in February 2010,[223] illustrating how much they plan ahead and how much they are determined to have their way. This Bill would have imposed their agenda throughout the 2011 Budget period. There were over $8 billion in earmarks. In his campaign Obama said he would veto earmarks. The 2010 Budget that was proposed in December 2009 contained $4 billion of earmarks; he did not veto any of them.

If while in the midst of budget deficits Democrats want to raise taxes instead of cut spending, in order to continue funding social programs, there is nothing stopping them from paying in more than their regular tax amount. So put up and shut up!

Why do you Democrats need the Buffett Rule to force you to support all the social programs you treasure?

The Wisconsin Democrat elected officials that hid in Illinois instead of performing their duty are typical cut and run democrats.

Southern Democrats, it's a new era, the rest have switched to being Republicans.

A (D) by a political candidate's name means "Don't vote for this person, they are fiscally irresponsible."

An (R) stands for "Restore fiscal responsibility and rescue your freedom."

Bureaucrats

Bureau rats.

Fat, lazy, ugly, unproductive paper pushers.

Entrenched.

Liberals

Parasites.

Liberal traits:

"Liberal Paranoia", caused from taking drugs since the 1960's:

- Halliburton, Dick Chaney
- Inanimate objects – SUV's, guns
- Tobacco, the depiction of "smokers" in *Water World*; There are Tobacco Nazi's
- Pesticides
- Patriotic flag waiving Americans
- Christians, the Religious Right, and all religions except for Islam; They are "Christophobic"
- Republicans, Conservatives, a "Vast Right-wing Conspiracy", a Republican behind every Bush and vice versa.

Liberals are as paranoid about a vast right wing conspiracy as women are about mayonnaise going bad.

179

Idealistic.

Do-gooders.

Liberals are losers. Misfits.

Most Liberals are angry people.

Some have self hatred.

Liberal men are like women. A female trait is that they do not deal well with reality. They have idealistic expectations and hold things up to their fantasy world. Women buy things regardless of the cost, even if they can't pay off their credit cards. Whatever is convenient for them they do, regardless of the consequences. They want everyone to be as miserable as they are. The bleeding heart Liberal man's emotions are closer to that of women.

Liberals don't have a sense of humor and take themselves seriously, but what they say and believe is so ludicrous and contradictory, they are funny.

Liberals are challenged by no grasp of economics.

Liberals are removed from economic reality.

Liberals are reality impaired.

Liberals are unaware of reality.

Liberals are unable to face reality.

Liberals are deniers of reality.

Liberals are delusional.

Liberals are obsessed with race.

They have no morals.

Many Liberal's have white hair.

Many Liberal men have white hair and weak chins.

The Journal of Politics announced on October 28, 2010 that researchers at the National Science Foundation found there is a "Liberal Gene." People with a specific variant of the DRD4 gene are more likely to be Liberal as adults. Thank God, maybe they can be treated for it if they catch it early. They focused on dopamine which affects brain processes, emphasis on the dope. It is hereditary, so we are asked to not hold them responsible for their opinions, they can't help themselves.[224] Luckily they abort many of their offspring or there would be even more of them running around screwing things up. Preventative medicine. I have long maintained that there should be a genetic test to find out when a person is young if they will eventually have white hair, in order to know if they are likely to be Liberal. If we could identify both the white hair gene and DRD4, then maybe we would know with a very high probability who has this combined genetic defect that causes Liberalism, which until now defied logic.

Michael Savage repeatedly says, "Liberalism is a mental disorder." He's right, it's a congenital disorder.

Favorite Liberal past times: Yoga, Hacky sack, peace marches, protests, getting stoned, whining, and collecting government handouts.

Meditate on this, you are fluke of the universe, you have no right to be here.

When Liberals were kids, they were the dorks in school, the losers. They somehow worked their way into having power through politics, the media, and Charitable Foundations, but they are still loser types. We should not give their assertion of standing any legitimacy. Acknowledge they are still a joke and put them in their place both verbally and by ignoring them.

Liberals that accuse others of racism would enslave everyone, of any color.[225]

Liberals have been around since the snake in the Garden of Eden.

Liberal San Franciscan's at their annual "Black and White Ball" only see grey.

A gun and a SUV held up a gas station, no people were involved.

Liberals view anything barley right-of-center as Right-Wing, but anything from center Left to off the scale Left, as normal.

Liberals are intolerant hypocrites. They are intolerant of conservative points of view.

The Political Class.

Limousine Liberals, during the first two years of the Obama Administration, according to iWatch News, the number of limos owned by the government increased by 73 percent. Most of the increase was in Hillary Clinton's State Department.[226]

Ideological idiots.

Liberals are irrational.

Men are from Mars, Women are from Venus, Conservatives are from Earth, Liberals are from Uranus.

Liberal's loath winners, conservatives, religion, and America.

Liberals complain about the rich being the winners of life's lottery, because Liberals are the losers of life's lottery.

Margaret Thatcher said Liberals "would rather that the poor were poorer, provided that the rich were less rich. That is the Liberal policy."[227] Their envy overrides practicality. Although there is income inequality, isn't it preferable that the poor become better off, even if the rich do get richer?

A study in 2006 by Arthur Brooks indicated American liberal households earn more than conservative households but give less to charity. In addition, American conservatives donate more time and give more blood than American liberals.[228]

Some people want Big Government because their parents didn't teach them to be responsible adults, to be independent, self-reliant, nor have the strength of character to feel free to make their own decisions and lead their own life. A better choice for them is to have Big Brother or better yet prison decide and provide everything for them. To remain dependant, immature, and take orders from someone else.

Liberals resent the traditional family make up.

It is easier to tear down America and blame it for everything that is wrong with them.

Ask a Liberal if they are proud to be an American. If they have to think about it or say no, suggest they go live in a country suited to their values.

Liberal policies don't create wealth; they just feed off of it.

Liberal politicians aren't problem solvers, they are problem causers.

Some Liberals are so against Republicans and off balance that they do things like the lady in San Francisco that shot at President Ford.

I agree with what Ruhm Emanuel said in August 2009, Liberal Democrats are f#*king retards!

Humanitarian motives, often disastrous results.

Liberals' goal is world socialism.

"Give me liberty or give me death" was countered with "better red than dead." They wholeheartedly embraced the latter.

Most Liberals will not admit that they are very Left, while Christians in the Roman era allowed themselves to be eaten by lions rather than deny what they believed in. I have utter contempt for people that do not stand up for what they believe in. They have no fortitude to admit their beliefs.

Conservatives proudly proclaim who they are. Liberals hide what they are. Liberals are against traditional American values and they don't want others to know they are working against the rest of us to change our country.

Seemingly in search of a new image and title a few years back, some Liberals proclaimed to be "Progressives", but that infers progress, NOT! It is interesting they chose the name of one of the leading Communist publications in this country to describe themselves. What it actually did was bring to light the true Progressive Movement that had been in the shadows for many decades.

Leftists

Leftists will use the Constitution to destroy the country, just like Lenin said the capitalist will sell the rope that hangs them.

184

The Left uses the trappings of the USA as a front.

Leftists have been conspiring to label people who identify a conspiracy as nuts. That is so when one of their conspiracies is exposed, the public is programmed to think the whistle blower is a conspiracy theory nut.

Leftists are agitators.

The Far-Left are atheist, so to have order, the authoritarian rulers act as God. They decide who lives and who dies.

Diabolical.

The Democrat candidate in Delaware that ran for the U.S. Senate in 2010 is a Marxist.

Some of their organizations in the USA are:
Workers World Party, League for the Revolutionary Party, Radical Student Union, The Democratic Left at George Washington University Destroy Industry, Fight Imperialism Stand Together, Freedom Socialist Party, Georgia State University Progressive Student Alliance, and Campus Anti-War Network.

Michael Moore, in February 2011 said, "There is a ton of cash in the country. What's happened is we've allowed a vast majority of that cash to be concentrated in the hands of just a few people and they're not circulating that cash. We've allowed them to take that. That's not theirs, that's a National Resource, that's ours."[229]

Fabian Socialists

The Fabian Society started in 1884 in England. Through incremental changes they sought nudge the masses towards socialism.[230] Instead of mass revolution, it followed a strategy of selective education of a powerful few to lead reforms in

185

government with the help of the few in media. They adopted the Doctrine of Inevitability of Gradualism. Its founder was General Quinton Fabian Maximus who learned to win through harassment and attrition.[231]

Their shield is a wolf in sheep's clothing and their logo is a turtle with the motto "When I strike I strike hard."[232]

Fabian Socialists founded the London School of Economics, which is the Think Tank behind the Labour party.[233]

From the Fabians the British Labour Party was formed, promoting 'social justice'.[234] All Labour Prime Ministers have been members of the Fabian Society.[235]

In America, the Council of Foreign Relations is a nongovernmental organization formed in 1921 on the principles of elitist in politics and the media directing events. When the media is working with government, there is no watchdog to keep government in check.

Saul Alinsky's *Rules for Radicals*' single formula for success seems to be agitate + aggravate + educate + organize. – Glenn Beck

Progressives

Progressives are the American version of Fabian Socialists that started in the USA in the early 1900's. Teddy Roosevelt's second run for President in 1912 was through the Progressive Party. He didn't win, but Woodrow Wilson, another Progressive did. Henry Wallace ran for President in 1948 under a national Progressive Party.

Progressivism advocates social, economic and political reform. Its implementation is developed gradually becoming more severe over time. Their insidious strategy and its sequence of actions are

186

planned out years, even decades in advance. They are the ultimate strategic planners.

They are using regulations to seize control.

Progressive revisionists reshape the past to justify policies for the present.[236]

Progressives believe things can be reformed to perfection.

Progressives, engineering society into their own perfect vision.

It was Progressives that ushered in Prohibition, that's another reason not to like them.

A Progressive is progressing left down the political spectrum from mere Democrat to full-fledged socialist.

The goal is control.

Progressives try to find ways around the Constitution.

Their beliefs are not compatible with the Constitution.

A relentless agenda.

They are like cancer cells that spread throughout every organ.

Incrementalism.

They present a clear and present danger.

In the 2008 Presidential campaign, Hillary Clinton identified herself as an early 1900's type Progressive.

<u>Socialists</u>

"They [socialist] always run out of other people's money." - Margaret Thatcher

Socialism doesn't work; it is just a slow bleed.

Socialism is an economic and political system in which the production and distribution of goods is controlled by a centralized government. It is a stage between capitalism and communism which advocates an end to private property.

In Greece, the radicals from the 1960's are running the government and allowed the Unions to have too much power, so it is no wonder the country is in financial collapse. That is what happens when socialists control government; it is the same situation in California.

National Socialist German Worker's Party, Nazi. My summary of some of their 25 point platform from 1920:

- We demand the formation of a strong central power in the Reich. Unlimited authority. The leaders of the Party promise, if necessary by sacrificing their own lives by the execution of the points without consideration.
- Demand the nationalization of all industries.
- Demand a land reform law for the free expropriation of land for public utility, abolition of taxes on land and prevention of all speculation in land.
- Demand the total confiscation of all war profits.
- Abolition of unearned income obtained without work or labor.
- Demand the State provides the opportunity for a livelihood for the Citizens.

188

- Demand the creation of a healthy middleclass, immediate communalization of the great warehouses and their being leased at low cost to small firms.
- Demand a division of profit of all heavy industries.
- Demand an expansion on a large scale of old-age welfare.
- Demand struggle without consideration against those whose activity is injurious to the common interest, punished with death.
- The State is to care for the national health. The legal establishment of a gymnastic and sport obligation.
- Demand the substitution of a German common law in place of Roman Law serving a materialistic World Order.
- The State is to be responsible for a fundamental reconstruction of our whole national education program. The concept of the State must be striven for by the school as early as the beginning of understanding. We demand the education at the expense of the State of outstanding intellectually gifted children of poor parents.
- Demand legal opposition to known lies through the press. Demand all writers of the newspapers appearing in the German language be members of the race. Publications which are counter to the general good are to be forbidden. Demand legal prosecution of artistic and literary forms which exert a destructive influence on our national life.
- Only a member of the race can be a citizen. No Jew can be a member of the race.
- Demand that every public office be filled only by citizens.
- Combat the Jewish materialistic spirit around us.[237]

The socialists today are the new NAZI's.

Hey, wake up, the socialists are taking over the country!

World Socialism

The Left refers to and blames things on a Vast Right-wing Conspiracy. There is no such thing. However, it is blatantly obvious that there is a vast Left-wing conspiracy!

There is an unwritten alliance for the common goals between the American Left and foreign Anti-Americanism.

The Green movement is a means to achieve the objective of world socialism.

Anti-War Movement

Regarding Nobel Peace Prize winner Obama and his unconstitutional attack on Libya in March 2011, the Anti-War Movement was a no-show. They didn't have a problem with the fact that only Congress can declare a war. Obama believes he gets his authority from the United Nations and not the United States Congress. Representative Dennis Kucinich thinks this over-reach of Executive authority is an impeachable offense. Then Senator Obama on December 20, 2007 said, "The President does not have power under the Constitution to unilaterally authorize a military attack in a situation that does not involve stopping an actual or imminent threat to the nation."[238] Then Senator Joe Biden said of President Bush, "If he takes the nation to war in Iran without Congressional approval, I will make it my business to impeach him."[239] Robert Gates, Secretary of Defense, when asked if Libya posed an actual or imminent threat to the United States said, "No, no, it was not – it was not a vital national interest to the United States."[240] Similarly, the Progressive President and Nobel Peace Prize winner Woodrow Wilson drew the U.S. into World War I when America had no national interest at stake.

Obama violated the War Powers Act by not going to Congress 60 days after engaging in the war with Libya.

190

Different branches of government can't trade powers, only Congress can declare war. The concept of the War Powers Act is unconstitutional.

The Responsibility to Protect Doctrine is promoted by Cass Sunstein's wife, Samantha Power, Obama's National Security Council special advisor, and sponsored by George Soros through the United Nations.[241] Under the guise of humanitarianism, the philosophy is that the international community has a responsibility to protect a people besieged by its government. This is an inroad for the U.N. to penetrate nation's sovereignty. Obama's use of it legitimizes the doctrine and puts it on a path for universal acceptability.[242] Libya is a trial run before the doctrine will be used against Israel by claiming the need to end its abuses in Palestine.[243] "War crime" has been applied to Israeli anti-terror operations in the Gaza Strip.[244] Obama ordered U.S. military intervention in Libya and justified it by obtaining a U.N. resolution; he did not get permission from our Congress which is required by law. This further gives the U.N. legitimacy and elevates the U.N.'s authority over our own. Obama is setting a calculated precedent. In Obama's address he said, the task that I assigned our forces ... to protect the Libyan people from immediate danger ... carries with it a U.N. mandate and international support. The doctrine's founder advocates a new world order.[245]

Obama studied under Edward Said at Columbia University. Said, photographed hurling rocks at Israelis, is an advocate for the rights of Palestinians.[246]

When the Obama Administration took office they stopped considering terrorists as "enemy combatants." If captured they would go before a U.S. court. The anti-war crowd has no outrage over Obama unilaterally sending a hit-squad into a sovereign country without their permission or knowledge to murder Osama Bin Laden, an unarmed and untried civilian. Where is the ACLU? Shouldn't the Left demand he be tried at The Hague as a war criminal? One of the principles that make our country so stable, minimizes corruption and attracts foreign investment is that the law applies to everyone. No one is above the law, not even the president. Obama continues to undermine the rule of law. He chooses which laws he will not enforce or abide by. He is eroding our stability and his credibility. Obama's Nobel Peace Prize increasingly becomes more of a joke.

The Iraq War protesters were completely ineffective in trying to prevent that war. They only identified themselves as being anti-American Leftists.

Pro-terrorist.

The Tea Party should mockingly carry signs reading: Stop Obama's illegal war in Libya!

Anti-American

People on the Left with a chip on their shoulder.

Anti-Capitalists

Anti-Capitalists are such hypocrites! They hate capitalists, yet probably everything they own was produced by multi-billion dollar corporations whose shares are traded on the New York Stock Exchange. Their possessions include: blue jeans, bicycles, cars, cell phones, computers, and other electronic devices. If they do not have apparel made by chain stores, then the cotton that the articles are made from was grown by subsidized farmers in every producing country and woven by large mills or by exploited third world children. A person would have to be living naked in a cave to not possess items made by capitalists, you hypocritical numb skulls.

In the Spring of 2009, Texas school books did not have the word capitalist in them.

192

Anti-Capitalists by their rhetoric are like al-Qaeda, that wants life like it was in the 7th century. That's about how basic the standard of living would be like without the benefits reaped from capitalism.

Communists

A word not often uttered in America anymore. We have been conditioned to associate the messenger as a nutty conspiritorist. However, in Europe communists are prevalent, there are even major political parties that are communists and openly use the title. Since the 1917 Revolution in Russia, there have been several communist organizations in America. With socialism on the rise since Obama took office, more communists in this country are emerging from the shadows.

Communism is a system described by Karl Marx and Friedrich Engels in various books starting with *The Communist Manifesto* written in 1848. Communism believes in and promotes an economic class struggle based on correcting exploitation, no private ownership of anything, abolition of all religions, overthrow of the capitalist system through revolution, and abolition of all non-communist States to bring about a world-wide Communist society.

Contrary to idealistic beliefs, Communism is out "to enslave the common man morally, mentally and physically for its own ... purposes."[247]

Marxism-Leninism plans communism to develop through two stages: first there will be socialism with a dictator; the main principle will be "from each according to his ability, to each according to his work." As people become indoctrinated, all capitalistic characteristics will disappear. The second stage will be stateless, classless, godless, where all property will be held in common and human activities will conform to the principle "from each according to his ability, to each according to his needs." The final stage of communist Utopia assumes voluntary work.[248] Russia's full-fledged attempt for 74 years failed.

They believe in the collective, not individual responsibility.

It makes us "all equal, equally miserable." - Rush Limbaugh

It is based on class envy.

It believes in cooperation rather than competition.

Communists are just Liberals that aren't lying.

As best illustrated in North Korea, Socialists and Communists demand conformity, uniformity, and control.

Marxism is based on class struggle. They want to get rid of all rulers. They want the workers to take over industry. They believe wealth belongs to the people. They believe in a work environment without divisions of labor. There would be a new ruling class, the ones organizing the revolution, like union bosses. This naive idealistic situation has never worked and could never work. There is no incentive to work.

Maoism was named after Mao Tse-tung, 1893-1976, who was the Chinese dictator from 1949-1976. He implemented: the dictatorship of a military-bureaucratic clique, depreciating the role of the people, anarchism, permanent revolution, revisionism, and repeated total purging. The preservation of poverty and backwardness allowed for diverting maximum resources to building up their military machine. He said, "Power grows out of the barrel of a gun." Right out of the book *1984,* Mao practiced the "need to constantly create contradiction", which led to a continual state of tension in society. To distract the working masses from serious internal unsolved problems, he organized mass campaigns aimed at intimidating the population with "threats from abroad" and domestic purges. Maoists proceed from the premise of an eventual world war and regard it as a source of world revolution.[249]

The Khmer Rouge that ruled Cambodia from 1975 to 1979 led by Pol Pot, was a replica of the Maoist regime. Their policy of social engineering led to genocide; their attempts at agricultural reform led to widespread famine; arbitrary execution and torture was carried out against perceived subversives; and there were thousands of deaths from treatable diseases. Peru's Shining Path embraced the tenets of Maoism. The Communist Party of India formed in 2004 is Maoist and aims to overthrow the government of India. The Maoist Party won the elections in Nepal in 2008. How would you like to live in those conditions? When you are controlled by a dictator, you don't know how tyrannical they will be.

Since Communists are atheists and don't believe in God, they have no moral qualms about committing unimaginably inhumane acts. Chinese Communist Chairman Mao insisted on collective farms. The program known as the Great Leap Forward from 1958 to 1961 banned privately owned farms. Collective Farms were a disastrous failure. The system caused three to five million of his people to starve to death the first year, approximately 10 million the second year, and 20 million the third year before he changed his mind. In total, an estimated 30 to 45 million of the population in China died.[250] Similarly, the Environmentalist in California don't care that they are depriving 23 million people of water and putting 400,000 acres of farmland out of production in the name of protecting the non-native Delta Smelt.

Mao said the communists were prepared to sacrifice 300 million Chinese for the victory of world revolution.[251]

Bill Ayres and the Weather underground expected to kill 25 million Americans after a successful revolution.[252]

The Chinese government harvests organs from their prisoners.

With China's wealth and Russia's weak economy, let's hope they don't buy Russia's nuclear weapons.

China's so called State Capitalism is just a better image name for National Socialism.[253]

The Black Panther party is profoundly influenced by Maoist thought. Former head of the Black Panthers, Khalid Abdul Muhammad, advocated killing all Whites – men, women, and babies.

In a move reminiscent of a scene in *Dr. Zhivago*, ACORN members lately are moving into and living in foreclosed homes, claiming the collective has a right to do that.

Ethel and Julius Rosenberg, convicted of espionage in 1951, were proven to be working for the Soviets, when the files were opened in Russia, after the collapse of the Soviet Union, and confirmed in 2008 by co-conspirator Morton Sobell.

In the USA, in 1918, the Communist Propaganda League was formed. In 1919, the National Conference of the Left-Wing of the Socialist Party adopted the Left-Wing Manifesto. In 1919, the Communist Labor Party of America formed. In 1921 the Workers Party of America formed.[254]

China

China is positioning itself to eventually take over the world, and we are not only just watching and doing nothing to prevent it, but in many ways we are helping them along; i.e., Jimmy Carter and later Bill Clinton basically allowing China to control the Panama Canal. Our top universities are not only educating Chinese nationals here, who take their gained knowledge home, but the

U.S. universities are also transferring their technology and professors to Chinese universities.

China produces approximately 97% of the global supply of "rare earth minerals," ingredients used in high tech gadgets. In early 2011 they plan to sharply reduce their export.[255] When they hoard limited natural resources that they control the majority of, they can exert an inordinate amount of influence on others.

The book Unrestricted Warfare explains how China's strategy is to defeat the U.S. on a new battlefield, through economic sabotage by computer hacking. China knows it cannot match U.S. militarily, so it will turn America's strengths against itself, like a judo artist does. China can launch a high tech cyber war using viruses against our financial institutions, communications network, and electricity network causing a financial crisis via paralysis.[256] The philosophy is, the best way to achieve victory is to control, not to kill. In that way infrastructure stays intact[257] and there remains a population of slave labor.

The "President" (Chairman of the Communist Party) of China is named Hu, so China could be referred to as Hu-ville.

Anarchists

Would you trust your car to "Anarchy Valet Parking?"

If the economy gets so bad you need gold to buy things, people will instead get what they want using lead, in the shape of bullets.

Global revolution may be coming our way in the wake of unrest that Wikileaks hath wrought.

The Left's Formula to Control the World

The formula the Left is currently using comes from the Liberation Theology model, which is:

197

1. Identify what you want to control. It is the world's economic engine. They will do this through Cap and Trade, and all the environmental laws and regulations.
2. Use Marxist techniques and strategies.
3. Identify victims using groups large enough to give power, i.e., Hispanics, Unions, unemployed workers, and Blacks.
4. Use, infiltrate or corrupt the most powerful institution at your disposal. The Education system, the Media, churches, the Democrat Party, and Leftist organizations like the Tides Foundation which is using capitalism.[258]

The main obstacle to any group wanting to rule the world is the United States of America, and that is why there are so many groups trying to destroy us. Everyone knows we cannot be defeated militarily; the only way we will fall is from within, like ancient Rome.

Different Leftist factions have directed their minions to methodically adopt laws that diminish our stability and our strength. They have been directing the U.S. towards socialism so we at least will conform to their way of thinking if they can't cause our utter disintegration. They have successfully dumb downed our educational system; degenerated our youth with drugs and pornography; desensitized people with excessive violence in the media; taken God out of everything they can that is related to the public; through over regulation they have made many geographic areas not business friendly, which stymies productivity; created a Welfare State that promotes a dependent lazy population and diminishes a strong work ethic; and used case law, which takes us ever further from the original intent of the Founders of the country.

The most likely way for them to succeed is to cause financial instability and possibly financial collapse. Using the Cloward and Piven strategy of over burdening the system has been very effective. The Cap and Trade scam would certainly cause massive financial hardship for businesses, but what Obama has orchestrated

198

has rapidly brought the U.S. to the precipice of the abyss, and that is massive unaffordable debt. The Health Care legislation, TARP, the Stimulus Bills, deficit spending, the Financial Reform Bill, AIG bailing out foreign financial institutions, the IMF bailing out foreign countries, the Federal Reserve bailing out foreign countries, lending to foreign banks and monetizing our debt is likely to bring America to its knees. Erskin Bowles, co-chair of the Deficit Commission said, "this deficit and this debt is like a cancer and is going to destroy our country from within."[259] The Pentagon's war game titled Unified Quest 2011, has the Army studying implications of large scale economic breakdown, keeping order amid Civil unrest and how to deal with fragmented global power, amid drastically lower budgets.[260]

Once the U.S. is no longer strong enough to be effective, the planet is likely to rapidly end up under a one world authoritarian rule.

Organized Anarchy

Wade Rathke of ACORN and Drummond Pike of the Tides Foundation along with labor, community organizers, and activists, met in Cairo prior to the revolt in Egypt to discuss leadership transition, succession, and democracy issues in the coming election.[261] These people strategically plan in advance and don't miss a thing.

A Shadow Legislature was formed by the Muslim Brotherhood, union leaders, and activists from meetings held in the Middle East.[262] The coming insurrection is being coordinated and prepared.[263]

The U.S. State Department used an idea from Jared Cohen, now at Google, to fund the Alliance Youth Movement, AYM, in 2008. It is made up of various activist youth organizations around the world and private sector partners like Google, Facebook, and YouTube. They produced a manual for worldwide distribution.[264]

Two activists from AYM created the "Operation Room" 15 days before the protests began in Egypt.[265]

When an Egyptian Google executive was asked in Egypt if he planned the revolution, he said, "Ya, we did. The plan was to get everyone on the street."[266]

Facebook was credited for the coordinated revolts through their "Solidarity Demonstrations" site. There are postings of planned dates for riots in several vulnerable countries.[267]

Iran's Ayatollah Khomeini wrote in a letter to Mikhail Gorbachev, after the collapse of the Soviet Union, that he predicted Islam would fill the ideological vacuum left by the collapse of Marxism.[268]

According to Paul Bremer, former Ambassador At Large for Counterterrorism, "Islamic extremists are a threat not only to the U.S., but to the entire globe. These extremists have a vision of a world converted to Islam and an established universal Caliphate. They seek to destroy everything that America and her ideals of individual freedom and democracy stand for."[269]

Islamic Socialism is promoted by Tariq Ramadan, grandson of the founder of the Muslim Brotherhood. As Tariq professes in his book, he is a militant anti-Western anti-Israeli anti-capitalist.[270] Tariq had been banned from the U.S. since 2004 for supporting Hamas,[271] but his Visa was restored in January, 2011 by Obama through Hillary Clinton as Secretary of State.[272]

Obama as a candidate said, "We will change this country and we will change the world."[273] Obama wants fundamental transformation, not just in America, but throughout the world.

It is telling that Obama did nothing to support the masses revolting against the anti-Israeli Iranian Islamic theocracy and the anti-

Israeli Syrians, but encouraged Egypt's pro-Israeli President Mubarak to step down during their revolt. Egypt's army, the strongest in the region, has kept Israel safe. If the Muslim Brotherhood controls the country, it will probably turn the army against Israel, and the U.S. will be sucked into the war in defense of its ally.

In mid-February 2011, Obama met with Eric Schmidt of Google, Mark Zuckerberg of Facebook, Steve Jobs of Apple and others in the technology industry with the ability to dramatically influence major events.

In May, 2011 Zuckerberg and Eric Schmidt were guests at the G8 summit in Europe.

The IAC, International Action Center, was founded by Ramsey Clark, former U.S. Attorney General[274] under LBJ in 1992. The IAC has communist roots and is anti-capitalist and anti-imperialist. It is eye-opening to discover that former high ranking officials in our government are anti-American. John Podesta, President of Center for American Progress – a Progressive think tank, was Clinton's White House Chief of Staff, and Co-Chairman of the Obama Transition Project.[275] Phil Angelides, Chairman of the Apollo Alliance was California's State Treasurer.

ANSWER, Act Now to Stop War and End Racism, formed after 9/11, it is considered to be a front organization for the Workers World Party,[276] Marxists advocating a socialist revolution.

Union riots are part of a grand plan. In 2007, Andy Stern said, "We're ... in the process of building a global union. We are beginning. We have ... offices now in Australia and in Switzerland and London, in South America and Africa. We've been working with unions around the world. And what we're working towards is building a global organization. ... workers of the world unite, it's not just a slogan ..."[277]

In England, there is the Red-Green Alliance. The Red is represented by communist and socialists, and the Green by radical Islamists. Their common enemies are the capitalists, the U.S. and Israel. They have joint anti-war efforts.[278]

Occupy Wall Street

The discontent over the financial condition that much of the world is facing first manifested itself in the form of riots in Greece that started in 2008. The EU, European Union countries are socialists. Rather than adopt a sensible balanced budget approach to government spending, the Leftists in government have promised benefits to government employees and union members that are unrealistic and unachievable. Faced with economic realities and pressure from member nations in the EU, austerity measures were implemented. Fanned by union agitators and anarchists, the anti-austerity demonstrations sprang up.

Following the anarchist's lead in Greece, public sector union members protested in a very hostile, uncivil manner after Wisconsin's Governor Scott Walker(R) proposed reasonable measures to solve the budget deficit in February 2011. Attempting to make it a national issue, the AFL-CIO president Richard Trumka went there to whip up the crowd. Van Jones, trying to come up with a catchy name that many people could identify with, inaugurated The American Dream Movement there. Of the deceptively named movement Jones said, "over the next hours and days, all who love this country need to do everything possible to spread the 'spirit of Madison' (Wisconsin) to all 50 States ... MoveOn.org and others have issued just this kind of call to action; everyone should prioritize responding and turning out in large numbers on Saturday (2/26/11), the powers-that-be should see a rainbow force coming together: organized workers, business leaders, veterans, students and youth, faith leaders, civil rights fighters, women rights champions, immigrant rights defenders, LGBTQ stalwarts, environmentalists, academics, artists, celebrities, community activists, elected officials, and more – all standing up for what's right."[279] Wisconsin was a trial run for what the Leftists here hoped would spread throughout America. That didn't catch on.

Stephen Lerner, former SEIU Director of Banking and Finance, on March 19, 2011, speaking at the "Left Forum 2011" said,

> "There are actually extraordinary things that we could do right now that would start to de, destabilize the folks that are in power and start to rebuild a movement. ... A quarter of the people who own a home are underwater. ... Ten percent of those people are now in strategic default, meaning they're refusing to pay but they're staying in their homes. ... If you could double that number, you would you could put banks at the edge of insolvency again. ... If we could organize in mass to do a mortgage strike. ... It would literally cause a new financial crisis. ... Things we can do that could really upset Wall Street. ... If city and state and other government entities demanded to renegotiate their debt. ... A third of bank profits generate from dealing with cities and states. ... What would happen if students said we're not going to pay? It's a trillion dollars. ... If public employee unions ... demand as a condition of negotiation that the government renegotiate. ... It's a strike issue for us. We will strike unless you force the banks to relieve the debt of the city. ... Moving to the kind of disruption in Madison, but moving that to Wall Street and moving that to other cities around the country... you've impoverished us and we're going to make it impossible for, for you to operate. ... Labor can't lead it, but we can be a critical part of it.   We do have money, we have millions of members who are furious, ... We're in a

transformative stage and what's happening in capitalism, ... What does the other side fear most? They fear disruption, they fear uncertainty. ... We need to have a simply strategy, how do we bring down the stock market, how do we bring down their bonuses, how do we interfere with their ability to be rich. ... You have to politically isolate them, economically isolate them and disrupt them. ... They have the money; we need to get it back; ... The JP Morgan shareholder meeting, ... there's going to be a ten state mobilization to try to shut down that meeting. ... We hope to sort of inspire a much bigger movement about redistributing wealth and power in the country."[280]

Occupy Wall Street is an offshoot of that movement.

Harkening back to 1969 when Bill Ayres of the Weather Underground staged the Days of Rage in Chicago, there is a coordinated world-wide plan to have potentially violent demonstrations in as many places as possible.

The Movement needs muscle. The AFL-CIO president, Richard Trumka, was appointed in February 2009 to Obama's Economic Recovery Advisory Board. Trumka said, "I'm at the White House two or three times a week. I have conversations everyday with someone in the White House or in the Administration."[281] Undoubtedly strategically planning the takeover of America. As some background to his demeanor, in 1993, Trumka instructed more than 17,000 striking union coal miners to "kick the sh-t out of every last one" of their fellow employees who resisted union demands. The Virginia Supreme Court concurred that "the union never represented ... that it regretted or intended to cease its lawless actions." He focused on recruiting government workers who would benefit from higher taxes and bigger government and who therefore would reliably support socialism and the pro-big government Democrat Party. He promotes anti-capitalism and class-warfare rhetoric. His aim is to radically transform society. He stated that he got into the labor movement "as a vehicle to do massive social change." Trumka rescinded the AFL-CIO rule that banned Communist Party members from leadership positions. Trumka works collaboratively on political campaigns with the Communist Party USA. President Obama has spent most of his time with his radical Czars and union leaders. Obama hasn't spoken with a half dozen of his cabinet members during the first two years in office.[282] Do you think Obama may be strategizing events to take place with unions?

Unions have smartly unionized the vital services: police, fireman, nurses, teachers, government employees, etc. When directed, they are expected to rise up in their millions.

On September 8, 2011 in the state of Washington, more than 500 Longshoremen with baseball bats overpowered security guards and held six guards hostage. They broke down gates, damaged railroad cars, and dumped grain. They believe they have the right to work there instead of another union. They warned that this was only the start.[283]

The Occupy Wall Street movement that began on September 17, 2011 is the vehicle that caught on. And the "99%" slogan is one that many people can identify with. It supposedly represents everybody except for billionaires. There is a counter group calling itself "the 53%." That is the percentage of Americans that pay all the income taxes and support the 47% that have a free ride. Only about 30% of the U.S. population is Far-Left. The unions and the Left are trying to co-opt the moderates among the Occupiers. Vladimir Lenin would have referred to the participants in the Occupy Wall Street movement as "useful idiots". The crowd of mostly Leftists suffers from economic illiteracy. They do not realize that what they are protesting about is the detrimental effects of government injecting itself in business, which is socialism, and they have been indoctrinated to be socialists. So the fools are protesting against what they were led to believe is what they stand for. "Crony capitalism" is the real culprit. And don't confuse Crony capitalism with true capitalism. The laissez faire aspect of capitalism means government noninterference with business, that's a good thing. As protection money, businesses now necessarily contribute to both political parties. During the last Presidential campaign, Obama received more money from Wall Street than any other politician.[284] Obama has inflicted the country with Crony capitalism through: bailouts of financial institutions, like banks, Freddy Mac, Fanny Mae, and AIG; acquiring car manufactures, then giving special treatment to union workers over bondholders, which violated the rule of law; subsidizing green energy, like risky loans to Solyndra while offshore oil wells were having permits denied; and having the Federal Reserve give billions to favored banks and trillions to foreign socialist governments. There is no transparency with the Obama Administration. People on the Right believe in free market capitalism. Government should not be choosing winners and losers. There should be open access to markets, not only to those who contributed to a politician's campaign or only to favored industries. Supply and demand in the free market should determine success or failure. Interest rates will find their own equilibrium; the Federal Reserve shouldn't be artificially setting them at the behest of the President. The Libertarian's fiscal principals are exactly right, keep government out of our lives. The Occupiers should be protesting in front of the White House and the Federal Reserve building. They have misidentified who is causing the financial problems.

As explained in Part 4 of this book, the Obama Administration has set provisions in place that would enable him to assume the role of a dictator. Be wary that Obama may be waiting for an event that would enable him to impose Marshall Law before the elections in November, 2012.

George Soros

The puppeteer. The man pulling the strings.

Uber Progressive.[285]

He is a Fabian Socialist[286] and an atheist.[287]

He is 7th on the 2011 Forbes 400 list of richest Americans with an estimated fortune of $22 billion.

In the guise of philanthropy, he has been buying up media outlets for years in order to, as Richard Poe writes; undermine America's traditional Western values. Soros provides funding for abortion rights, atheism, drug legislation, sex education, euthanasia, feminism, gun control, globalization, mass immigration, gay marriage and other movements in social engineering.[288]

George Soros has donated approximately $8 billion over a 30 year period[289] for various nefarious causes. He used nearly $5 billion to promote "democracy" in Russia, Africa and Asia. His main philanthropic arm is the Open Society Institute Foundation, which dolls out between $400-$500 million each year[290] and is headed by the creator of the radical SDS, Students for a Democratic Society. He committed $10 million to (ACT) Americans Coming Together, and a Democrat Party get-out-the-vote group. He has awarded over $8.7 million in grants to the (ACLU) American Civil Liberties Union. He pledged $5 million to MoveOn.org. He gave $3 million for the Center for American Progress, which is the liberal answer to the Heritage Foundation. He funds Human Rights Watch, Amnesty international, Arab American Institute, NAACP, La Raza, ACORN, Media Matters, (NPR) National Public Radio, Free Press, Sojourners, Planned Parenthood, the Tides Foundation, (NRDC) Natural Resources Defense Council, and many, many more leftist organizations. He also provides campaign contributions, among which went to Hillary Clinton and Al Gore.[291]

He intimidates through the Leftist organizations he funds.

Soros wrote, "The main obstacle to a stable world and a just society is the United States." He is a real life version of Dr. Evil. He stated in an interview for *The Australian*, America as the center of the globalized financial markets ... of the world. This is now over ... the time has come for a very serious adjustment in America's consumption habits.[292] We are next on his list.

Soros is named at least a half-dozen time as one who has waged financial terrorism in East Asia.[293]

He created a Shadow Party within the Democrat Party. Richard Poe, author of *Soros Influence* wrote, "Soros has spent 25 years recruiting, training, indoctrinating, and installing a network of loyal operatives in 50 countries, placing them in positions of influence, and in power in media, government, finance and academia." He is behind radicalizing the Democratic Party by packing it with radicals while causing the ousting of moderates. He is actively working to destroy America from the inside for years.[294] Realizing the most effective way to control political advertizing is to control soft-money, Soros spent seven years and millions of dollars pushing a soft-money ban through Congress resulting in the McCain-Feingold Act in 2002. By forming the Shadow Party, for which John McCain was the keynote speaker at its Convention in 2000, Soros offered the Democrats an alternative money spigot which he controlled and was a power play to gain control of the Democrat Party.[295]

One dealing Soros had with Obama was with Petrobras, Brazil's state-controlled oil company. Soros' hedge fund invested hundreds of millions of dollars into it,[296] and days later Obama gave billions of taxpayer's dollars to Petrobras to expand their offshore oil fields.[297] The Obama Administration is banning offshore drilling to American oil companies crippling them as competitors.[298]

208

In 2009, Soros said, I think you need a new world order, which China has to be part of the process of creating it.[299]

In 2004, he said, "When you try to improve society, you affect different people and different interests differently. And they're not actually commensurate. So you very often have all kinds of unintended adverse consequences. So I had to experiment. And it was a learning process. The first part was this subversive activity, disrupting oppressive regimes. That was a lot of fun. And that's what actually got me hooked on this whole enterprise."[300]

In Thailand he was called an economic war criminal.[301]

Although a Jew, he was raised as anti-Semitic.[302]

He said of himself that he harbored messianic illusions.[303]

He will probably end up being the Hitler of our time, for all the persecution he will be responsible for.

Google

Google has the potential, if used for nefarious purposes, to be a major component of the all-seeing, all-knowing Big Brother type government structure. As stated in Part 4, Google keeps a record of everything ever searched for through them on the internet.

Google's Chairman/CEO, Eric Schmidt, when asked in August, 2010 about Google's future, he said "We know roughly who you are, roughly what you care about, roughly who your friends are, Google also knows to within a foot, where you are. I don't think society understands what happens when everything is available, knowable and recorded by everyone all the time."[304] In October, 2010 he said, "We don't need you to type at all, because we know where you are, with your permission. We know where you have been, with your permission. We can know more or less what you're thinking about."[305] Similarly, Apple's iphones and ipads

209

keep detailed data in an unencrypted file on tracking the device's location.[306]

Google has a close relationship with the U.S. government through the National Security Agency, law enforcement, NASA,[307] the General Services Administration,[308] and the National Geospatial Intelligence Agency.[309] Eric Schmidt is on the White House Council for Science and Technology[310] thus giving him privileged access to NASA airfields.[311]

Google gave over $1 million to the ultra-left wing MoveOn.org to create support for Net Neutrality.[312] Eric Schmidt is on the advisory board of The Politics of Trust Network, which promotes social responsibility, with Van Jones, Nancy Pelosi, Drummond Pike, and Tom Hayden.[313] Google, in 2010, gave over $145 million to non-profits and academic institutions through their charitable giving fund,[314] an arm of The Tides Foundation.

As of mid-February 2011, two Google executives have ties with the Egyptian revolt. Al Gore, long involved with global change, is on Google's board. Obama met with Google's former Chairman/CEO, Eric Schmidt, in mid-February, 2011.

Facebook

Facebook has been critical to the spread of coordinated revolts in the Middle East and North Africa.

Putting information about yourself on social networks is like getting a tattoo, it might seem like a good idea at the time, but it is next to impossible to get rid of.

9/11/01

In essence, 9/11 was a report card on how the Left has done to influence the principles and values of Americans for the generations since 1933. They have failed miserably. What the Liberal Media never stated was that 9/11 revealed that the propaganda from teachers, the Liberal Media, left-of-center politicians, Unions, Political Correctness, Court decisions, Social Engineering, etc, to promote and instill Socialism in this country since 1933, when Franklin D. Roosevelt became President, has not been embodied in the majority of the citizens. It appeared that immediately after 9/11/01, 99.9% of the country was patriotic.

The citizens love this country. Countless true heroes emerged that flag, felt connected to one another, even if they lived thousands of miles away. People realized we share many of the same values. Citizens are willing to fight to defend our freedom. Then the Left slowly started coming forward to oppose the patriotic sentiments, blaming America. They claim we brought this on ourselves. When they fully understood that the vast majority of the population loves this country, they gave up their veiled practice of subtle, incremental persuasion, and exposed their true beliefs. These beliefs run the spectrum from just left-of-center, to seething anti-American, anti-capitalist anarchist. Many who were viewed as just regular Democrats, with a legitimately different political outlook, were exposed as either, extremely Liberal, Leftist, Socialists, anti-American, anti-capitalists or worse. Some of these extremists are potential domestic terrorists. Because of 9/11, the un-Americans lost all the ground they thought they had won forever to our patriotic spirit. The Thought Police lost a lot of work it thought it had cemented through brainwashing the public.

Shortly after 9/11, when it seemed like the other half of the country became patriotic; remember, the Republicans always have been.

As a result of 9/11 and Obama, there are born-again patriots.[315]

Jamie Gorelick, known as "The Mistress of Disaster," when acting as the U.S. Deputy Attorney General under Clinton, placed a wall between agencies so the FBI and the CIA couldn't share information with each other. Attorney General John Ashcroft asserted that "The single greatest structural cause for September 11 was the wall that segregated criminal investigators and intelligence agents." The wall surpassed the requirements of the Foreign Intelligence Surveillance Act.[316] She should have not been on the 9/11 Commission. The 9/11 Commission Report was a white-wash to protect people like Gorelick and to not let Americans know what happened leading up to the event.

Operation 'Able Danger' that had been tracking al-Qaeda in the U.S. was mysteriously disbanded in January 2001.[317]

An approach to a solution is Pax Romana Americana. Kill all your enemies. Hey al-Qaeda, as Donald Rumsfeld said, we are going to kill you.

Multiculturalism gave way to patriotism right after 9/11.

9/11/01 made the "no profiling" issue nonsensical.

Liberals want to go back to a time before 9/11/01.

After 9/11, the US citizens cannot trust the security of this country to the Democrats.

The Liberal media did not call the Terrorists, Terrorists, but referred to them as hijackers.

What if the Black Box's revealed that in the two airplanes that crashed into the World Trade Center buildings, the passengers were Peace-nicks and their way of dealing with the high-jacking was to hold hands and sing "Give Peace a Chance". Then Flight 93's approach was more deliberate and purposeful.

The terrorists piloting the planes, as they were crashing into their targets, were yelling that they were doing it for Islam. There was no universal condemnation from the Islamic leaders of the world.

212

The Democrats are either in denial about how they think the public perceives them or they decided to just keep spouting their doctrine through their usual propaganda tactic.

Which group would you feel more comfortable protecting your safety, your family's safety, and the safety of the country, the Democrat Dukakis in a tank surrounded with Clintons Cabinet of mongrels or the Republican George W. Bush on the flight deck of an aircraft carrier surrounded by his Cabinet of experienced veterans?

It took nearly 10 years, but Osama Bin Laden is dead!

Just as Osama Bin Laden misjudged America, assuming the country would fold and do nothing after the attack on 9/11. He may have assumed if captured our soldiers would not shoot an unarmed man. Guess again mother f#*ker!

Terrorists

Terrorist attacks on the United States around the world since 1979, from a speech given by U.S. navy Captain Dan Quimette:

- Iranian students seized the American Embassy in Tehran. The inept President Jimmy Carter was unable to have them freed for the last 443days of his presidency. Our military had been downsized and we were perceived to be a paper tiger by our enemies.
- Shortly after the Tehran incident, Americans began to be kidnapped and killed throughout the Middle East.
- April 1983, a car bomb exploded at the U.S. Embassy in Beirut, Lebanon killing 63 people.
- Six months later a car bomb exploded at the U.S. Marine Corps headquarters in Beirut killing 241.
- Two months later in December 1983, a car bomb was driven into the U.S. Embassy in Kuwait.

- In September 1984, a car bomb was driven into the gates of the U.S. Embassy in Beirut.
- In April 1985, a bomb explodes at a restaurant frequented by U.S. soldiers in Madrid, Spain.
- In August 1985, a car bomb explodes at the U.S. Air Force Base at Rhein-Main, Germany killing 22.
- 59 days later the cruise ship Achille Largo is hijacked and an American in a wheelchair is executed.
- In April 1986, the bombing of TWA Flight 840 killed 4.
- In 1988, the bombing of Pan Am Flight 103 over Lockerbie, Scotland killed 259.
- In January 1993, two CIA agents are shot and killed at CIA headquarters in Langley, Virginia.
- In February 1993, a car bomb exploded in the underground parking in the World Trade Center in New York City killing 6 and injuring over 1,000 people.
- In 1995, a car bomb explodes at a U.S. military complex in Riyadh, Saudi Arabia killing 7.
- In 1996, a car bomb explodes at the U.S. military compound in Dhahran, Saudi Arabia killing 19 and injuring over 500.
- In 1998, simultaneous attacks on two U.S. embassies in Kenya and Tanzania killing 224.
- In 2000, a small boat exploded alongside the USS Cole docked in Aden, Yemen killing 17 sailors. Attacking a U.S. War Ship is an act of war, yet President Clinton sent the FBI to investigate it as a crime.
- On September 11, 2001, four civilian aircraft were hijacked, two were flown into and demolished the two World Trade Center Towers in New York, one was flown into and damaged the Pentagon in Washington, D.C. and one was intended to destroy either the U.S. Capitol or the White House in Washington, D.C. Approximately 3,000 innocent Americans were murdered. The terrorists expected the Towers, which each house 60,000 workers, to

tumble over destroying other skyscrapers and result in 250,000 deaths.

For our Intelligence Agencies, Military and political leaders to not see a pattern over a 23 year period as Middle East terrorists being engaged in a war against the USA is hard to understand. U.S. embassies are sovereign, they are considered to be on U.S. soil. Continuing to treat terrorists as criminals, as Obama is doing, demonstrates an utter lack of comprehending the reality of the situation. America not responding decisively encourages further attacks. The world has changed forever and the Democrats in office need to deal with the problem in a responsible way.[318]

"We are up against a vicious enemy, the radical Islamists are there, they intend to try to create a Caliphate in this world and fundamentally alter the nature of nation states, and we're reluctant to engage in the competition of ideas and point out what they really are and how vicious they are."[319]

The Panty Bomber on the airplane on Christmas of 2009, and the UPS planes with bombs in the cargo being shipped to America in the Fall of 2010, are just a couple of incidents demonstrating the never ending attempts to attack us here and abroad.

If Obama goes through with trying the Terrorists held at Guantanamo in U.S. Courts instead of through the military, the estimated cost for security alone is $200 million.

Put Obama in Guantanamo.

The Left and Islam know the USA stands in their way to achieving their goals, and both are against freedom. These enemies of the state are both foreign and domestic. They aren't always working together, but they are striving to reach the same end. We need to fight both in order to retain our freedom.

On October 27, 2010, Pierre Thomas on ABC News said in the past 18 months 40 American citizens have been arrested for terrorist plots.

We are living in a new ear. The country needs to reassess and redefine what it means to be a citizen.

The massacre at Ft. Hood in November 2009, was not prevented because of Political Correctness. More information about the assailant, Major Nidal Hasan, was not investigated because he is a Muslim.

Janet Reno, Attorney General and a stooge for Bill Clinton, in 1993 ordered the assaults on a Seventh Day Adventist religious sect in Waco, Texas that killed approximately 84 including 25 children. The FBI used tanks and .50 caliber rifles. It was an extreme case of government abuse of power. It violated citizen's rights and freedom of religion.

The distinction between Foreign Terrorists and the Oklahoma City Bomber: Foreign Terrorists are anti-American; they want us to abide by the prescripts of their religion. The Oklahoma City Bomber became anti-Government, after the Government killed its own citizens for practicing their religion.

Environmentalism is Domestic Terrorism.

Republicans will take the war to the Terrorists. Democrats will allow the Terrorists to bring the war home to us.

The country cannot risk having a Democrat as President in this age of terrorism. Your life depends on it.

Big cities that are predominantly Liberal are inviting terrorist attacks if they vote for Democrats.

216

North Korea. Oh goody, a 27 year-old dough-boy with nuclear weapons.

Cyber terrorism from hacktivists through Operation Payback from Wikileaks supporters is the latest threat. The future threat will especially be from China. Julian Assange said, "It is not our goal to achieve a more transparent society; it is our goal to achieve a more just society." He wants the U.S. to lock down internally so there is less communication. Libertarians want transparency, the Left wants chaos.[320]

Iraq

Sadam's Insane

After Sadam Huessein's Regime fell, Iraqis, not Americans, did all the looting. For such a religious people, they weren't following their version of "thou shall not steal", if they have that precept.

Based on the looting in Iraq after Saddam's ouster, they need a dictator to control them. Based on the Russian Mafia being so dominant after the Communist Party fell, in lieu of a dictator,

Russians apparently feel comfortable with any strong corrupt control.

Human Shields! Free airfare to Iraq! Place an apple on your head and we will try to knock it off with a cruise missile.

Tom Daschle's most useful function would be to act as a Human Shield in some anti-American country.

The coordinated worldwide "peace marches" in February 2003 proves there is a communication network between different Leftists groups around the planet.

To the "Peace Activists", your side lost.

If you think we went to Iraq for its oil, then use the same logic and ask what did we go to Afghanistan for? They didn't have oil or any known valuable resource at the time.

People against the war, must therefore support: mass graves, torture chambers, rape, a dictatorship, corruption, etc.

U.S. soldiers sacrificed their lives so Iraqis can vote.

After all we do for them, Mexico's president, Vicente Fox, would not support the US war in Iraq. The Environmentalist Green Party in Mexico is allies with Fox.

OPEC, Oil Producing Economic Council, should be referred to as OPECkers.

The Democrats found themselves caught between Iraq and a hard place. Senator Harry Reid said the war was lost.

It is a "religious war" to the Muslims.

Afghanistan

Remember when an Afghan was a blanket or a tall shaggy dog?

Mr. Taliban.

The Mosque at Ground Zero

Just because they have a right to build a mosque at Ground Zero, doesn't make it right.

If their reason for building the mosque were true, to unite people, they would be sensitive to Americans opposed to it and build it further away.

218

Named Cordoba after the place in Spain that celebrates the conquering of Christianity there around the 8th century. This will be another "victory mosque" symbolizing the conquering of America by toppling the World Trade Center Towers. Muslims have a history of erecting mosques in places that they have conquered.

They blew up the Towers, let's blow up their Mosque.

We should make a stipulation that we will allow a mosque to be built at Ground Zero after we build a 9/11 memorial near the Rock at Mecca. Oh, I forgot, non-Muslims are not allowed to even set foot in Mecca.

MoveOn.org

When President Clinton was being impeached, this group encouraged everyone to just "move on." What is so funny and ironic is they just can't seem to move on; they kept rehashing it for years. Whenever you hear the name, always think of them as "Just-can't-seem-to-MoveOn.org".

They have five million members and their Political Action Committee is one of the largest in the country. Their aim is "to fight for a more progressive America and elect Progressive candidates."[321] They supply ActionForum software to their members to organize quick action on issues.

They oppose the repeal of the estate tax.

They get funding from George Soros.

The Apollo Alliance

Started in 2001, the Apollo Alliance is a coalition of environmental, labor and community leaders to promote a "clean energy revolution," with the intent to create green-collar jobs.

They want to reduce carbon emissions and oil imports. They intend the changes to be "so profound that it will touch literally every quarter of American life." They have the "ability to mobilize a coalition unprecedented in its strength and diversity."[322]

With the advent of the Obama Administration coming into power, in 2008 The New Apollo Program identified priorities for federal action and investment, including a 'cap and invest' program that plans to invest $500 billion in clean energy to "transform America into the global leader of the new green economy." They accomplished "gaining inclusion of $25 billion in the 2008 federal economic rescue package for low interest loans to auto manufacturers." They "are working with several Midwest senators to incorporate these recommendations into recovery and stimulus packages." They are co-convening with Communist Van Jones' Green For All.[323]

The Apollo Alliance has strong political connections. The Chairman of the Board is Phil Angelides, former California Treasurer, who got California's two largest public pension funds to commit to invest $1.5 billion in clean energy. The Board includes

John Podesta, founder and President of the Center for American Progress, which is funded by George Soros and advocates progressive policy. Podesta had served as Clinton's Chief of Staff and co-chaired Obama's transition. Other board members are the Sierra Club Executive Director, the NRDC's President Frances Beinecke, the United steelworkers International President, the President of Laborers International Union, a former Executive V.P. of SEIU, the Chairman of the National Wildlife Federation, a former EPA administrator, and Joel Rogers, co-founder and first chairman of the Apollo Alliance, whom Newsweek identified as among the 100 Americans most likely to shape U.S. politics and culture in the 21st century.

So they are politically tapped in to the billions of taxpayer dollars provided by the stimulus slush funds and are using the new clean energy environmental movement schemes to access it.

The 2,000 plus page Stimulus Bill document was ready to distribute seemingly so quickly because it had been formulated and worked on for years by the Apollo Alliance,[324] a Leftist organization.

They are a project of the Tides Center.

The Tides Foundation

The Tides Foundation was founded in 1976 by Drummond Pike. Its stated purpose is to promote progressive environmental and social change. According to the Tides website, the foundation has granted more than $500 million to over 800 projects.[325]

The Capital Research Center's 2003 newsletter, Foundation Watch, carried an article titled "The Tides Foundation," that exposed that this foundation, along with the Tides Center, effectively launders donor's money so that donors cannot be linked to the ultimate recipient. It stated that The Foundation awards grants to groups that promote environmental extremism, opposition to free trade, anti-war protest, banning gun ownership, abolition of the death penalty, abortion rights, gay advocacy, and exclusion of humans from wildlands.[326]

The article also revealed that in 1994, the Clinton Administration transferred control of the Presidio in San Francisco from the Defense Department to the Interior Department. It explained how at the same time Drummond Pike had also created Highwater, Inc., a company that signed a 55-year lease with the Interior Department for a 12-building complex including the Letterman Hospital. Highwater, it said, renovated the buildings into modern office space, then renamed it the Thoreau Center for Sustainability. It further stated that The Tides Foundation occupies the office space

221

rent-free for 10 years while collecting rent from the 63 Left-leaning tenants.[327]

According to the Tides website, in 2005, the Tides Foundation's, Groundspring.com, merged with Network for Good to form the largest nonprofit provider of Internet-based fundraising.[328]

Network for Good is a not-for-profit organization co-founded by AOL, Yahoo! and Cisco Foundation to make it as easy as a few mouse clicks online to donate, volunteer, and get involved with issues people care about.[329]

According to the Foundation Watch article, "Money is to the Tides Foundation and Center what water is to the tide. … And there is an ocean of it."[330] Apparently, it rolls in and out. According to the Tides website, Tides is an appropriate metaphor, tides are connected around the world, they constantly change the landscape,[331] and they are relentless.

Most of the large Charitable Foundations were started by conservative businessmen. The Left shrewdly positions themselves where they can exert the most influence, so they become involved in these foundations and eventually take them over. That is why old conservative wealthy family-named foundations now support Left-wing causes.

Capital Research Center's 2003 newsletter, gives The Pew Charitable Trusts, whose $4 billion is from the Sun Oil fortune, as just one example. The Foundations contribute to the Tides Foundation and direct the money to radical projects with anonymity. From 1993 to 2003, 91 Foundations made grants to Tides. Donors include: The Rockefeller Foundation, the Ford Foundation, the Heinz Endowments, the Bank of America Foundation, John D. and Catherine T. MacArthur Foundation, the David & Lucile Packard Foundation, The Bill and Melinda Gates Foundation, and Lucent Technologies Foundation.[332]

What is really alarming, the Foundation Watch article revealed, is that the federal government grants them millions of taxpayer dollars from: the Fannie Mae Foundation, Department of Interior, EPA, Department of Housing and Urban Development, Department of Health and Human Services, Department of Energy, Department of Agriculture, and Centers for Disease Control.[333]

The Tides Center chairman is Wade Rathke, president of an SEIU chapter, and founder of ACORN.[334]

According to the Foundation Watch article, "The Tides Foundation", The Tides Foundation has funded Greenpeace, Friends of Earth, MoveOn.org, Environmental Working Group, (EWG), and Environmental Media services, (EMS). EWG's goal is to cripple agribusiness. They attack modern farming methods. EMS has ads warning of "Frankenfood", genetically modified food products.[335]

My summary of the three Tides-supported environmental groups described in the Foundation Watch article are:

- The Ruckus Society. Co-founded in 1995 by radical Mike Roselle of Earth First! This group has trained volunteers for protest demonstrations against the World Bank, globalization and biotechnology. They make no apologies for violence. They use vandalism strategically. They train for police confrontation, street blockades and using the media to their advantage. They were part of the World Trade Organization riots in Seattle in 1999, where shop windows were smashed and vehicles overturned.
- Union of Concerned Scientists; it has a political agenda. In 1997, it claimed most scientists agreed with the theory of global warming, when only 1,600 scientists did and 40,000 scientists signed a petition citing the absence of any proof that global warming was caused by humans. They use scare tactics by making doomsday predictions. They would deprive the world of cars, computers and airplanes.

- California Wildlands Project, founded by Earth First! Founder, Dave Foreman; it advocates permanent protection on both public and private wildlands by legislation or deed restrictions making the land off-limits to humans. CWP wants 50% of the continental United States off-limits to humans. The Clinton-era proposal, "Roadless Rule," forbade road-building on over 50 million acres of public land. A federal court threw it out.[336]

The most notable nonprofit funded by Tides is the NRDC, see below.

NRDC, Natural Resource Defense Council

The NRDC has surpassed the Sierra Club as the biggest most dangerous a&sholes advocating for extreme environmental causes. It is a very large, powerful and influential organization.

Founded in 1970, it now has 1.3 million members with offices in San Francisco, Beijing, Washington, New York, Los Angeles and

Chicago. It is the country's most effective environmental action group employing more than 350 lawyers and scientists. Its priorities are global warming, preventing pollution, and improving ocean governance. NRDC lawyers helped write some of America's bedrock environmental laws. It "strives to help create a new way of life for humankind."[337] It solves problems on a global scale. It has a strong presence in government and the entertainment industry. Board members include: Leonardo DiCaprio, Robert Redford, and James Taylor. It has an unparalleled arsenal of capacities that allows it to attack an issue from every angle and with maximum force.

In 1989, the Alar pesticide scare pushed NRDC into national prominence. They leaked a false report that Alar, a pesticide widely used by apple growers, caused cancer, particularly in children. Originally, the report was never reviewed by scientists, but was subsequently proven wrong. However, the damage was done. Alar was withdrawn from the market, as apple sales plummeted and many innocent farmers suffered great financial losses. These staged events are designed so that money flows to the NRDC and other fundraising environmental groups from donors who reward them for attacking the establishment.

The bulk of The Department of Agriculture's budget funds food stamps, so don't be mislead by its title. So while the Department of Agriculture is supporting farmers it is also giving money to the Tides Center, the Tides Center gives money to NRDC, and the NRDC maliciously causes farmers to go broke. The U.S. government is funding both the promotion and demise of agriculture.

The NRDC also receives millions of taxpayer's dollars from the EPA and the Department of Energy.

Their NRDC Action Fund supports pro-environment legislation through advertising and by mobilizing Astroturf pressure.

They provide up-to-the-minute dispatches through their Switchboard blog and web site and have a network of members that "take to their phones and computers when we need to hold lawmakers accountable."

In 2003, the NRDC ran TV ads that claimed "poisonous emissions" from electric utilities threatened "mass destruction." They promoted a Bill which put costly restrictions on carbon dioxide emissions, much like the rejected Kyoto Protocol would have done.

Even though the NRDC is flatly opposed to oil drilling, Frances Beinecke, the female President of the NRDC, was appointed to Obama's Commission dealing with the Gulf Oil Crisis during the summer of 2010.

Obama named John Bryson, co-founder of the NRDC, as the new Commerce Secretary in May, 2011. He will undoubtedly promote green technology.

NRDC's goals in the next 5 years are: set a cap on carbon emissions to allow investments in clean energy to grow by hundreds of billions of dollars as part of the Cap and Trade scam, get rid of all dams, and spread propaganda to convince the public that economic prosperity and environmental protection are not at odds as it has proven to be at odds in Europe.

ACOE, Army Corp of Engineers

The ACOE is headed by the Secretary of the Army, which is within the Department of Defense. Senator Joseph McCarthy was right about subversives in our government. They certainly have taken over that section of our Army.

Who would have thought that the ACOE has environmental sustainability as a guiding principle? That they should be protecting and restoring the Nation's environment and be cleaning contaminated sites to sustain the environment. They also provide environmental management products.[338]

The ACOE has continued to not abide by Supreme Court decisions like in Rapanos v. United States. The Left gets laws adopted that initially seem benign, but are later enhanced to be used for nefarious goals. The Clean Water Act is being interpreted to further the Left's agenda. The ACOE continues to illegally assert jurisdiction on isolated bodies of water as small as mud puddles and claim they are "Waters of the United States", which are suppose to only be navigable waterways. Why is a government agency anti-property rights, one of the cornerstones of our Republic? Why is the Department of Defense defying Supreme Court decisions? And why is it outrageously exceeding its authority? Chief Justice Roberts said of the ACOE, "its essentially

226

boundless view of the scope of its power."[339] The Environmentalists believe the public's interest should not be subordinate to private property rights.

The U.S. government owns nearly 30% of its total territory. They own approximately 84.5% of Nevada, 69.1% of Alaska, 57.4% of Utah, 53.1% of Oregon, and 50.2% of Idaho.[340] There has been a big land grab going on. They own much of the land in the Western states. In 1980 they added 53 million acres of land.[341] Aside from the 650 million acres they own fee simple, they also control vast amounts of land's development rights through restrictions, easements or determinations from a permitting process. They keep finding ways to control more land mass.

The concept of Mitigation is a complete scam, it is just a way for the government to extract more money out of people and businesses. They set up a permitting process that identifies habitat that they say they do not want destroyed, then if you pay them, you can go ahead and destroy it. The area destroyed is supposedly off-set by not destroying like habitat in an area that is not threatened and would never be destroyed anyway. The net result is, you destroy what you want, where you want, as long as you pay the government first, and everything else stays the same. The down side is, the bureaucrats take years to finalize the process, unless you pay more to speed it up.

On October 20, 2007, in the State of Georgia, while running out of water for people, the ACOE was still sending water down river for mussels and sturgeon. Georgia sued the ACOE asking for Federal interdiction, which never came.

Fish and Wildlife Service

Fish and Wildlife Service assumes responsibility for administering the Endangered Species Act. It uses the ESA to control private property.

The Brown Shirts.

Agriculture

America doesn't manufacture much anymore, the Financial Markets create nothing but digitized money.[342] Ag produces food and fiber and a lot of ancillary businesses. Ag in California for instance, has always been its number one industry, producing over $36 billion annually.[343] Ag has been the backbone of America. Ag has made us strong and independent, and that is why it is a prime target for the Left to destroy. The Left don the guise of Environmentalists in this effort. They want to destroy the USA so there can be world socialism. Their actions are not just a result of stupidity, although there is strong evidence of that also.

As Vice President, Al Gore told a young person there is no future in Ag in the United States and to find a different job.

It is unpatriotic to weaken the USA by destroying Ag. We certainly do not want to rely on other countries to supply our food, especially in time of war and in this era of bio-terrorism. To be a strong nation we need to be able to feed our own population.

After the first time Terrorist contaminate our food supply, people will want all of our food to be produced in America.

An honest man without food for one day will lie to get it, after two days without food he will steal to get it, and after three days and with no hope of ever getting food, he will kill to get it. Mayhem happens quickly.

When it becomes scarce, food will become the pre-eminent strategic commodity, more so than gold. You can't eat gold.
Here is a tip for the Liberals; the fastest way to put farmers out of business is to stop eating.

228

Talk about biting the hand that feeds you.

It is too bad Ag does not have the ability to not sell food to those who are out to destroy it.

Is there anything more essential than eating? Why then shouldn't protecting our Ag Industry be of the upmost importance? It should be considered a National Security issue. Shouldn't people that provide the food and fiber be shown some respect and appreciation? The country in general marginalizes and has no respect for the industry they rely on the most. In Japan farmers are practically revered because they feed the multitudes.

In 2009, world hunger affected over one billion people, one-sixth of the world's population.[344] The Environmentalists keep trying to take farmland out of production. From a group that always says they are doing things "for the children" they sure do not care about people starving.

From 2004 - 2006 the USA came close to being a net importer of food.[345]

The Environmentalists that are trying to destroy America are doing their best to deprive farmland of water. In California, they are using the Endangered Species Act to protect the tiny non-indigenous Delta Smelt as a reason to shut off the pumps from the Delta that supply 23 million Californians their water. For three years ending in 2010, that decision put 400,000 acres of farmland out of production. It killed permanent crops; orchards had to be bulldozed down. Some multi-generation farms went broke. Unemployment was 40% in a couple of towns. Fresno's Mayor Gene Autry correctly identified this man-made drought as eco-terrorism. The water allocation that was five percent of normal during the three years of drought was increased to 50% because two Representatives bargained the increase for their vote for the Health Care Bill. Even though 2011 started off as a very wet year, the initial water allocation was 25%.[346] After there was over twice the normal rain accumulations, the allocation only rose to 50%. When 2011 was on track to be the second wettest year on record, the allocation was set at just 70%.[347] It is clear they are trying to put the farmers out of business and reduce America's food supply.

Starving children are a result of Environmental Terrorism, let's preserve Ag.

In California, environmentalists, the media and some politicians are always against Ag. Whenever there is an environmental problem, they always blame Ag. The decline in the Delta Smelt population was immediately blamed on the pumps supplying water to Ag, but it is likely caused by numerous non-Ag factors including the daily dumping of millions of gallons of ammonia from partially treated sewage from the many cities that surround the Delta.

The Leftist Environmentalists that are trying to bring America to its knees have focused their attention on destroying Ag in California because the San Joaquin Valley, SJV, is the largest Mediterranean growing region in the world. California produces more than 400 commodities.[348] They have been able to get laws in place that use 1.2 million acre feet of Ag water annually, off the top without regard to drought years, to be used for environmental purposes. Environmentalist and Democrat politicians have blocked construction of new storage facilities for about 40 years. California's water storage is designed for a population was about half its current size. California's population is now 37.3 million people.

One of the tactics that undermines Ag's ability to operate economically is through air quality restrictions. The SJV Air Pollution Control Board blames Ag for the air pollution trapped in the valley. It is obvious that the majority of the air pollution is caused by cars owned by the millions of non-Ag related people that live there. Ag and truckers are forced to purchase expensive new diesel engines if theirs were manufactured before a certain date. Ag was in the Valley first and its existence is essential. The San Joaquin Valley should be treasured and restricted to be used as a growing region to provide food for a growing world population, not as a bedroom community for urban areas. Air pollution from non-Ag related vehicles are diminishing the yields of crops; the SJV Air Pollution Control Board has it backwards. Restrictions should be placed on all non-Ag infringements of Agriculture.

Growing food is not like manufacturing products; you cannot relocate just anywhere and start growing food. Growing crops requires adequate water and the right climate and soil. Not all soil was created equal. Particular crops grow in different climates. Also, to produce food on a commercial scale requires a lot of space.

Environmentalists, Developers and Agriculture all have starkly different visions for the San Joaquin Valley.

Gov. Schwarzenegger had a task force with development type people to chart the future of SJV. They are paving it over. It is clear that Ag is just in a holding period until its farmland will be developed. There is absolutely no respect for nor appreciation of Ag in California.

Prior to 1951 Los Angeles County was the number one agriculture producing county in the USA. They paved it over.

Another strategy used by the Environmentalists to destroy Ag in the SJV is through water quality restrictions. They have set unattainable salt level thresholds for the San Joaquin River so Ag will be prohibited from draining its water into the river.

The NRDC, Natural Resource Defense Council, originally through a lawsuit, which was later legislated, has a Restoration Project for the San Joaquin River that is funded by the Department of the Interior. This project will take thousands of acres of prime farmland permanently out of production, farmland that could be feeding countless numbers of people in perpetuity. Their reason for the project is to reintroduce salmon, which some experts believe cannot be achieved due in part to non-attainment of sufficiently cold enough water temperatures. The NRDC stated that they will consider the billion dollar effort a success, if they can maintain a 500 fish population; that works out to $2 million per fish. This is your money. This is your food. And this is outrageous!

On February 9, 2009, environmentalist Lloyd Carter, director of the California Water Impact Network, conveyed the notion that fish are more important than humans.

Instead of the old 'guns or butter' choice, now it is 'fish or butter' or 'fish or water'. In the case of the San Joaquin River Restoration Project, it's '$2 million fish or butter'.

Grapes of Wrath II, with not enough of a reliable supply of water to grow crops in California, there may be a reverse commute back to Oklahoma.

High Speed Rail in California is on a very fast track to the elimination of Ag. It will make the San Joaquin Valley a bedroom community of Los Angeles and the San Francisco Bay Area. With an estimated cost of $45 billion, this boondoggle isn't likely to ever make a profit. If High Speed Rail made economic sense, private enterprise would have provided it. The Left just thinks the U.S. should have mass transportation like Europe has.

Environmentalists continually add to the Endangered Species list. The listing of Fairy Shrimp, located mostly in California's Sierra Nevada foothills, has caused 1.7 million acres to not be allowed to be developed. The obvious observation is, how can 1.7 million acres of something possibly be endangered? This designation has confined development to the SJV floor where the farmland is located. The houses sprawling from towns should be built in the foothills on the poor soil, not on farmland, a finite resource.

Because Prop. 65 restricts more pesticides than anywhere else on the planet, food grown in California it is the safest food in the world. You don't need a Geiger-Counter with you to go shopping.

The EPA in early 2011 are treating spilled milk the same as an oil spill.[349] Huh? The Environmentalists are anti-Ag. This will be another financial burden on struggling dairies.

Farming is not a crime.

The media propaganda that most of Agriculture is composed of "corporate farms" is a myth. At least in California there are only a few true corporate farms. Some farmers have incorporated for tax reasons, but in no way fit the image of a large corporate farm.

If you don't have enough food, you are calorically challenged or food insecure.

The names of Subdivisions and streets on converted agricultural land should be required to be referred to in the past tense i.e., Used to be Countryside Drive, Used to be Vineyard Estates, Used to be Green Meadows, etc.

Along the Klamath River the Environmentalists want all dams removed and farmland to be permanently taken out of production. This is referred to as farmland retirement. Go ahead and approve this if Environmentalists first sign an agreement that their descendants are the first to be denied food when demand exceeds supply. Farmer's descendant's belief in the Second Amendment will surely enforce the agreement over the Environmentalists descendants' opposition using the First Amendment.

Irrationality and hypocrisy are both rampant with regard to the Hetch Hetchy Dam in California. This is the dam that supplies all

233

of San Francisco's drinking water. Many environmental organizations, including the Sierra Club, want to tear down the dam, and all dams for that matter. Most of these idiots live in San

Francisco and they have no clue how things work. All they know is, you turn on the faucet and water comes out. The hypocrisy in this case comes the Left's leaders, like Senator Diane Feinstein, and then House Speaker, Nancy Pelosi, that while promoting Restoring the San Joaquin River by taking water from farmland, they refuse to use their city's water to restore the Tuolumne River below Hetch Hetchy Dam.

It is ironic that clothes made in the USA sell in China for a premium, while only 2% of clothes worn in the U.S. are made in America.

The liberal press for years has denigrated cotton being grown in California, complaining that it uses too much water. In fact it uses an average amount and there are many crops that use a lot more water. In the summer of 2010 the author of the Washington, D.C. publication *Congressional Quarterly* linked the modern-day cotton industry with slavery. This vindictive association is the smoking gun, and is why the Left has a problem with cotton. Slavery ended 146 years ago, but the Left just can't seem to move on.

State of California

State of Confusion.

The Peoples Republic of California.

The Socialist Republic of California

How California was run after the 2002 election, when both Houses, the Governor, and all but one elected official were Democrats, demonstrates the failure of Socialism. In the

234

November 2, 2010 mid-term elections The Democrats swept every office. The proposition vote requirement to pass a budget from a 2/3 vote to a simple majority was approved. The only reason the deficit has not been bigger is because the Republican minority kept the Democrats somewhat restrained as to the size of the budget. Now there is no check. Hold on to your wallets Californians. This is a frigid-blue State.

In 2010 it was the 7th year in a row that California ranked the worst State in the country to do business. It's expensive and it's hostile to business.[350] The criteria voted on by CEO's was tax policy, workforce quality and quality of living and infrastructure.

In June, 2011 the state legislature foolishly decided to collect on-line sales taxes, which could cause approximately 10,000 Amazon.com affiliates to go out of business, thereby increasing unemployment.

The Cloward and Piven strategy of flooding the welfare system with more applicants than they could possibly afford to carry, has certainly worked in California. Their break-the-bank strategy is intended to force the Federal government to bail out the overburdened state welfare system with a federally guaranteed annual income. The idea was to consciously create a fiscal crisis by putting unmanageable strains into the capitalist system, strains that precipitate an economic and/or political crisis. The disgruntled entitlement recipients deprived of their promised payments are expected to revolt.[351]

California's State Budget has been late 25 of the last 30 years. The Democrat legislators are inept and incompetent. The 2010 Budget was 100 days overdue and still did not address a multi-billion dollar deficit.

Regarding balancing budgets, Legislators should be required to at least be able to perform basic arithmetic.

While the Budget goes unresolved, the Democrat legislators spend their time introducing the most ridiculous Bills, like banning cosmetic surgery for dogs, requiring public buildings to accommodate feng shui – a Chinese design for harmonious energy flow, designate the banana slug as the state mollusk, and granting a liquor license to a nudist colony.

California's public employee pensions are approximately $500 billion underfunded.

The average person is being raped financially and being made a fool of by unions. Government employee's salaries are approximately twice that of the private sector, plus they have lavish pensions, while most people have none. In some small towns the most expensive buildings are government courts and administration offices.

As of the first half of 2009, California in eight years had lost 1/3 of its manufacturing jobs, which brought in $75 billion per year, because of environmental and work related regulations, and higher taxes imposed by the State Legislature.

California Propositions equal direct democracy, but we are supposed to be a representative democracy. This over use of and reliance on ballot measures was started by the Progressive California Gov. Hiram Johnson, 1911 - 1917.

California has 1/3 of all welfare cases in the U.S., but only has 12% of the U.S. population.

California is a Welfare State, so it is obviously going to have a lot of Democrat voters.

In 2008, the California Senate passed SB1322 introduced by Alan Lowenthal (D), which allows communists to teach and public employees no longer have to take an oath of office to defend the

Constitution of the U.S. or California, and can be in an organization that advocates the overthrow of the government by violence. Gov. Schwarzenegger didn't sign the Bill, but people in the media supported it. California has laws that are still relevant: the state "faces a clear and present danger" that is "great and imminent" that communists will "infiltrate and seek employment" in public jobs. The aim of these people is to "establish a totalitarian dictatorship" based on Marx, Lenin or Stalin. I wish they would enforce the law and prevent these Commies from indoctrinating our youth.

On July 14, 2011 Gov. Jerry Brown signed a law requiring text books include the study of Lesbian, Gay, Bisexual and Transsexual Americans.

The California Secretary of Agriculture under Schwarzenegger had a ponytail. There aren't any real farmers that have ponytails, although some Organic growers may. California is the main commercial producer of food in the USA, and this is who they put in charge?

Former Governor Gay Davis looks like a gay High School principal.

Gov. Davis said, "there are people here from every planet". It sure seems that way. And he is trying to get drivers licenses for them so they can vote for him. They are beyond illegal aliens.

He presided over a $38 billion deficit.

The California Recall was a bloodless revolution. Democracy in its truest form.

Gov. Arnold Schwarzenegger could have borrowed Julius Caesar's line from ancient Rome: "I came, I saw, I conquered". Gov. Gray Davis response would be, "I had it, I spent it, it's gone".

237

The head of the California Teachers Association told a fiscally responsible Democrat Legislator that he runs California's government. The newly elected Gov. Schwarzenegger found out the hard way that the Unions have the most power in California.

In 2003, Gov. Gray Davis signed a Bill that would have given illegal immigrants the chance to obtain driver's licenses, to make it easier for them to vote for Democrats. Fortunately, it did not become law.

Lieutenant Governor Cruz Bustamante is a member of MECHA, Movement of Chicano Students, a radical organization trying to return Southwest America to Mexico. He took an oath to uphold the U.S. Constitution. These two facts are incompatible. This is sedition bordering on treason.

Cruz Bustamante's American is having the Southwest revert to Mexico.

Cruz Boost-your-taxes.

Cruz Bustamante has made a political alliance with the Indian casino tribes in exchange for political contributions which will help denigrate California.

Proposition 54 on the special Recall ballot of October 7, 2003, promoted a color-blind society approach in dealing with people. It was defeated. The Democrat majority wants to keep a policy of tracking race in order to divide us. African-American Ward Connerly introduced the proposition which would forbid government from categorizing citizens by race or ethnicity. Lt. Gov. Cruz Bustamante illegally used $3.8 million from his campaign war chest to purchase advertizing and personally denounced Prop. 54 using scare tactics.

238

A cyst is a small infection which attaches itself to something far more significant than itself. Politicians name public works projects after other politicians. Just one example was the removing of a historic Spanish name and replacing it with a politician's, named Sisk. There should be a "cyst" law preventing replacing historic names with current politicians names.

California allows approximately 25,000 illegal aliens to not only knowingly attend public colleges but gives them the discounted in-state tuition rate. At a time when California's deficit is about $25 billion annually, it cost the taxpayers $208 million per year for this gift. Its own citizens lose those slots at the colleges to illegals. [352]

The Commission that operates the Golden Gate Bridge in San Francisco broke even in 1971, meaning the tolls collected, paid off in full the debt that it took to build it. The bridge could have been free to cross after that point, if the maintenance costs were picked up by the highway system, or tolls would have been negligible if the Commission had to cover the cost of maintenance. But the Liberals controlling the commission, eager to grow government services, branched out into other transportation modes like buses, which run at a deficit. By 2006 the operating deficit was $80 million. Because of this, the toll to cross the bridge has been $6 since 2008. Typical Liberalism.

The California Teachers Association spent the most of all lobbyists, $212 million since 2000.[353]

California does not have a Planning Department, and it shows. Most of the growth is allowed to develop on farmland, that's your food supply! The Liberal's policies in California are going to directly affect you or your descendants when there is not enough food to go around.

Representative Gary Condit (D) was a "Blue Ball" Democrat.

France

Those f#*king French.

The "F" word = Frenchmen.

The Taliban in Afghanistan blowing up 165 foot tall 1,700 year-old historic Hindu statues carved into the cliffs[354] was almost as outrageous an act against the world's monuments as when the French blew the nose off the Sphinx in Egypt. It shows how arrogant and self-centered some groups are. Thank goodness they didn't attach an ugly large French nose to it.

It is not surprising that French Kings in the DaVinci Code thought they were descendants of Jesus. It seems like most of the French think they are God.

Cone heads.

The French, during WWII in Tunisia, North Africa, for 10 days fought against the American troops trying to land, killing 700 Americans.

Who would have believed that France led the way militarily, or at least verbally, into the war with Libya.

To the Liberals - if capitalism isn't your bag, why don't you move to France.

Japan

In 2001, an American submarine accidentally ran into a Japanese ship and sunk it. The Japanese government demanded an apology from the USA. Correct me if I'm wrong, but Japan never apologized to America for attacking Pearl Harbor did they?

Space Program

On April 15, 2010, Obama changed NASA's, National Aeronautics and Space Administration, mission. He isn't allowing them to go to the moon. They had planned to have projects in a certain sequence, in order to learn from using landing and temporarily living on the moon as practice to land and temporarily live on different astrological bodies as staging areas, leading up to having enough experience to successfully be able to inhabit Mars. Obama interjecting his inexperience into this field is analogous to politicians making decisions for the military in time of war. Liberals have always rejected the idea of going into space, wanting to wait until all problems on Earth have been solved, meaning never. If Liberals had their way, in 1492 Columbus would not have been allowed to try something new, because there were still poor people in Spain. Obama, referring to the moon, said "We've already been there." What if the King of Spain told Columbus after a few trips to the Americas, "that's enough, been there done that, nobody's going back?" NASA said there is a treasure chest of water and gases to use on the moon. Just like the early Americas had a treasure chest of natural resources. Forward looking people realize the great benefit of Space Exploration, Liberals never have. It is Trickle-Down Economics that people benefit from. Let the best and brightest among us go as far as they can and as a result everyone benefits. Liberals use the lowest common denominator as the base line and pull everyone down to that level, so the advancement of the human race is slower and hampered.

The commander of the last Space Shuttle flight on July 8, 2011 said, "The shuttle was a reflection of what a great nation can do when it dares to be bold."[355] Our Space Program provided the country with pride and esteem. It inspired many of our youth to excel in science and math, which resulted in great advanced in technology. The program's termination by Obama is emblematic of his orchestrating the decline of American exceptionalism. He is directing the U.S. towards mediocrity. An estimated 9,000 jobs will be lost when NASA's shuttle program ends.[356] Just what the economy doesn't need now.

Obama wants privatization of the space program. In order to gain revenue from advertizing, I'd like to see a lunar rover shaped like the Oscar Myer hot dog vehicle.

On the Left there are moon landing deniers that don't believe it ever happened.

It is ironic that Obama changed NASA's mission from planetary exploration to observing Global Warming on Earth in the year 2010, the same year as in the title of the sequel to *Space Odyssey*, about futuristic space exploration. It is like the Taliban wanting to still live in the 7th Century.

Class Action Settlements

The Politically Correct issues like being against the Tobacco Industry are awarded outrageously high settlements. The settlements that are supposed to fund improvements are just big slush funds that states use to squander the money on unrelated pet projects.

Drugs

I wouldn't be surprised if Doctors started prescribing anti-drug pills.

Just like Terrorists, drugs are an attack on the USA. See what happens when dope smokers, like the Clintons, Gore and Obama are running the country. There isn't enough effort made in preventing drugs from being brought in.

The War On Drugs – our military's technology detects all planes illegally crossing our boarders, but because of Government policies, it does nothing about it.

The U.S. Border Patrol – should use each states National Guard to protect our borders. In California, before the Iraq War, all they did was caravan up and down the highways on weekends.

Republican Screw-Ups

Get a spine. Stop compromising! Stand up for the principles you believe in.

Not correcting misinformation put out by Democrats. When Democrats lie and the Republicans don't call them on it, the general public can only assume what was said is true. Obama said that Social Security payments may not go out if the debt ceiling wasn't raised by August 2, 2011. Social Security is supposed to be solvent for many more years, so that is a fear mongering lie! The Republicans response after Obama's speech to the Nation, should have refuted that claim and stated the facts.

Not educating the public about fiscally conservative principles.

Not explaining the reasons why they vote for particular Bills, nor the long term ramifications of Leftist laws if enacted.

When the debt ceiling issue had a supposed deadline of August 2, 2011, the Republicans should have agreed to all support their Cut, Cap and Balance plan that passed the House. That moment provided fiscal conservatives with the most leverage over the Democrats and the President they had had to that point. In the long run, it would have been better to allow the deadline to expire without raising the debt ceiling. The government has more than enough revenue to pay its debt obligations. The other budget items would then need to be prioritized by those in government. It would be revealing to know what their priorities are. Most importantly, all citizens would finally understand what being deeply in debt really means. The government borrows approximately 40% of what it spends, that is unsustainable. It would have demonstrated that we need to live within our means. Standard & Poor's gave a wake-up call when it lowered the government's credit rating on August 5, 2011.

Republican Progressives that vote for over-spending.

RINO's = Republicans In Name Only.

Country Club Republicans that bash conservatives.

When in power they didn't dramatically reform or repeal the income tax structure or estate taxes.

In June 2010, the Republicans should have filibustered Supreme Court nominee Elena Kagan so the public would have had time to see how unqualified she is. For such an important position and all the damage to the country she will wreak, that was an inexcusable dereliction of duty.

The Republican leadership is comprised of weak-spined compromisers. It should be replaced with determined fiscally conservative limited government types.

Revisionists

Hijacking history. By using propaganda, they alter the way things were, by stating it the way they want everyone to think things were.

Painfully Correct Revisionism

So try this on, if we were to use *Painfully* Correct Revisionism: Our country values morality and strives for excellence. Because there is separation between School and State, we lead the world in having well-rounded graduates. Parenting classes, economics, ethics, U.S. History and understanding the Constitution are required courses. After college there is a two year compulsory enlistment in our military. Combat troops can vote at the age of 18, property owners can vote at the age of 25. Because our military is involved with other government agencies in preventing illegal border crossings, there is no illegal drug use. There are sniper towers located along our southern border manned by those State's National Guards to keep out and stop all attempts of illegal entry. The policy of automatic citizenship for babies of non-citizens has long since been abolished. There are strict anti-pornography laws. Child molesters are castrated and given long sentences. The Death Penalty is used in every State and a speedy trial and carrying out of the judgment is a high priority. There is now justice from the judicial system. Continually furthering advancements in Space exploration is a national priority. We use all of our natural resources, including oil and coal, from all of our territories, including Alaska and off-shore. There is widespread prosperity because the Federal government is small, in keeping with the founding principles, and the Mellon/Harding/Coolidge economic policies are followed. We finally paid off the national debt. The IRS was abolished with the adoption of a small national sales tax. That tax plus local sales tax and use taxes are all that is needed to fund the limited governmental functions. There is no foreign aid. We do not contribute to the IMF or the World Bank. We long ago dropped out of the United Nations. There are few obstacles to starting and running businesses. Because everyone has a firm understanding of economics and business, learned in school, the only ones proposing fiscally irresponsible policies are those with the "Liberal Gene" and are dismissed after trying to explain the consequences of their irrational suggestions. Legal immigration has long been limited to mainly Europeans with a strong preference of Scandinavian females.

A *Painfully* Correct solution to create jobs, eliminate terrorism, and reduce gas prices. Create jobs by mass producing neutron

245

bombs, drop them on Muslim nations, then send their oil here. Problems solved.

PART 9

CRITIQUE OF SELECTED PRESIDENTS

George Washington, 1st President 1789 - 1797

A truly great man, in the right place at the right time and guided by Divine Providence.

Honesty is the best policy.

Thomas Jefferson, 3rd President 1801 - 1809

A founding father of the USA. The author of the draft of the Declaration of Independence.

He sent Lewis and Clark to map the newly acquired western territory. He was a legislator, lawyer, inventor, architect, writer, agriculturist, and diplomat.

Abraham Lincoln, (R) 16th President, 1861 - 1865

The first Republican President.

He freed the slaves.

He didn't allow States to secede from the United States as they have a right to do.

Article III, Section 3. of the Constitution defines treason as levying war against the States, or giving aid and comfort to their enemies.

Theodore Roosevelt, (R), 26th President 1901 – 1909

Teddy was a great individual, but unfortunately became a Progressive.

With an energetic personality he was a hunter, explorer, author, outdoorsman, conservationist and soldier. As a Rough Rider in the Spanish-American War he charged up San Juan Hill in Cuba.

With the Assassination of President McKinley, Teddy became the youngest President at the age of 42.

Teddy had the White House rebuilt adding the West Wing.

In keeping with his motto of "Speak softly and carry a big stick", he modernized and dramatically increased the size of the Navy. He felt that the Panama Canal was his most important and historically significant international achievement. His settlement of the war between Japan and Russia led to him winning the Nobel Peace Prize. He was the first American to win one.

Woodrow Wilson, (D), 28th President 1913 – 1921

He preceded FDR as the first president with socialistic programs and policies. He was one of the most damaging presidents to our country.

He had been a college professor and a college president, never a good idea for either occupation to be in a position to run the country and affect the economy.

His re-election slogan was "He kept us out of war", one month after being re-elected he had the U.S. enter the war. He founded the League of Nations, devoted to world peace. It was proven a failure when World War II began.

In 1913, he enacted income taxes, created huge federal bureaucracies, including the Internal Revenue Service and the Federal Reserve, and incurred a $25 billion debt.

Wilson's State sponsored "Committee on Public Information" propaganda was so affective that the NAZI minister of Propaganda Joseph Goebbels presumably used it as his model.[357] Wilson employed tens of thousands to spread propaganda. Wilson instituted the Espionage Act and the Sedition Act and interned Americans of German descent during WWI.[358] It empowered government to suppress and punish disloyalty and subversion, ban all seditious materials from the mail, which was anything that might impugn the motives of the government. Progressive California Senator Hiram Johnson said, "You shall not criticize anything or anybody in the government any longer or you shall go to jail." The Committee of Public Information made lists of dangerous Americans, set up prison camps, attempted to register all German aliens, arrested more than 6,300 people, banned books, banned teaching the German language in schools, some states banned teaching all foreign language in schools, monitored suspected disloyalty, called the German language hate speech, read peoples mail, spied on Americans, and the 4 Minute Men infiltrated citizen groups.[359] That's what you can expect from Progressives. Not only can it happen here, it did happen here!

Prohibition started during Wilson's term.

Calvin Coolidge, (R), 30th President 1923 -1929

A very popular president.

Recovering from the Depression of 1920-1921, he drastically reduced the size of government. The economic policies advocated by Secretary of the Treasury Andrew Mellon that were a continuation of President Harding's strategy and started while Coolidge was Harding's Vice President, were perhaps the most successful of any Administration. Government spending was greatly reduced and the top marginal tax rate was cut from 58% to 25%.[360] Their economic policies were responsible for the Roaring Twenties, a time of unprecedented prosperity, which dramatically raised the standard of living and expanded the Middle Class. Industrial production grew dramatically, unemployment dropped in 1926 to 1.8%,[361] GNP increased by 4.2% per year through the 1920's, they reduced the National Debt, and by 1926 only about the top 10% of the population were subject to Federal income tax[362] and there was no inflation. The Mellon/Harding/Coolidge policies should be used as the blueprint to recovering from economic hard times.

A conservative, he said, "The business of America is business."

"In a free republic a great government is the product of a great people. They will look to themselves rather than government for success.[363] The destiny, the greatness of America lies around the hearthstone (what is being taught at home around the fire). If thrift and industry are taught there, and the example of self-sacrifice oft appears, if honor abide there, and high ideals, if there the building of fortune be subordinate to the building of character, America will live in security, rejoicing in an abundant prosperity and good government at home and in peace, respect and confidence abroad. If these virtues be absent there is no power that can supply these blessings. Look well to the hearthstone, these in all hope for America lies.[364]

He was known as Silent Cal. History about him has remained mostly silent because in order to build up FDR, the New Deal historians have denigrated Coolidge[365] as well as Andrew Mellon.

250

Franklin D. Roosevelt, (D) 32nd President, 1933 -1945

The similarities with Obama are truly frightening.

FDR was the second president with socialistic programs and policies.

He is the only president to serve more than two terms. He died in office during his fourth term. He might still be President if he were a younger man and in better health, or is that referred to as a dictator?

During the Great Depression he enacted The New Deal, some think of it as a Raw Deal. The only thing we have to fear is, Franklin himself. He took the country off the gold standard, allowed deficits, tripled taxes, placed new controls over banks and utilities, started Social Security, started unemployment insurance, and gave concessions to Labor including forming the WPA, which became known as Workers Poke Along. His Secretary of the Treasury testified, "We are spending more money than we have ever spent before and it does not work." The economy went into a second depression and the US economy was worse than the rest of the world's economies.

The Supreme Court was invalidating New Deal measures, so FDR sought legislation to enlarge the courts size so he could appoint enough of his supporters to have a majority. He was unsuccessful, but changed constitutional law enough so the government could legally regulate the economy.

In 1935, he taxed undistributed profits, preventing businesses from saving money and keeping a cash reserve. He kept changing the rules creating instability. Businesses refused to invest in that environment, so unemployment steadily rose. In 1936, the Stock Market crashed losing 49% of its value, starting a double dipped depression. FDR said of businessmen and bankers, that he welcomed their hatred because every time they made an attack on him he gained votes.[366] He waged class warfare.

The economic measures taken in the Depression of 1920 worked well, but FDR's approach was the opposite strategy. So in an attempt to destroy and discredit Andrew Mellon, the architect of the 1920 recovery, he was falsely accused of being a tax cheat.[367]

It took business demand from WWII to bring us out of the Depression, not baseless government spending.

FDR sought neutrality legislation to keep the US out of the war in Europe.

Some believe he knew in advance that the Japanese were going to attack Pearl Harbor but kept quiet and allowed it to happen.

FDR had 100,000 Americans of Japanese descent sent to Internment Camps. They were imprisoned without any due process, many lost their property and had their lives destroyed. There were curfews on Germans and Italians from 8:00 PM to 6:00 AM and they were prohibited traveling over five miles from home.

The government confiscated: guns, shortwave radios, cameras, and flashlights. People of those ethnic groups were evacuated from coastal towns. Broad subpoenas were issued to quiet grassroots opposition groups. There were boycotts of businesses without a 'Blue eagle' poster.[368] That's what you can expect from Socialists. Not only can it happen here, it did happen here!

The Office of War Information reviewed and edited text books and Hollywood scripts.

FDR helped plan the United Nations.

In 1933, FDR banned private ownership of significant amounts of gold coin. Violations could be fined up to 10 years in jail.[369]

252

In FDR's 1944 State of the Union speech, he proposed a second Bill of Rights. He said, "And after this war is won we must be prepared to move forward, in implementation of these rights." His list is eerily similar to the NAZI's list in the Socialists section of Part 8. It includes the right: of every family to a decent home; to adequate medical care; to a useful and remunerative job; to earn enough to provide adequate food, clothing and recreation; of every farmer to sell his product at a return which will give his family a decent living; to adequate protection from the economic fears of old age and unemployment; to a good education; and of every businessman to trade in an atmosphere of freedom from unfair competition. The legislative movement to enact them into law through a universal health care Bill, the Full Employment Bill and later the Housing Act of 1949,[370] were fortunately blocked in Congress. In 2004, Cass Sunstein published *The Second Bill of Rights: FDR's Unfinished Revolution* ... arguing that citizens rights only exist to the extent that they are granted by the government.[371]

Wife and cousin, Eleanor, along with Rosalynn Carter are among the ugliest women you've ever had the misfortune to see.

Harry Truman, (D), 33rd President 1945 – 1953

A little man in every sense of the word. He relieved of duty the great General Douglas MacArthur.

He authorized dropping two atomic bombs on Japan, causing the most collateral damage from anyone in U.S. history.

In 1950, he sent US troops to Korea entering into the Korean War.

There are two good things about Truman, his saying "the buck stops here", and his presidency led to the first Republican sweep in 20 years.

Dwight D. Eisenhower, (R), 34th President 1953 - 1961

I like Ike.

He was the Supreme Allied Commander during WW II.

In 1953, he help end the Korean War.

In 1954, he helped integrate public schools.

In 1956, he initiated the construction of the U.S. Highway System.

He was the first president to appoint a Black person to a White House executive position. He was the first president since Reconstruction to meet in the White House with Black civil rights Leaders. He was the first combat commander to incorporate Blacks into White units on the battlefield. In 1957, he pushed to get Civil Rights past.[372] The irony is that LBJ was the Senate Majority leader who watered down the bill and wouldn't allow it to pass because it desegregated schools, yet LBJ got the credit when it did pass in 1964.[373]

John F. Kennedy, (D), 35th President 1961 – 1963

The only Democrat worth having as President. By today's standards he would never have been the Democrat nominee, he was too fiscally responsible.

The first Catholic President.

At 43 years old, he was the youngest person elected President.

He was a WWII war hero.

He advanced the space program and achieved his goal of putting a man on the moon by the end of that decade.

254

He cut taxes.

He was assassinated on November 22, 1963.

Lyndon B. Johnson, (D), 36th President 1963 -1969

LBJ was the third president with socialistic programs.

Through his Great Society he declared War on Poverty and enacted the Welfare system, Medicare and Medicaid. His programs have been immensely expensive and very unproductive. In September, 2011 there were more people in poverty than 1965.

He escalated the Vietnam War.

Richard Nixon, (R), 37th President 1969 -1974

A terrible president.

He was called "the last liberal president". It has been said that he expanded the role and size of government more than any president since FDR. He started the Environmental Protection Agency and signed OSHA into law. He called for comprehensive health insurance. He imposed wage and price controls for nearly 1,000 days, unprecedented in peacetime.

On August 15, 1971 by Executive Order he took the U.S. off the gold standard.

He ended the Vietnam War.

He was the first president to resign from office. He was complicit in a misdemeanor crime called Watergate and his covering up of his involvement was blown out of proportion by the Democrats, which forced him out of office.

Jimmy Carter, (D), 39th President 1977 – 1981

He was probably the most incompetent president ever.

He epitomized what Democrats are like in their lack of understanding economics. He drove the economy into the ground with increased taxation and regulation. Interest rates were at historic highs. The Federal Funds Rate was at 19%. The Prime Rate went to 21.5%. There was stagflation, which is rising prices with stagnant wages. His policies caused double-digit unemployment and double-digit inflation. The term coined to measure the shape of the economy was "the misery index", which is the unemployment rate plus the rate of inflation. There was economic malaise.

There were very unpopular, horrendously long gas lines.

He created a situation that allowed Communist China to control the Panama Canal, one of the most dangerous strategic blunders for our country.

American embassy personal in Iran were held hostage for 444 days throughout the end of his term. It wasn't until Ronald Regan became president that they were released.

In an interview in 2004, he said "the American Revolution could have been avoided ... had the British Parliament been a little more sensitive to the colonist's ... we would have been a free country now as is Canada and India and Australia in a nonviolent way."[374]

In 1977, Carter gave millions of undocumented illegal aliens amnesty. They would eventually be eligible to vote. Guess who they would likely vote for?

He boycotted the 1980 Olympics. The Olympics have always been non-political and he ruined all the dreams, aspirations and hard training of our American athletes for his own shortsighted political reasons. Shame on you!

Ronald Reagan, (R), 40th President 1981 – 1989

One of the best presidents ever.

His policies brought about the demise of the Soviet Union. Communism does not work, so their economy was on the verge of collapse. Reagan deliberately set out to bankrupt the Soviet Union to push it into financial collapse.[375] His Star Wars, SDI, Strategic Defense Initiative, was just too expensive for them to compete against, so they folded their hand and terminated the government of the Soviet Union.[376]

He asked for and got the communists to tear down the Berlin Wall.

His economic programs and policies like lowering the tax rate spurred prosperity. The top tax rate was lowered from 70% to 28%. The Seven Fat Years were the longest economic expansion in peacetime history.

Understanding the difference between Carter and Reagan, resulted in the Iranian leaders freeing the American hostages held in Iran just minutes after Reagan was sworn in as President.

He had terrorists in Libya bombed by an air strike.

He was the face of Republicans: patriotic, principled, good values, integrity, dignity, decency, strength, courage, conviction, vision, action, and leadership. A determined leader, he inspired by example.

He connected with the American people like no other President.

Reagan said, "Government is not the solution to our problems, government is the problem."

257

George H. W. Bush, (R), 41st President 1989 -1993

He didn't destroy Russia's nuclear missiles and warheads after the Soviet Union's collapse. He should have paid for or done whatever it took to have their entire nuclear arsenal destroyed. This was probably the most serious missed opportunity in our country's history.

He shut down nuclear warhead production, and according to Michael Savage, had our neutron bombs deactivated.

He foolishly signed a law requiring 800,000 acre feet of water each year in California go to environmental uses regardless of drought conditions.

Bill Clinton, George W. Bush, Barack Hussein Obama

See Part 1.

PART 10

RANDOM THOUGHTS

Kids used to play Doctor, they now play TSA Agent.

Men, join the Peace Corp to get a piece.

Today there are TV shows like: "My Big Fat Obnoxious Gay Midget Bachelorette Survivor".

Have a real Survivor show, put them in Afghanistan.

The Dixie Chicks said they were embarrassed that President Bush is from Texas. Just so you know, we're ashamed the Dixie Chicks are from Dixie!

Communist countries take children away from their parents at three years old to prepare them for the Olympics, and still loose. It is not necessary. By separating them from their families, they lose out on a normal life even if they win the competition. They do not want there to be strong family ties, just allegiance to the government.

It is such a coincidence that Farrah Fawcett died the same day as Michael Jackson, because Farrah is who Michael wanted to end up looking like.

The past is memories, the future is expectations, life is now.

Michael Moron.

Shoeless Joe Jackson vs. Clueless Jesse Jackson.

If it weren't for ex-wives and taxes, I'd be a rich man.

Because there have been so many suicides, San Francisco Liberals want to spend $50 million to place a net under the Golden Gate Bridge. Using that same twisted logic, since some people commit murder using things other than guns, i.e., strangulation, doesn't it follow that hands need to be banned. Hands have been used to strangle people and what is worse, hands are what hold guns, fingers pull triggers. We have a Right to Bare Arms, but we should ban hands.

Two dogs looking in a bedroom window chuckling, "they're doing it people style again".

When the Liberals convince everyone just how dangerous sports are to one's health, we will be a nation reduced to playing hacky sack and pocket pool.

In Genghis Kahn's era, they played polo with the conquered's head. What if their national past time was hacky sack? What part of the anatomy would they use?

With modern technology, the obese need a refrigerator that won't let them open the door.

Don't let other people tell you what to do. If someone says, "have a nice day", and you don't want to, tell them to go to hell.

Brittany spears, a Mouseketeer gone bad.

Life is full of highs and lows, ebbs and flows.

It is remarkable that just before the 100th anniversary of the first flight at Kitty Hawk, the spacecraft Pioneer 10 left the Solar

System. Both endeavors were by Americans.

He was such a loser instead of holding up a gas station, he held up an ATM.

The USA gave charities 75% of all giving in the world in 2002.[377]

Be a registered organ donor upon your death.

Unfortunately Americans have a strong yen for Japanese cars and products.

The Lorena Bobbitt doll – a knife in one hand and the bobbed-it in the other.

Tiger Woods new sponsors should be Trojan, Viagra, an escort service, and car insurance.

On July 18, 1969 Teddy Kennedy leaves Mary Jo Kopechne in a car to drown, then swims away to hide. Why would voters keep re-electing someone that would do that? Who wouldn't swap Teddy Kennedy for JFK or Teddy Roosevelt for FDR?

PART 11

SOLUTIONS, MAKE CHANGES

America's most recent golden age was the 1950's. It was a time when the last thing a child heard their mother say as they were leaving home in the morning was, "Be home by dinner." How far away from those insulated, safe, carefree days our society has fallen. It seems the damage done will never be reversed. Our children are no longer safe to roam their own neighborhood alone. The perverts, drug pushers, kidnappers, and drive by shooters are just too prevalent nowadays. Moral decay is the cause. Lenient liberal judges appointed by Leftist legislators voted in by Democrats are facilitators of street crime. It is time to clean up the country. Get rid of the Leftist agenda and restore our values. The majority of Americans do have good values and want that type of lifestyle back again. We need to stop allowing Liberals to have their way. Don't put up with it anymore!

So much of what has been institutionalized since 1913 needs to be changed; the goals and principles of the tax structure, estate tax, the 17th Amendment, what the Federal government spends tax dollars on, separation of school and state, The Federal Reserve, etc. Encourage politicians to not resign to, as fact, that all the socialistic programs Woodrow Wilson, FDR, and LBJ created need to be permanent and try instead to now eliminate as many as possible. States can nullify all laws the Congress has written that aren't based on the Constitution. We are playing by the Liberal's rules, if we accept the premise that they will always be in place. If we do, only minor adjustments can be made, but what is needed is sweeping change.[378] We need to rebuild America.

Face the fact that approximately 30% of the U.S. population are Liberal nuts that are so different from normal reasonable people that their beliefs are incomprehensible.

Understand, identify, expose, and then deal with the Far-Left Socialist Movement.

In order to improve our quality of life, actions need to be implemented. This is up to you, not just others!

The historic mid-term elections on November 2, 2010 that produced the biggest Party turnover in 70 years was just the beginning. The citizens need to keep pressure on the Republicans to roll back the draconian Obama agenda. The General Election in 2012 needs to really cement our liberties and freedoms by voting out everyone up for election that is not doing what is best for our country. America is at a crossroad. What the Tea Party and conservatives do during 2011 and 2012 is pivotal. Be part of the solution!

"Eternal vigilance is the price of freedom." - Thomas Jefferson.

The answer lies with the truth.

Glenn Beck's 8/28/10 Rally in Washington, D.C. was reportedly the fifth largest event held on the Mall. The Rally was a faith based, family oriented, patriotic, peaceful gathering. It showed how many people care and want change.

As explained in the book *Paradigm Shift*, knowledge is disseminated, and then possessed by everyone all at once. It isn't about one person or one group. It is beliefs in ideals, values and principles i.e., honor and one's sacred honor, that multitudes posses and will go out to live and spread the message by setting an example that commands emulation.

Glenn Beck, for example, understands that the country is in trouble and he is willing to do and say the hard things to try to rectify the situation. Glenn's message is, each individual must take personal responsibility to better themselves and thereby bettering the country. Belief in Devine Providence is exposing you to these truths for a reason.

Do something to improve yourself, the country you live in, and our children's future. If America loses its freedom, the world will rapidly fall into a totalitarian nightmare.

You need to step out of your comfort zone and force yourself to do more, complacency isn't working. The Left is relentless and has been achieving their agenda for many decades. You will lose your freedom and your descendant's freedom if you don't do everything you can to prevent it now.

We are witnessing history. We are in the beginning of the Second American Revolution.

Take personal responsibility.

Pray for and defend freedom and liberty for all.

Be part of the solution. The following are things you can do.

Self Education:

"Let us dare to read, speak, and write." - John Adams

Educate yourself about our country and what the Left has been up to. Read the Constitution. If you have children, most schools study the Constitution in 8th grade, have them also read it with you at home and discuss it. If they are older, ask them to re-read it. Together with your family watch shows that pertain to pertinent events like Glenn Beck on TV. Watch Fox TV. Watch movies that provide insight into what totalitarianism is like, *The Last Emperor*, *Dr. Zhivago*, etc. Also listen to conservative radio shows.

Read books relating to government and freedom like *Animal Farm*, *Brave New World*, *1984*, *Fahrenheit 451*, and Ayn Rand's books.

The two most important things ever written are the Bible and the U.S. Constitution, read them both and abide by them.

Knowledge will prevent us from being slaves. - attributed to John Adams.

Question everything. "Question with boldness" - Thomas Jefferson.

Rush Limbaugh

Attila the Tongue.

Listen regularly to his radio show. He has done more for the conservative movement than anyone in the country.

Glenn Beck

If there are reruns, watch his TV Show on the Fox channel. If you can, follow his GBTV on his website and listen to his radio show. He serves as an educator and a history professor.

Education

Stop standing silently on the sidelines while the Left indoctrinates our kids.[379]

There should be a separation of School and State. For more information, contact Alliance for the Separation of School & State

266

at www.schoolandstate.org. Until then, advocate for vouchers and charter schools.

Free Market Education, there needs to be more competition in the choice of education than just a State-run monopoly. [380]

Encourage your elected representatives to abolish the Department of Education.

If you are not inclined to be a teacher, as a start, please vote for Republican School Trustees, pressure Trustees to not hire Liberals.

Get together with like-minded people in your community and with an organized and well thought out plan go about getting rid of Liberal teachers. This probably needs to be a top down ousting. Investigate candidates running for elected Trustees. Be involved in campaigns to not elect Liberal Trustees so they do not hire a Liberal college president who in turn hires Liberal teachers and professors who in turn try to indoctrinate your kids into becoming Liberal.

Get involved in the process of selecting the curriculum and textbook choices for your community's schools. The disinformation, propaganda, and indoctrination seriously affect our country and the next generation.

Refute misinformation.

Do not endow even your Alma Mater unless they make lasting changes to eliminate Professors that promote or condone Political Correctness. If your Alma Mater refuses to change, endow a conservative College like the Institute of World Politics in Washington, DC.

Promote the concept that Political Science majors should be required to have a minor in Economics, and not Sociology

267

emphasized Economics classes, but true business education, so politicians will understand the ramifications of their votes.

There should be an outreach project to educate Liberals about fiscal responsibility and economics, but not through a government program. Maybe retired businessmen would want to do this for our legislators. It would be very helpful.

Encourage open discussions about bringing sanity back to public policies, like letting kids walk to neighborhood schools instead of busing them across town. In February 2011, in Wake County, North Carolina, the school board voted to put an end to using race and income to determine which school the kids would attend, allowing them to go to their neighborhood school. Martin Luther King Jr. would be proud.

When writing or referring to anyone in a Government bureaucracy or to Democrats, use the term Comrade in order to get the point across that the country is becoming increasingly communistic. For example, when referring to a problem with the Post Office, "It must have gotten lost in the mail or from some other bureaucratic inefficiency, comrade".

Local Government

Get involved in citizen advisory committees that do things like review your community's budget or the salaries and pensions of elected officials.

Federal Government

If you disagree with something the government is doing, tell your U.S. Representative and U.S. Senator directly to do something about it and get results. For example, if you do not want the Department of Interior to take thousands of acres of farmland out of production and waste $1 billion trying to reintroduce 500 fish, tell your representatives to defund the project.

States can nullify unconstitutional laws imposed by the Federal Government. Encourage your Representatives to purse that course of action to eliminate bad laws.

Tell your representatives to treat the food supply as a National Security issue and to prevent farmland from being paved over.

As a safeguard from bio-terrorism, don't allow food to be prevented from being grown in California, not just because of the enormous variety of different crops but because it is the safest food in the world because Prop.65 restricts more pesticides than anywhere else.

Encourage your Representatives to privatize as many government functions as possible, and to induce limited government. We need Entitlement reform.

Encourage your Representatives to pass legislation that will allow for the extraction of oil, natural gas, and coal from all U.S. territories.

Encourage your Representatives to replace the Obama appointed heads of regulatory agencies and cut their funding. Obama has greatly expanded the budgets of the EPA, OSHA, etc., and staked them with Leftist ideologues.

There are two ways to deal with Special Interests: control the effects or remove the causes. A caution about the later, it can destroy liberty, so the cure may be worse than the disease.

National Debt

Support Representative Ron Paul's effort through H1207, to audit

269

the Federal Reserve, so we know what they are up to. Insist on transparency in government versus secrecy.

The Federal Reserve, established in 1913, can be abolished and replaced with free-market banking. The government gets around taxing and borrowing by just having the Federal Reserve print or create the money it needs. There are no elected officials in the Federal Reserve. The workers there are not government employees. The general public does not know who owns this "quasi-private" institution. There is no accountability to anyone. Wasteful spending has to be a thing of the past.

Statements by Obama and the Secretary of the Treasury, Timothy Geithner, in 2011 about the country defaulting if the debt ceiling is not raised, is irresponsible and dishonest. The government collects enough tax revenue to easily make the debt payments. This is the same kind of fear mongering as local communities make about cutting police and fire department personnel when there are needed budget cuts. They say the only cuts will be to the most essential services, not to all the bloated give away programs. The Mainstream Media repeats and spreads this lie about defaulting on the debt.

When the National Debt is increased the Federal Reserve creates money by selling Treasury Bonds which it has to pay back and is paying interest on them during the life of the bond. This is inflationary. The Quantitative Easing scam is even worse, it creates money out of thin air. That "money" is used by the Federal Reserve to buy the Treasury Bonds. That is really inflationary. When there is more money it has less value. The government is robbing you of your hard earned nest-egg.

Encourage your representative to follow the Mellon/Harding/Coolidge approach to improving the economy.

270

Unions

Collective bargaining with government employees is not allowed at the Federal level. States must pass laws that allow workers to have "right to work" protections for public sector employees. Encourage your representatives to legislatively discontinue this practice.

When you see union protesters, say to people walking by to support capitalism by purchasing the product that the business is selling. Help make unions irrelevant by ignoring their boycotts and picketing.

Courts

If you are unhappy with the legal system, and you ever voted for a Democrat, you are part of the problem. Do not vote for Democrats, they appoint Liberal judges who make rulings that are against the values of pro-life, religion, marriage, property rights, the Second Amendment, water rights, etc.

Encourage and support legislators that want to retract the law that being born in this country grants automatic citizenship. Illegal alien mothers purposely bare an 'Anchor baby' here to tie them to this country. The ramifications of this policy costs us billions of dollars annually.

Encourage and support legislators to enact Tort reform.

The public, from a financial perspective as well as a deterrent to crime, should have the right to a fair and speedy execution of capital punishment crimes.

The Left claims the gas chamber is cruel and unusual punishment. California's left argues it is cheaper to sentence capital punishment criminals to life imprisonment than to be on Death Row for 20-30 years. The Justice system needs to go in the opposite direction.

271

Condemned criminals should be hung in short-order after sentencing. Rope is cheap and can be re-used multiple times. The cost and length of time for appeals is ridiculous and was designed to get to this point where it is not worth the cost.

Rights

The Federal government has violated States Rights. The Federal government has over stepped its authority. Support efforts by Gov. Rick Perry and others to reassert their State's Rights and force the Federal government to confine itself to the limitations defined in the Constitution.

Support efforts to repeal the 17th Amendment.

Taxes

The Fair Tax Act, HR 25, would abolish the IRS because with only a national sales tax the IRS would not be needed.[381] The current progressive income tax rate schedule is grossly unfair, and although a flat rate sounds great, a consumption tax is an even fairer way to collect revenue. If there were no income tax at all and the only tax was a national sales tax, then everyone would pay based strictly on what they purchase. You determine how much tax you pay based on your consumption decisions, not the government by imposing a progressive rate structure. There wouldn't be any loopholes for people to avoid paying taxes, even illegal drug traffickers would pay for their purchases here. Taxing would be spread out to include everyone, so the base would be enormous thereby making the rate low. The proposal is at 23%, but after put into practice, my guess is it could be in the low teens with a smaller government model. High income people make larger purchases, like yachts and planes, and so would pay in a lot.

Low income people would only be paying on their basic necessities like food, beer, cigarettes and lottery tickets.

272

Support any effort to repeal Inheritance Tax, known as Estate Tax, which is actually a Death Tax.

The Capital Gains Tax should be eliminated in order to stimulate investment.

United Nations

Encourage legislators to propose the USA drop out of the U.N. Support any effort for the USA: to not fund it or withdraw from it. The League of Nations dissolved, why not the U.N.

Foreign Aid

"Foreign aid might be defined as a transfer (of money) from poor people in rich countries to rich people in poor countries." - Douglas Casey

Most other countries hate us, so why give them money?

We send billions of dollars to Israel which they use in part to build settlements, then later they use more U.S. aid money to tear down the settlements.

Foreign Aid is nothing more than bribes.

The fashionable thing the Limousine Liberals to do now is to send money to Africa. Billions of taxpayer's money and billions of private philanthropy money has gone there recently. With the current economic crisis America is in, it would be better to keep the money in our own country. Products produced by businesses like Microsoft are purchased by American consumers, a portion of the profit goes to Bill Gates, he is giving some of that money to other countries. It would help our economy if the money stayed in America and was reinvested here to create more jobs. When it leaves the country it is an amount that is taken out of our financial system which is detrimental to our economy. It is an unpatriotic act and redistributes our wealth globally.

IMF, International Monetary Fund

Encourage legislators to propose the USA drop out of the IMF.

Support any effort for the USA: to not fund it and withdraw from it.

World Bank

Encourage legislators to propose the USA drop out of the World Bank. Support any effort for the USA: to not fund it and withdraw from it.

Boycotts

Use the free market and vote with your dollars to defeat Liberals.

The Leftist Cesar Chavez boycotted grapes in the 1960's. Patriotic Americans need to exercise their right to boycott people and organizations that are un-American: Liberal media, movie stars, Universities, etc. They are so entrenched in our society it is the only way to curb their activities. Voting with your dollars will cause sponsors to stop supporting them with advertising, which allows them to have a voice in the media.

Boycott businesses that advocate environmental extremism. In the Spring of 2010, American Express had a TV commercial favorably recognizing a guy causing dams to be torn down. Boycott sponsors with gays on TV.

Boycott Action Comics for indoctrinating children into believing the Leftist globalization view that the United Nations is a higher authority than the United States of America by having Superman denounce his American citizenship.

Boycott the approximately 165 cities and counties that have passed laws against the Patriot Act.

Boycott Sanctuary Cities.

We could make each December 7th, the anniversary of the bombing of Pearl Harbor, a day when people put notes that say "Buy American" on Japanese cars and other foreign made products. You could even sneak up on the cars while no one is looking.

Delta Airlines in June, 2011 made a deal with Saudi Arabia that people could not fly if wearing non-Muslim religious artifacts or if Jewish. They are putting money before our principles of freedom of religion.

When you find out that a company either directly or through a subsidiary donates to Liberal causes, i.e., General Electric owns NBC News, then not only boycott the parent company and its subsidiary, but spread the word among your friends and others.

If there are liberal inspired laws or ordinances that by violating them doesn't infringe on other people's rights, like smoking out of other's range, you can employ civil disobedience in protest and go ahead and conduct the prohibited act.

Abortion

When someone says Pro-Choice, immediately say the Devil's Choice. Say it frequently enough that it becomes associated in everyone's mind with the Pro-Choice term. Make people realize who is really behind it.

<u>Voting</u>

Be sure you vote and try to help get at least one other likeminded voter to the polls. Overcompensate for others apathy.

Volunteer for a position that prevents voter fraud.

The eligibility requirement should be ownership of real estate and be at least 25 years old, a criteria based on age indexing since 1776. The exception would be those serving in the military who could vote at age 18.

Strongly oppose passage of the Dream Act.

Encourage friends you may have that are Democrats to form a Third Party of fiscally responsible Democrats.

If someone is elected under suspicious circumstances, try to recall them like Gov. Gray Davis was in California.

Vote RINOs out of office.

Elect fiscal conservatives.

Let your elected representatives know you will not vote for them, if they do not support issues that are important to you.

If you are an employer that has a TV in a waiting area for your customers, have the channel set to Fox News. The other networks spew propaganda that may lead susceptible clients to vote for fiscally irresponsible politicians that will increase your taxes and impose restrictive regulations that will directly impact you. Likewise, if you are a customer, ask that the channel be changed to Fox News. Similarly, turn off NPR and tune into conservative talk radio.

If you have been voting for Democrat candidates but the things they stand for, namely: Big Government, tax the rich, dumb down education, no individual ownership of guns, don't punish criminals, very limited property rights, and being anti-capitalists is not what you believe in, please stop voting for them. Their policies are ruining the country!

We need to resurrect the 1946 slogan "Had Enough? Vote Republican!"

Immigration

Encourage legislators to propose immigration policy be changed. With so many illegal Latinos entering and residing in the U.S., the demographics of the population has changed to the point that in 2011 the majority of children born are to non-whites. For the sake of strengthening the population's skill level, exceptional foreign students earning degrees in selected needed fields of study, that would commit to residing here for a minimum of 10 years, should be the only ones granted citizenship for a period of time. Even though new citizens should prove that they will not be a burden on society, we have enough people to take care of for the foreseeable future. If we do open up immigration at some point, it should be strictly to Caucasians. No more Latino or Muslim immigrants.

Encourage legislators to propose that the North American Free Trade Agreement, NAFTA member nations standardize their immigration laws to match Mexico's stringent immigration law.

Drugs

There should be an all out war on drugs. Encourage abolishment of the absurd policy of not using our military to fight drug trafficking. Drugs are destroying so many lives in this country. Use our military's extensive capabilities to detect everything crossing our borders and have them prevent drugs from entering and seize what is here.

277

Agriculture

The Environmentalists are causing farmland to be deprived of water. Foolish policies are causing farmland to be paved over. Encourage legislators to protect our farmland and food supply.

Tea Party

The modern-day Tea Party movement was sparked by CNBC Business anchor Rick Santelli's televised rant on February 19, 2009. Patriots around the nation spontaneously communicated through the internet and organized rallies in various cities around the country, which took place on February 27, 2009. On April 15, 2009, concurrent with the income tax due date, large rallies were held in many locations. In the Summer of 2009 there were town hall meetings about socialized medicine. Taxpayers had enough of Obama forcing a program against the will of 70% of the voters, and similar to the Boston Tea Party in 1773, the people peacefully rebelled. The Tea Party is comprised of patriots defending America's values, principles, and original intent.

Ron Paul had a celebration of the 134th anniversary of the Boston Tea Party on December 16, 2007.

Be a government by the people, take back our government. The Tea Party is a grassroots movement to take back our government. You can't afford to be apathetic or we'll lose the country.

The core values of all Tea Party groups are: fiscal responsibility, constitutionally limited government, and free markets. What's not to like? They advocate non-violence and do not condone racism.

The Tea Party Movement is the Second American Revolution.
If you are so inclined, join a Tea Party group and/or contribute to one, the extra support will be useful and meaningful.

278

The Tea Party is comprised of constitutionalists.

The Tea Party Movement will set the course for Congressman Paul Ryan's path to prosperity.

The Tea Party's Taxpayer March on Washington drew an estimated one million people to the Mall on September 12, 2009.

The Left wants and needs the Tea Party to be violent. The Tea Party is not inclined to play their game. There was a saying in the 1960's, "suppose they gave a war and nobody came." By not doing what they expect, it defuses them, it takes away their power and their argument.

The Tea Party formed to get the USA back on track. The country isn't over, this is the beginning of a bright new future!

Share the ideas found in this book

The information contained in this book will provide an excellent education for the Occupy Wall Street types, students and Democrats. Liberals are hopeless and humorless, but it will be fun to infuriate them with it.

Fiscally Conservative Organizations

Support, join or contribute to groups like the Heritage Foundation at heritage.org; Hillsdale College at hillsdale.edu; The Cato Institute at cato.org; Americans for Prosperity americansforprosperity.org; for private property rights the Pacific Legal Foundation at community.pacificlegal.org; for privacy and civil liberties issues the EPIC, Electronic Privacy Information Center at epic.org; for Agriculture the American Farmland Trust at farmland.org, and for property rights American Stewards of Liberty at americanstewards.us and for lists of conservative organizations FreeRepublic.com.

<u>America</u>

America is not like the rest of the world. America is not just buildings or a location; it is a wonderful experiment, a concept of self-government by the common man which provides liberty and the opportunity for advancement through capitalism in the pursuit of happiness. There is hope for everyone evidenced by countless success stories. During challenging times there is a patriotic feeling, a sense of standing together and fighting for a set of ideals and principles, fighting for the best hope for the world to have a future that includes individual freedoms, laws, justice and democracy; everything dear to the American character. Few want to live in or bring children into a world of total totalitarianism, no freedom, no justice, unfair laws, with a bleak future. The human race has evolved a governing and economic structure to this point where we now have a Republic with democracy, freedoms and capitalism. Let's pray people won't allow the world to slip back to the dark ages.

Every loyal American, including descendants of the Confederates, should agree with Abraham Lincoln's words in the Gettysburg Address, "It is ... for us here to be dedicated to the great task remaining before us ... devotion to that cause ... that we here, highly resolve ... that this nation, under God, shall have a new birth of freedom and a government of the people, by the people, for the people, shall not perish from the Earth.

The U.S. is the most powerful economic engine on the planet. If sound economic policies were reinstated, we would once again be the envy of the world instead of being on the brink of financial collapse. We need new management, a fiscally conservative President and Senate and House of Representatives that will eliminate restrictive financial and environmental regulations and allow the free market system to thrive.

If there is great civil unrest, go and protect your church because a strategy of the radicals is to burn the churches so people won't have a place to go for spiritual refuge and guidance.

Restore the Republic, win back America!

Painfully Correct

If you are sick and tired of political correctness, the best way to put an end to it is to combat it by being *Painfully* Correct each and every time you are subjected to political correctness. We have all accepted political correctness for far too long, it is time to do away with it. It just takes you to say NO to it. This has to be a national movement carried out by each individual. Remember the old adage, "If you aren't part of the solution, you are part of the problem." The more people that are *Painfully* Correct the more prevalent it will become, until the accepted practice will be, being *Painfully* Correct. Use ideas in this book to combat political correctness. When you hear someone state something in politically correct terms, say "Let's be *Painfully* Correct", then tell them like it is and set the record straight. Liberalism doesn't work. The things Liberals believe in are absurd. These lunatic Liberal losers are a joke. We need to first mock this insidious disease called political correctness, and then make it irrelevant!

PART 12

CONCLUSION

If you have read the entire book, you must realize that in this era a vote for a Democrat is a vote for socialism. If you do not want America to be a socialist country, even if you and your family have voted Democrat for generations, don't vote for Democrats.

Connect the dots. Whether coincidence or not, regarding predictions from various sources that the world will end in December of 2012, we are at a pivotal point in time, when the world could rapidly fall under Totalitarian Rule. The number of countries simultaneously experiencing civil unrest may be unprecedented. Over the last 100 years, the Progressives have gradually and methodically put all the pieces in place. A revolution in the United States could be launched at any time now. The Devil's claw is around us, about to clench his fist. The only hope is that patriotic Americans will exert sufficient determination to defeat the beast and that God will help us in the endeavor.

Obama has assigned his appointed cronies and advisors, which are mostly Leftist radicals, to strategic government positions (details in Part 1, Obama). They have rapidly enacted laws that are following the Cloward and Piven economic collapse strategy and have changed laws that could create a dictatorship (details in Part 4, Purpose). They have enacted the Financial Reform Bill, Health Care, have proposed Cap and Trade, which would control Industry, and are close to implementing the Food Safety Bill, which will control our food supply. The Leftists have organized and prepared their radicals for revolution. There are millions of willing dupes: in Unions, in extreme environmental organizations, from the anti-American segments of the Latino and Black communities, in the civil rights movement, Left-leaning clergy, feminists, gays, Leftists academics, community activists, to the proverbial college malcontents, and from many of the people dependant on Entitlement programs. It is obvious from Obama's rhetoric of fundamental transformation, his use of Czars, the fast pace of having legislation enacted, and the massive debt incurred, that the Left is poised for a takeover of the United States. Thankfully, patriots have risen up in the form of the Tea Party Movement to oppose the fundamental transformation of America.

It is a volatile time. The worldwide Environmental Movement with their Cap and Trade scheme, fueled by the Global Warming hoax, is the longer term instrument that will give Leftists enough global power to control every aspect of the world's population (details in Part 7, Cap and Trade). Their immediate vehicle is through financial collapse (details in Part 8, The Left's Formula to Control the World). The final step of their strategy is to silence the opposition, the conservative media, and to then control all media (details in Part 4, Purpose). Because they know their influence is on the decline because of the results of the 2010 mid-term elections, they may revolt sooner rather than waiting for ideal conditions. The Left has all the legislative pieces in place for taking control, one way or the other. They have never been closer to achieving their goal and won't stop until they get their way. They realize their Czars may lose their power soon and be replaced. The public is on to them. The U.S. is vulnerable financially. George Soros, for instance, could persuade China to call the U.S. debt, which would result in us defaulting. China could determine that in the long run they would benefit if America could be caused to collapse now. So even though the Republicans were able to establish a majority in the House of Representatives, conservatives will have to be ever vigilant to fend off a total take over by the Left at any time.

Our freedom and liberties are too precious to risk losing. We need to take back the country, and soon! We need to instill limited government. The new Congress should adopt the Mellon/Harding/Coolidge policies as a template to maintaining a sound economy (details in Part 9, Presidents).

Just as Russia tried Communism for 74 years and found it doesn't work, then changed systems, America has tried mild socialism from 1913 through 1920 and from 1933 until now, and it doesn't work. We need to once again practice what was the original intent of the Founders, which does work. 1776 was an outstanding year which marked the inception of Adam Smith's free market capitalism and the concept of a self-governing free citizenry, through the U.S. Constitution. Our country is now on the brink of financial collapse, Democrats need to be told that the country can no longer afford to indulge their fiscally irresponsible whims; we just can't support their foolish policies any longer.

Don't allow the Left, that only comprises approximately 30% of the population, to highjack our country by imposing laws and regulations that go against your values. Put Liberals on a collision course with reality. Let's destroy Multiculturalism and Political Correctness like we are going after Terrorism. We finally got the balls to fight Terrorism, let's fight PC, drugs, illegal immigration, and un-American activities with the same vengeance.

Be morally correct. Go forth and spread the truth! But even more importantly, put the words into action.

To Politically Correct practitioners and enforcers, let me extend to you a sincere and heartfelt F#*K YOU A&SHOLE !!! for trying to destroy our country and for imposing all your Leftist views on everyone else.

My epitaph should be: They f#*ked with the wrong guy.

Let's all be *Painfully* Correct!

Painfully Correct may be purchased at https://www.createspace.com/3720939

For more information, and where to purchase humorous bumper stickers and other *Painfully* Correct products, go to http://www.painfullycorrect.com

PAINFULLY CORRECT

SOURCES

"2008 Presidential Election Finance/Insurance/Real Estate Sector Totals to Candidates." *Open Secrets.* July 13, 2009. http://www.opensecrets.org/pres08/sectors.php?sector=F (accessed October 20, 2011).

"34 Years of Tides." *Tides.* http://www.tides.org/about-us/history/index/ (accessed October 7, 2010).

ABC News Political Punch. February 18, 2008. http://blogs.abcnews.com/politicalpunch/2008/02/michelle-obam-1-2 (accessed September 13, 2010).

ABC Nightly News. February 18, 2011.
"About the Fabian Society." *The Fabian Society.* http://www.fabians.org.uk/about-the-fabian-society (accessed September 16, 2011).

"About the MoveOn Family of Organizations." *MoveOn.org: Democracy in Action.* http://www.moveon.org/about.html (accessed September 29, 2010).

Adams, J. Christian. "Doing the DOJ's Job for Them: Demanding Valid Voter Rolls Before November." *Pajamas Media.* September 7, 2010. http://pajamasmedia.com/blog/doing-the-dojs-job-for-them-demanding-valid-voter-rolls-before-november (accessed October 1, 2011).

Aim Report. "Is Barack Obama a Marxist Mole?" *AIM*. March 18, 2008. http://www.aim.org/aim-report/is-barack-obama-a-marxist-mole/ (accessed November 2, 2010).

Alinsky, Saul D. *Rules For Radicals*. Random House, 1971.

Allahpundit. "Obama's Turnout Pitch to Latinos: Get Out There and Punish Your 'Enemies'." *Hotair*. October 25, 2010. http://www.hotair.com/archives/2010/10/25/obamas-turnout-pitch-to-latinos-get-out-there-and-punish-your-enemies (accessed November 26, 2010).

Allan, Alasdair, and Pete Warden. "Got an iPhone or 3G iPad? Apple is Recording Your Moves." *O'Reilly Radar*. April 20, 2011. http://radar.oreilly.com/2011/04/apple-location-tracking.html (accessed April 26, 2011).

Allen, Vanessa. "Outrage as Agony Aunt Tells TV Audience 'I Would Suffocate a Child to End Its Suffering'." *Daily Mail*. October 5, 2010. http://www.dailymail.co.uk/news/article-1317400/Virginia-Ironside-sparks-BBC-outrage-Id-suff (accessed November 26, 2010).

Ambinder, Marc. "What Hillary Clinton Didn't Do." *National Journal*. November 30, 2010. http://www.nationaljournal.com/whitehouse/hillary-clinton-didn-t-turn-diplomats-into-spies-2010 (accessed December 4, 2010).

American Broadcasting Companies, Inc. "World News with Diane Sawyer." *Lexis Nexis News.* February 25, 2011. http://www6.lexisnexis.com/publisher/EndUser?Action=UserDisplayFullDocument&orgID=574&topic (accessed March 28, 2011).

"American Jobs Act." *The White House Office of the Press Secretary.* April 27, 2009. http://www.whitehouse.gov/the_press_office/President-Obama-Announces-Members-of-Science-and-Technology-Advisory-Council/ (accessed September 23, 2011).

Anders, Jarolsaw. "United States is Largest Donor of Foreign Aid, Report Says." *US Department of State Bureau of International Programs.* May 24, 2007. http://www.america.gov/st/washfile-english/2007/May/20070524165115zjsredna0.2997553.html (accessed November 29, 2010).

Andrea. "Moammar Kadafi Praises Obama in Speech to United Nations General Assembly." *Renovomedia.* September 23, 2009. http://www.renovomedia.com/politics/moammar-kadafi-praises-obama-in-speech-to-united-nations-general-assembly-video/ (accessed October 19, 2010).

Andrews, Sean. "Tariq Ramadan and Islamic Socialism." *LBO-Talk.* February 16, 2007. http://mailman.lbo-talk.org/2007/2007-February/003211.html (accessed September 29, 2011).

Angle, Jim. "British PM Decries Multiculturalism, Warns of Danger." *Fox News.* February 8, 2011. http://www.foxnews.com/world/2011/02/07/multiculturalism-europe-blamed-extremism-british-bp/ (accessed February 15, 2011).

"Apollo Alliance Background." *Apollo Alliance.* http://apolloalliance.org/about (accessed October 8, 2010).

"April 6 Youth Movement." *Frontline PBS.* February 22, 2011. http://www.pbs.org/wgbh/pages/frontline/revolution-in-cairo/inside-april6-movement/ (accessed September 16, 2011).

Balz, Dan. "Obama's Debt Commission Warns of Fiscal 'Cancer'." *The Washington Post.* July 12, 2010. http://www.washingtonpost.com/wp-dyn/content/article/2010/07/11/AR2010071101956.html (accessed December 10, 2010).

Beck, Glenn. "Glenn Beck Quote of the Day: America Makes Nothing of Value." *Fox News Insider.* October 18, 2010. http://www.foxnewsinsider.com/2010/10/18/glenn-beck-quote-of-the-day-america-makes-nothing-of-value (accessed December 3, 2010).

—. "Glenn Beck: America's Banker: How Will China Treat Deadbeat Borrowers?" *Fox News.* January 18, 2011. http://www.foxnews.com/on-air/glenn-beck/transcript/americas-banker-how-will-china-treat-deadbeat-borrower? (accessed February 7, 2011).

—. "Glenn Beck: America's Stretch of Stability the Exception, Not the Norm." *Fox News.* December 13, 2010. http://www.foxnews.com/on-air/glenn-beck/transcript/americas-stretch-stability-exception-not-norm (accessed December 16, 2010).

——. "Glenn Beck: Clear Choice From National Mall." *Fox News.* October 5, 2010. http://www.foxnews.com/story/0,2933,601803,00.html (accessed November 24, 2010).

——. "Glenn Beck: Founders' Fridays: James Madison." *Fox News.* June 11, 2010. http://www.foxnews.com/story/0,2933,594542,00.html (accessed December 3, 2010).

——. "Glenn Beck: Fundamental Transformation of America." *Fox News.* April 22, 2011. http://www.foxnews.com/on-air?glenn-beck/transcript/beck-fundamental-transformation-america (accessed April 26, 2011).

——. "Glenn Beck: George Soros' Mr. Potter Moment." *Fox News.* October 20, 2010. http://www.foxnews.com/story/0,2933,6019725,00.html (accessed November 29, 2010).

——. "Glenn Beck: Indoctrination in America." *Fox News.* March 5, 2010. http://www.foxnews.com/story/0,2933,588338,00.html (accessed December 3, 2010).

——. "Glenn Beck: Left's Egypt Conspiracy Accusations Lack Facts." *Fox News.* February 8, 2011. http://www.foxnews.com/on-air/glenn-beck/transcript/lefts-egypt-conspiracy-accusations-lack-facts (accessed February 10, 2011).

——. "Glenn Beck: Meet the Radicals: Warning Signs of Revolution." *Fox News.* December 20, 2010. http://www.foxnews.com/on-air/glenn-beck/transcript/meet-radicals-warning-signs-revolution? (accessed February 7, 2011).

——. "Glenn Beck: Republic vs. Democracy: What Did Our Founders Truly Intend?" *Fox News.* August 6, 2010. http://www.foxnews.com/story/0,2933,598802,00.html (accessed November 24, 2010).

——. "Glenn Beck: Restoring History." *Fox News.* July 9, 2010. http://www.foxnews.com/story/0,2933,596523,00.html (accessed November 30, 2010).

——. "Glenn Beck: Soros Exposed: Research on the Progressive Puppet Master." *Glenn Beck.* November 11, 2010. http://www.glennbeck.com/content/articles/article/198/478 56/ (accessed November 29, 2010).

——. "Glenn Beck: The Puppet Master." *Fox News.* November 9, 2010. http://www.foxnews.com/story/0,2933,602142,00.html (accessed February 8, 2011).

——. "Glenn Beck: The Revolution is Now." *Fox News.* December 9, 2010. http://www.foxnews.com/on-air/glenn-beck/transcript/revolution-now (accessed December 11, 2010).

——. "Glenn Beck: Three Reasons to Be Wary of Google." *Fox News.* February 16, 2011. http://www.foxnews.com/on-air/glenn-beck/transcript/beck-three-reasons-be-wary-google (accessed February 17, 2011).

Glenn Beck: Union Protestors Promise to 'Release All Hell'. Performed by Glenn Beck. Fox News. March 23, 2011.

——. "Glenn Beck: What is the Red-Green Alliance?" *Fox News.* February 11, 2011. http://www.foxnews.com/on-air/glenn-beck/transcript/what-red-green-alliance (accessed February 14, 2011).

——. "Glenn Beck: Who Are Fabian Socialists?" *Glenn Beck.* October 6, 2010. http://www.glennbeck.com/content/articles/article/198/463 61/ (accessed November 26, 2010).

——. "Glenn Beck: Who Is Organizing Against Free Speech?" *Fox News.* October 22, 2010. http://www.foxnews.com/story/0,2933,601982,00.html (accessed November 24, 2010).

——. "Glenn Beck: Who Wants a Califphate in the Middle East?" *Fox News.* February 3, 2011. http://www.foxnews.com/on-air/glenn-beck/transcript/who-wants-caliphate-middle-east (accessed February 8, 2011).

Liberation Theology and the Political Perversion of Christianity. Performed by Glenn Beck. Glenn Beck. July 13, 2010.

Meet Glenn's Mentor (Repeat). Performed by Glenn Beck. Glenn Beck. December 29, 2010.

Netroots Targets Glenn. Performed by Glenn Beck. Glenn Beck. July 26, 2010.

Truth About Church and State. Performed by Glenn Beck. Glenn Beck. September 27, 2010.

Beckerman, Gal. "The 'Answer' Question Poses Difficult Choices for Liberals." *Forward.* September 30, 2005. http://www.forward.com/articles/1985/ (accessed September 16, 2011).

Beisner, Calvin, and David Barton, interview by Glenn Beck. *Glenn Beck: Dangers of Environmental Extremism* (October 15, 2010).

Beres, Robin. "Our Enemies Are Still Plotting Against Us." *Richmond Times-Dispatch.* November 29, 2009. http://www2.timesdispatch.com/nws/2009/nov/29/ed-beres29_20091127-194201-ar-21367/ (accessed February 9, 2011).

"Bill Ayers: Any Country With a US Military Base Should Be Able To Vote In American Elections." *I Hate The Media.* March 30, 2011. http://www.ihatethemedia.com/bill-ayers-any-country-with-us-military-base-should-vote-american-elections (accessed September 24, 2011).

Blodget, Henry. "CAUGHT ON TAPE: Former SEIU Official Reveals Secret Plan to Destroy JP Morgan, Crash The Stock Market, And Redistribute Wealth In America." *Business Insider.* March 22, 2011. http://www.businessinsider.com/seiu-union-plan-to-destroy-jpmorgan (accessed September 23, 2011).

Bloom, Ron. "Ron Bloom: Mao and Free Market 'Nonsense;." *Freedom Eden.* October 20, 2009. http://freedomeden.blogspot.com/2009/10/ron-bloom-mao-and-free-market-nonsense.html (accessed July 11, 2011).

Blount, Jeb, and Miles Weiss. "Soros Hedge Fund Bought Petrobras Stake Worth $811 Million." *Bloomberg.* August 15, 2008. http://www.bloomberg.com/apps/news?pid=newsarchive& sid=aFHPjfeUvtl8 (accessed September 22, 2011).

Blume, Howard. "Los Angeles School Named After Al Gore." *Los Angeles Times.* September 5, 2010. http://articles.latimes.com/2010/sep/05/local/la-me-gore-school-20100906 (accessed September 9, 2010).

Booker, Christopher. "Climate Change: This is the Worst Scientific Scandal of Our Generation." *The Telegraph.* November 28, 2009. http://www.telegraph.co.uk/comment/columnists/christoph erbooker/6679082/Climate-change-this-is-the-worst-scientific-scandal-of-our-generation.html (accessed October 19, 2011).

Freedom Watch. Performed by Neal Boortz. Freedom Watch. December 2, 2010.

Boulton, Clint. "GSA Picks Google Apps Cloud Over Microsoft, IBM." *E Week.* December 2, 2010. http://www.eweek.com/c/a/Messaging-and-Collaboration/GSA-Picks-Google-Apps-Cloud-Over-Microsoft-IBM (accessed September 24, 2011).

Bovard, James. "Money: The Great Gold Robbery - The Foundation for Economic Education." *U.S. Rare Coin Investments.* http://www.usrarecoininvestments.com/coin_articles/The_ Great_Gold_Robbery.htm (accessed November 29, 2010).

Brayton, Ed. "Obama Wants Access to Facebook, Skype, Others." *Science Blogs.* September 29, 2010. http://scienceblogs.com/dispatches/2010/09/obama_wants_access_to_facebook.php (accessed December 3, 2010).

Brody, David. "All the President's 'Czars'." *CBN News.* September 28, 2009. http://www.cbn.com/cbnnews/politics/2009/September/All-the-Presidents-Czars/ (accessed September 26, 2011).

Bruck, Connie. "The World According to Soros." *The New Yorker*, January 23, 1995: 54-78.

Buchanan, Patrick. "Obama's Choice - FDR or Reagan." *MSNBC.* January 9, 2009. http://www.msnbc.msn.com/id/28579400/ (accessed July 7, 2011).

Bullock, John. "Eco Warrior Sterilizes Herself to Save the Planet." *Tiger Weekly.* November 28, 2007. http://tigerweekly.com/print/11-28-2007/7091 (accessed December 10, 2010).

Burton, Katherine, and Roben Farzad. "Soros Goes Private as Golden Era of Rock Star Traders Concludes." *Bloomberg.* July 28, 2011. http://www.bloomberg.com/new/2011-07-28/soros-goes-private-as-golden-era-of-rock-star-traders-ends-with-dodd-frank.htm (accessed September 22, 2011).

Buruma, Ian. "Tariq Ramadan Has An Identity Issue - Europe - International Herald Tribune." *The New York Times.* February 4, 2007. http://www.nytimes.com/2007/02/04/world/europe/04iht-web.0204tariq.4461545.html (accessed September 29, 2011).

Bush, President George W. "George W. Bush Speech to Congress September 20. 2001." *The History Place.* September 20, 2001. http://www.historyplace.com/speeches/gw-bush-9-11.htm (accessed December 9, 2010).

Byrne, John. "Shocking Cable: US Says Saudi Donors Are Chief Financiers of al Qaeda." *Raw Story.* November 29, 2010. http://www.rawstory.com/rs/2010/11/shocker-admits-saudi-donors-chief-financiers-al-qaeda-leaked (accessed December 10, 2010).

California Department of Food and Agriculture. "California Agricultural Production Statistics 2009-2010." *CDFA.* 2010. http://www.cdfa.ca.gov/Statistics/ (accessed November 20, 2010).

Canfield, Clarke. "Portland, Maine, Weighs Letting Noncitizens Vote." *Boston.* October 23, 2010. http://www.boston.com/news/nation/articles/2010/10/23/portland_maine_weighs_letting_noncitizens_vote (accessed November 24, 2010).

Carter, Jimmy. "Hardball with Chris Matthews for Oct. 18." *MSNBC TV.* October 19, 2004. http://www.msnbc.msn.com/id/6281085/ (accessed December 2, 2010).

"Cass Sunstein." *Discover The Networks.* 2010. http://www.discoverthenetworks.org/individualProfile.asp?indid=2422 (accessed July 11, 2011).

Chief Financial Officer, Revenue Financial Management OS:CFO:R. "Table 6. Internal Revenue Gross Collections, by Type of Tax, Fiscal Years 1960-2007." In *Internal Revenue Service Data Book 2007.* 2009.

Choudary. "This Week Transcript: Holy War: Should Americans Fear Islam?" *ABC News.* October 3, 2010. http://abcnews.go.com/ThisWeek/week-transcript-holy-war-americans-fear-islam/story?id=11786745 (accessed December 10, 2010).

Clabough, Raven. "Beck's Founders' Fridays Attempts to Undo Revisionists' Damage." *The New American.* June 1, 2010. http://www.thenewamerican.com/index.php/culture/37-history/3678-becks-founders-fridays-attempts-to-undo-revisionists-damage (accessed September 24, 2011).

—. "U.S. Military Prepares for Economic Collapse." *The New American.* December 7, 2010. http://www.thenewamerican.com/index.php/usnews/politics/5418-us-military-prepares-for-economic-collapse/ (accessed September 16, 2011).

Clark, Stephen. "DREAM Act Would Cost Taxpayers $6.2 Billion Per Year, Group Says." *Fox News.* December 2, 2010. http://www.foxnews.com/politics/2010/12/02/dream-act-cost-taxpayers-billion-year-group-says/ (accessed December 4, 2010).

Cobiella, Kelly. "Shuttle Program End May Cost Florida 8,999 Jobs." *CBS News.* July 7, 2011. http://www.cbsnews.com/stories/2011/07/07/earlyshow/main20077478.shtml (accessed July 18, 2011).

"Collective Bargaining Impact on State Budgets." *Nightly Business Report.* March 7, 2011. http://www.pbs.org/nbr/site/onair/transcripts/collective_bargaining_impact_110307/ (accessed March 25, 2011).

Condon, Stephanie. "Stimulus Bill Includes $7.2 Billion For Broadband." *CNET News.* February 17, 2009. http://news.cnet.com/8301-13578_3-10165726-3/.html (accessed September 27, 2010).

"Congressional Record (Bound Edition), Volume 146 (2000), Part 12 - Social Security Benefits." *GPO.* 2000. http://www.gpo.gov/fdsys/pkg/CRECB-2000-pt12/html/CRECB-2000-pt12-Pg16583-2.htm (accessed July 7, 2011).

Coolidge, Calvin. "Nominating Speech for Calvin Coolidge." *Calvin Coolidge.* April 27, 1920. http://www.calvin-coolidge.org/html/nominating_speech_for_calvin_c.html (accessed May 7, 2011).

Coulson, Andrew J. "Markets Versus Monopolies In Education." *School Choices.* 1998. http://schoolchoices.org/roo/fm.htm (accessed July 6, 2011).

Coulter, Ann. "Pretend To Be All That You Can Be." *World Net Daily.* October 3, 2007. http://www.wnd.com/news/article.asp?ARTICLE_ID=57971 (accessed May 14, 2011).

Cover, Matt. "EPA Contest Seeks Videos Promoting Government Regulations." *CNS News.* April 16, 2010. http://www.cnsnews.com/node/64297 (accessed September 24, 2011).

Cravatts, Richard L. "All Campus Free Speech is Acceptable - Except About Islam." *American Thinker.* October 9, 2009. http://www.americanthinker.com/2009/10/all_campus_free_speech_is_acce.html (accessed September 18, 2011).

D'Aleo, Joseph. "Climategate: NOAA and NASA Complicit in Data Manipulation." *Pajamas Media.* January 29, 2010. http://pajamasmedia.com/blog/climategate-noaa-and-nasa-complicit-in-data-manipulation?singlepage=true (accessed July 7, 2011).

Democracy Corps. "Frequency Questionnaire." *Democracy Corps.* June 19-22, 2010. http://www.democracycorps.com/wp-content/files/dcor062210fq6.web_.pdf (accessed October 27, 2010).

Department of Water Resources California State Water Project. *Notice to State Water Project Contractors.* DWR9625, Sacramento: State of California, 2011.

DePaul, Jennifer. *The Fiscal Times.* April 14, 2010. http://www.thefiscaltimes.com/IssuesBudget-Impact/2010/04/14/USDA-Will-Spend-63-billion-On-Food-Stamps-This-Year.aspx (accessed October 27, 201).

Dinan, Stephen. "Obama Climate Czar Has Socialist Ties." *The Washington Times.* January 12, 2009. http://www.washingtontimes.com/news/2009/jan/12/obama-climate-czar-has-socialist-ties/ (accessed September 20, 2011).

Dolan, Maura, and Larry Gordon. "Illegal Immigrants Can Qualify for In-State College Tuition, Court Rules." *Los Angeles Times.* November 15, 2010. http://articles.latimes.com/2010/nov/15/local/la-ne-illegal-students-20101116 (accessed December 11, 2010).

Domenech, Ben. "How Donald Berwick Will Run Your Health Care." *Big Government.* May 13, 2010. http://biggovernment.com/bdomenech/2010/05/13/how-donald-berwick-will-run-your-health-care/ (accessed July 11, 2011).

D'Souza, Dinesh. "How Obama Thinks." *Forbes.* September 27, 2010. http://www.forbes.com/forbes/2010/0927/politics-socialism-capitalism-private-enterprises-obama-business-problem.html (accessed May 4, 2011).

D'Souza, Dinesh, interview by Glenn Beck. "The Roots of Obama's Rage." *The Glenn Beck Program.* (September 15, 2010).

Eaton, Joe. "The Center for Public Integrity: Limousine Liberals? Number of Government-Owned Limos Has Soared Under Obama." *Huffington Post.* May 31, 2011. http://www.huffingtonpost.com/the-center-for-public-integrity/linousine-liberals-number_b_868922.html?ncid=webmail (accessed June 1, 2011).

Eilperin, Juliet. "Bolivia, Ecuador Denied Climate Funds." *The Washington Post.* April 9, 2010. http://views.washingtonpost.com/climate-change/post-carbon/2010/04/bolivia_ecuador_denied_climate_funds.html (accessed May 14, 2011).

Eisenhower Memorial Commission. "Dwight D. Eisenhower Memorial Commission." *Eisenhower Memorial.* http://www.eisenhowermemorial.org/Civil-Rights.htm (accessed October 28, 2010).

"Estate Tax Exemptions and Rates Over Time." *Journal of Accountancy.* November 2007. http://www.journalofaccountancy.com/Issues/2007/Nov/Est ateTaxExemptionsAndRatesOverTime (accessed December 4, 2010).

"FBI Captured Muslim Brotherhood's Strategic Plan." *Big Peace.* October 26, 2010. http://bigpeace.com/teamb/2012/10/26/fbi-captured-muslim-brotherhoods-strategic-plan/ (accessed May 25, 2011).

"FDR's Second Bill of Rights and the Progressive Mission." *The Realignment Project.* July 4, 2009. http://realignmentproject.wordpress.com/2009/07/04/fdrs-second-bill-of-rights-and-the-progressive-mission (accessed November 24, 2010).

Finnegan, Leah. "Tariq Ramadan, Muslim Scholar Formerly Banned From U.S., Returns To Country." *Huffington Post.* April 8, 2010. http://www.huffingtonpost.com/2010/04/08/tariq-ramadan-muslim-scho_n_531207.html (accessed September 29, 2011).

Fish and Wildlife Service. "Origins of the U.S. Fish and Wildlife Service." *Conservation History.* May 21, 2009. http://training.fws.gov/History/TimelinesOrigins.html (accessed November 8, 2010).

Fletcher, Michael A., and Jonathan Weisman. "Bush Signs Bill Authorizing 700-Mile Fence for Border." *The Washington Post.* October 27, 2006. http://www.washingtonpost.com/wp-dyn/content/article/2006/10/26/AR2006102600120.html (accessed December 9, 2010).

"Flight Safety Digest." *Flight Safety Foundation.* July-August 1996. http://flightsafety.org/fsd/fsd_july-aug96.pdf (accessed April 28, 2011).

Folsom, Burton, interview by Glenn Beck. "Glenn Beck: Obama and FDR." *The Glenn Beck Program.* (February 10, 2009).

Folsom, Jr., Burton. "Three Myths of the Great Depression." *The Foundation for Economic Education.* September 2004. http://www.fee.org/pdf/notes/NFF_0904.pdf (accessed September 20, 2011).

Foundation, The Heritage. "The Unsustainable Growth of Welfare - Solutions for America." *The Heritage Foundation.* August 17, 2010. http://www.heritage.org/Research/Reports.2010/08/The-Unsustainable-Growth-of-Welfare (accessed September 27, 2010).

Franklin, Benjamin. "On The Price of Corn and Management of the Poor, 1776." *Founding.com: A Project of the Claremont Institute.* 1776. http://www.founding.com/founders_library/pageID.2146/default.asp (accessed May 9, 2011).

Friel, Brian, Richard E. Cohen, and Kirk Victor. "National Journal 2007 Vote Ratings." January 31, 2008.

"From Astronauts To The Boss, Thoughts On Shuttle." *AZ Central.* July 8, 2011. http://hosted.ap.org/dynamic/stories/U/US_SHUTTLE_QU OTES?SITE=AZPHG&SECTION=HOME&TEMPLATE =DEFAULT (accessed July 19, 2011).

Fuller, Jacquelline. "Spreading Holiday Cheer With Charitable Donations." *Google Blog.* December 17, 2010. http://googleblog.blogspot.com/2010/12/spreading-holiday-cheer-with-charitable.html (accessed September 28, 2011).

"G-8 Pledges $40 Billion for 'Arab Spring'." *The Wall Street Journal.* May 28, 2011. http://online.wsj.com/article/SB100014240527023045208 04576348792147454956.html (accessed July 6, 2011).

Gaffney, Frank. "The 'End of the Beginning' on Shariah?" *Townhall.* August 24, 2010. http://townhall.com/columnists/frankgaffney/2010/08/24/th e_end_of_the_beginning_on_sharia/ (accessed September 18, 2011).

Garrettson, Jim. *Executive Gov - Ninth Circuit Court: Secret GPS Tracking is Legal.* August 11, 2010. http://www.executivegov.com/2010/08/ninth-circuit-court-secret-gps-tracking-is-legal/comment-page-1/ (accessed October 28, 2010).

Gaynor, Michael. "What Did Wade Rathke Know About Egypt That the CIA Didn't and What Will Obama Do Now?" *Emerging Corruption.* February 9, 2011. http://emergingcorruption.com/2011/02/what-did-wade-rathke-know-about-egypt-that-the-cia-didnt-and-what-will-obamb-do-now/ (accessed September 16, 2011).

Genova, Windsor. "Abortion Doctor Arrested for Murder of Mother and Seven Babies." *All Headline News.* January 19, 2011. http://www.allheadlinenews.com/briefs/articles/90031406 (accessed January 20, 2011).

"George Soros." *Discover The Networks.* 2011. http://www.discoverthenetworks.org/individualProfile.asp?indid=977 (accessed September 15, 2011).

"George Soros: Top 10 Reasons He Is Dangerous." *Human Events.* April 2, 2011. http://www.humanevents.com/article.php?id+42674 (accessed September 15, 2011).

"Get It Straight: Consumer Spending is *Not* 70% of GDP." *Business Week.* August 2009. http://www.businessweek.com/the_thread/economicsunbound/archives/2009/08/get_it_straight.html (accessed September 19, 2011).

"Glenn Beck vs Fabian Socialism." *Right Pundits.* http://www.rightpundits.com/?p=7394 (accessed September 16, 2011).

Glover, Mark. "California is Worst State for Business, CEO Survey Says." *Sacramento Bee.* May 6, 2011. http://www.sacbee.com/2011/05/06/3606144/california-is-worst-state-for.html (accessed May 7, 2011).

Goodwin, George J.W. "The German Hyperinflation, 1923." *PBS.* 1981. http://www.pbs.org/wgbh/commandingheights/shared/minitext/ess_germanhyperinflation.html (accessed September 19, 2011).

Graves, Lucia. "Obama Looking For Ways Around Congreess On Gun Policy." *Huffington Post.* March 15, 2011. http://www.huffingtonpost.com/2011/03/15/obama-gun-laws-congress_n_836138.html (accessed September 19, 2011).

Gray, John. *Liberalism.* University of Minnesota Press, 1986.

"Great Leap Forward." *Encyclopedia of Marxism.* http://marists.org/glossary/events/g/r.htm (accessed June 4, 2011).

Green, Tanya L. "The Negro Project: Margaret Sanger's Eugenic Plan for Black Americans." *Black Genocide.* . http://www.blackgenocide.org/negro.html (accessed November 24, 2010).

Greenberg, David. "The Hidden History of the Espionage Act." *Slate.* December 27, 2010. http://www.slate.com/id/2278922/ (accessed June 4, 2011).

Groves, Steven. "Obama Wrongly Adopts U.N. "Responsibility to Protect" to Justify Libya Intervention." *The Heritage Foundation.* March 31, 2011. http://www.heritage.org/Research/Reports/2011/03/Libya-Intervention-Obama-Wrongly-Adopts_UN-Responsibility-to-Protect (accessed September 29, 2011).

Halsall, Paul. "Modern History Sourcebook: Ronald Reagan: A Time for Choosing Speech, 1964." *Fordham.* May 1998. http://www.fordham.edu/halsall/mod/1964reagan1.html (accessed November 2, 2010).

Ham, Mary Katharine. "Hammertime: Moore's National Resources." *The Daily Caller.* March 11, 2011. http://dailycaller.com/2011/03/11/hammertime-moores-national-resources/ (accessed March 25, 2011).

Hamden, Toby. "Barack Obama Vows to 'Change the World'." *The Telegraph.* October 17, 2008. http://www.telegraph.co.uk/news/worldnews/northamerica/usa/barackobama/3219308/Barack-Obama-vows-to-change-the-world (accessed February 14, 2011).

Harris, Malcolm. "Rising Tuition + Student Loans = Education Bubble." *The Fiscal Times.* May 9, 2011. http://www.thefiscaltimes.com/Articles/2011/05/09/Rising-Tuition-Student-Loans-Education-Bubble.aspx#page1 (accessed October 20, 2011).

Hatter, Karen. "The Voting Rights Act of 1965 Ended the Use of Literacy Tests." *Now Public.* February 9, 2010. http://www.nowpublic.com/world/voting-rights-act-1965-ended-use-literacy-tests (accessed October 31, 2010).

Heilemann, John. "The West Wing, Season II." *New York Magazine.* January 23, 2011. http://nymag.com/news/politics/70829/ (accessed October 14, 2011).

Hilton, Ronald. "The Collapse of the Soviet Union and Ronald Reagan." *Stanford University.* http://wais.stanford.edu/History/history_ussrandreagan.htm (accessed December 11, 2010).

"Historical Highest Marginal Income Tax Rates." *Tax Policy Center.* October 26, 2009. http://www.taxpolicycenter.org/taxfacts/displayafact.cfm?Docid=213 (accessed September 11, 2010).

"History of the United Nations." *United Nations.* 2005. http://www.un.org/aboutun/unhistory/ (accessed May 25, 2011).

Hitchens, Peter. "The Black Kennedy: But Does Anyone Know The Real Barack Obama?" *Daily Mail Online.* February 2, 2008. http://www.dailymail.co.uk/news/article-511901/The-Black-Kennedy-But-does-know-real-Barack-Obama.html (accessed July 19, 2011).

Holzer, Ben. "Political Vote Buying Statutes: Textual Limits, Enforcement Challenges, And The Need For Reform." *NYU Law.* www.law.nyu.edu/ecm_dlv2/groups/public@nyu_law_web site_journal_of_legislation_and_public_policy/documents/e cm_pro_062198.pdf (accessed September 26, 2011).

Hoover, J. Edgar. *Masters of Deceit.* New York: Holt, Rinehart and Winston, 1958.

Hopper, Reed M. "U.S. Supreme Court Rejects Unlimited Federal Control of Wetlands Ruling Reverses Decision in Michigan, Landowner's Case." *Pacific Legal Foundation.* June 19, 2006. http://www.pacificlegal.org/page.aspx?pid=912 (accessed June 28, 2006).

Horowitz, David, and Richard Lawrence Poe. "Part 3: The Shadow Party." *Richard Poe.* October 11, 2005. http://www.richardpoe.com/2005/10/11/part-3-the-shadow-party/ (accessed December 11, 2010).

The Way Forward: Regan's Resolve. Performed by Brit Hume. Fox News. December 12, 2010.
Ibid.

"Illegal Immigration a $113 Billion a Year Drain on U.S. Taxpayers." *Federation For American Immigration Reform.* July 6, 2010. http://www.fairus.org/site/News2?page=NewsArticle&id=2 3198&security=1601&news_iv_ctrl=1741 (accessed December 11, 2010).

"International Monetary Fund." *IMF.* http://www.imf.org/external/about/quotas.htm (accessed May 25, 2011).

Jacobs, Frank. "Federal Lands in the US." *Big Think.* June 16, 2008. http://bigthink.com/ideas/21343 (accessed November 14, 2010).

"James Glassman & Jared Cohen: On 2008 Alliance for Youth Movement Summit." *AnarchitexT.* May 20, 2011. http://anarchitext.wordpress.com/2011/05/20/alliance-for-youth-movement/ (accessed September 16, 2011).

Jefferson, Thomas. "Thomas Jefferson on Politics & Government: Educating the People." *University of Virginia.* http://etext.virginia.edu/jefferson/quotations/jeff1350.htm (accessed October 19, 2010).

Jenkins, Jr., Holman W. "Google and the Search for the Future." *The Wall Street Journal.* August 14, 2010. http://online.wsj.com/article/SB10001424052748704901104575423294099527212.html (accessed September 15, 2011).

"Jim Wallis." *Discover The Networks.* 2010. http://www.discoverthenetworks.org/individualProfile.asp?indid=1833 (accessed September 20, 2011).

"John Holdren, Obama's Science Czar, Says: Forced Abortions and Mass Sterilization Needed to Save the Planet." *Zombie Time.* http://zombietime.com/john_holdren/ (accessed September 20, 2011).

"John Podesta." *Change: The Obama-Biden Transition Team.* http://change.gov/learn/john_podesta (accessed September 15, 2011).

Jones, Van, interview by Uprising Radio. *Memphis Conference "The Dream Reborn".* (April 4, 2008).

—. "Introducing The 'American Dream' Movement." *Huffington Post.* February 22, 2011. http://www.huffingtonpost.com/van-jones/american-dream-movement_b_826477.html (accessed September 19, 2011).

Jordan, Eason. "The News We Kept To Ourselves." *The New York Times.* April 11, 2003. http://www.nytimes.com/2003/04/11/opinion/the-news-we-kept-to-ourselves.html (accessed December 4, 2010).

Kaplan, Jeremy A. "Researchers Find the 'Liberal Gene'." *Fox News.* October 28, 2010. http://www.foxnews.com/scitech/2010/10/28/researchers-liberal-gene-genetics-politics/ (accessed October 31, 2010).

"Kelo v. City of New London." *Conservapedia.* December 28, 2009. http://conservapedia.com/Kelo_v._City_of_New_London (accessed May 5, 2011).

Kerpen, Phil. "Sham Angelides Comission Will Protect ACORN." *Big Government.* September 17, 2009. http://biggovernment.com/pkerpen/2009/09/17/sham-angelides-commission-will-protect-acorn/ (accessed September 15, 2011).

Performed by Jeffery Khuner. Michael Savage Show. February 11, 2011.

Kincaid, Cliff. "Ex-Con Counts on "Faith Community" to Pass Health Care." *Romantic Poet.* November 30, 2009. http://romanticpoet.wordpress.com/2009/12/02/ex-con-counts-on-%e2%8 %9cfaith-community%e2%80%9d-to-pass-health-care/ (accessed July 11, 2011).

Klaus, Vaclav. "From Climate Alarmism to Climate Realism." *The Heartland Institute.* March 9, 2008. http://www.heartland.org/policybot/results/22902/From_Cli mate_Alarmism_to_Climate_Realism.html (accessed October 22, 2010).

Klein, Aaron. "Another Stunner Behind Obama's Libya Doctrine." *World Net Daily.* March 29, 2011. http://www.wnd.com/?pageId=281065 (accessed September 29, 2011).

—. "Bill Ayers, Communist Provided Arizona Shooter's Curriculum?" *World Net Daily.* January 10, 2011. http://www.wnd.cdom/?pageId=249429 (accessed January 19, 2011).

—. "Hamas Terrorists Make 2008 U.S. Presidential Pick." *World Net Daily.* April 14, 2008. http://www.wnd.com/index.php?fa=PAGE.view&pageId=6 1631 (accessed July 11, 2011).

313

—. "Obama Adviser: Amnesty to Ensure 'Progressive' Rule." *World Net Daily.* February 2, 2010. http://www.wnd.com/?pageId=123955 (accessed November 24, 2010).

Klein, Ezra. "The Case For A Temporary Extension Of All The Bush Tax Cuts." *The Washington Post.* August 17, 2010. http://voices.washingtonpost.com/ezra-klein/2010/08/the_case_for_a_temporary_exten.html (accessed December 9, 2010).

Klusendorf, Scott. "Peter Singer's Bold Defense of Infanticide." *Equip.* December 8, 2001. http://www.equip.org/articles/peter-singer-s-bold-defense-of-infanticide (accessed September 16, 2011).

Koch, Wendy. "Obama Bans Offshore Oil Drilling in Atlantic Waters." *USA Today.* December 2, 2010. http://www.usatoday.com/news/washington/environment/2010-12-02-oildrill02_ST_N.htm (accessed September 22, 2011).

Kolbert, Elizabeth. "Greening The Ghetto." *The New Yorker.* January 12, 2009. http://www.newyorker.com/reporting/2009/01/12/090112fa_fact_kolbert?currentPage=all (accessed May 14, 2011).

Kudlow, Larry. "Beware of Google." *Kudlow's Money Politic$.* May 23, 2006. http://kudlowsmoneypolitics.blogspot.com/2006/05/beware-of-google.html (accessed September 28, 2011).

Kurtz, Stanley. "Cloward-Piven Redux." *National Review Online.* December 30, 2010. http://www.nationalreview.com/corner/256112/cloward-piven-redux-stanley-kurtz (accessed January 25, 2011).

Kurtz, Stanley. *Glenn Beck: Radical in Chief.* Performed by Glenn Beck. Glenn Beck. December 29, 2010.

—. "Obama and Ayers Pushed Radicalism On Schools." *The Wall Street Journal.* September 23, 2008. http://online.wsj.com/article/SB122212856075765367.html #printMode (accessed January 26, 2011).

—. "Obama's Radical Past." *National Review.* October 12, 2010. http://www.nationalreview.com/articles/249390/obama%E 2%80%99s-radical-past-stanley-kurtz?page=1 (accessed July 11, 2011).

"Labor in a Global World with SEIU President Andy Stern." *NDN.* June 20, 2007. http://action.ndn.org/ct/-pLSSIF19mjf/ (accessed September 19, 2011).

Lake, Eli. "4 GOP Leaders Warn of Uranium Mine Sale." *The Washington Times.* October 5, 2010. http://www.washingtontimes.com/news/2010/oct/5/4-gop-leaders-warn-of-uranium-mine-sale/ (accessed September 26, 2011).

Lanman, Scott, and Jeannine Aversa. "Bernanke Leaves Door Open to More Stimulus Should Economy Fail to Rebound." *Bloomberg.* June 22, 2011. http://www.bloomberg.com/news/2011-06-23/bernanke-leaves-door-open-to-easing-if-economy-weakens-further.html (accessed July 5, 2011).

Levinson, Charles. "El Baradei's Roll Cast in Doubt." *The Wall Street Journal.* February 3, 2011. http://online.wsj.com/article/SB10001424052748704775604576120443506757576.html (accessed September 16, 2011).

Lewis, Laura. "NASA Takes Google on Journey into Space." *NASA Ames Research Center.* September 28, 2005. http://www.nasa.gov/centers/ames/news/releases/2005/05_50AR.html (accessed September 24, 2011).

Lifson, Thomas. "Eliminating 25 Million Americans." *American Thinker.* October 23, 2008. http://www.americanthinker.com/blog/2008/10/eliminating_25_million_america.html (accessed February 12, 2011).

Performed by Rush Limbaugh. The Rush Limbaugh Show. December 16, 2010.

Performed by Rush Limbaugh. The Rush Limbaugh Show. November 12, 2010.

—. "Desperate Democrats Cry Racism." *The Rush Limbaugh Show.* 17 November, 2010. http://www.rushlimbaugh.com/home/daily/site_111710/content/01125107.guest.html (accessed November 18, 2010).

Lindgren, Jim. "The Volokh Conspiracy - Funding Barack Obama's 'Civilian National Security Force'." *Volokh.* July 19, 2008. http://volokh.com/posts/1216451854.shtml (accessed January 22, 2011).

Lonergan, Sean. "The Sapir-Whorf Hypothesis." *Introduction to Cultural Psychology Forum.* April 11, 2000. http://www.psy.dmu.ac.uk/egi-bin/412/9900psyc1011.pl?read=42 (accessed July 7, 2011).

"Longshoremen Storm Wash. State Port, Damage RR." *Yahoo! News.* September 8, 2011. http://news.yahoo.com/longshoremen-storm-wash-state-port-damage-rr-144921214.html (accessed October 18, 2011).

Lord, Lewis. "An Eagle That Didn't Take Off." *US News.* August 10, 2003. http://www.usnews.com/usnews/culture/articles/030818/18 70thann.htm (accessed November 29, 2010).

Luhby, Tami. "Obama Looks to Help States with Jobless Aid." *CNN Money.* February 9, 2011. http://money.cnn.cdom/2011/02/08/news/economy/unempl oyment_insurance_relief/index.htm (accessed September 19, 2011).

Malveaux, Suzanne, and Ed Hornick. "Obama Aide Fires Back at Beck Over Mao Remarks." *CNN Politics.* October 16, 2009. http://articles.cnn.com/2009-10-16/politics/beck.dunn_1_mao-mein-kampf-lee-atwater?_s=PM:POLITICS (accessed April 21, 2011).

"Maoism." *Encylcopedia 2.* http://encyclopedia2.thefreedictionary.com/Maoism (accessed October 25, 2010).

"Mark Lloyd." *Discover The Networks.* 2009. http://www.discoverthenetworks.org/individualProfile.asp? indid=2411 (accessed September 20, 2011).

"Mass Immigration Reduction Act of 2001/Stealth Amnesty." *Balance.* October 2001. http://www.balance.org/alerts/alert102001.htm (accessed December 2, 2010).

Mataconis, Doug. "Senator Biden v. President Obama On The Use Of Military Force." *Outside The Beltway.* March 23, 2011. http://www.outsidethebeltway.com/senator-biden-v-president-obama-on-the-use-of-military-force/ (accessed March 25, 2011).

McCarthy, Andrew C. "Why Won't Obama Talk About Columbia?" *National Review Online.* October 7, 2008. http://www.nationalreview.com/articles/225910/why-wont-obama-talk-about-columbia/andrew-c-mccarthy (accessed July 11, 2011).

McChesney, Robert W. "The U.S. Media Reform Movement: Going Forward." *Monthly Review.* September 4, 2008. http://monthlyreview.org/2008/09/01/the-u-s-media-reform-movement-going-forward (accessed May 3, 2011).

McCormack, Richard. "The Plight of American Manufacturing." *Prospect.* December 21, 2009. http://prospect.org/cs/article=the_plight_of_american_man ufacturing (accessed October 31, 2010).

McGreevy, Patrick. "Teachers Union Tops List of State Political Spenders." *Los Angeles Times.* March 10, 2010. http://latimesblogs.latimes.com/california-politics/2010/03/teachers-union-tops-list-of-state-political-spenders.html (accessed December 2, 2010).

Meacham, Jon. "On His Own." *Newsweek.* August 23, 2008. http://www.newsweek.com/2008/08/22/on-his-own.html (accessed May 5, 2011).

"Michelle Obama's Old Law Firm Defends ACORN." *World News Daily.* December 23, 2008. http://www.wnd.com/?pageId=84434 (accessed July 11, 2011).

Miller, Joshua. "Defense Secretary: Libya Did Not Pose Threat to U.S., Was Not 'Vital National Interest' to Intervene." *ABC News.* March 27, 2011. http://abcnews.go.com/International/defense-secretary-libya-pose-threat-us-vital-national/story?id=13231987 (accessed March 29, 2011).

Mishak, Michael. "Unplugged: The SEIU Chief on the Labor Movement and the Card Check." *Las Vegas Sun.* May 10, 2009. http://www.lasvegassun.com/news/2009/may/10/stern-unplugged-seiu-chief-favor-movement-and-the-card-check/ (accessed November 24, 2010).

Moran, Rick. "Great News! NV Voting Machines Automatically Checking Reid's Name." *American Thinker.* July 28, 2011. http://www.americanthinker.com/blog/2010/10/great_news_nv_voting_machines.html (accessed September 24, 2011).

Morano, Marc. "'Execute' Skeptics? Shock Call To Action: 'At What Point Do We Jail or Execute Global Warming Deniers'--'Shouldn't We Start Punishing Them Now?'." *Climate Depot.* June 3, 2009. http://www.climatedepot.com/a/1096/Execute-Skeptics-Shock-Call-To-Action-At-what-point-do-we-jail-or-execute-global-warming-deniers-Shouldnt-we-start-punishing-them-now (accessed September 19, 2011).

Moyers, Bill. "Bill Moyers Talks with Andy Stern." *Bill Moyers Journal.* June 15, 2007. http://www.pbs.org/moyers/journal/06152007/transcript2.html (accessed September 16, 2011).

Murdock, Deroy. "MURDOCK: Death Threats From the Left." *The Washington Times.* March 18, 2011. http://www.washingtontimes.com/news/2011/mar/18/death-threats-from-the-left/ (accessed September 18, 2011).

Napolitano, Andrew P. "How Congress Has Assaulted Our Freedoms in the Patriot Act." *Lew Rockwell.* December 16, 2005. http://www.lewrockwell.com/orig6/napolitano2.html (accessed September 26, 2011).

Napolitano, J. A. "Liberty Forums." *Ron Paul Forums.* February 21, 2011. http://www.ronpaulforums.com/showthread.php?280931-Judge-Napolitano-s-closing-argument...&s=d.. (accessed February 23, 2011).

Freedom watch. Performed by Judge Andrew Napolitano. Freedom Watch. February 21, 2011.

Freedom Watch. Performed by Judge Andrew Napolitano. Freedom Watch. October 16, 2010.

Freedom Watch. Performed by Judge Andrew Napolitano. Fox News. December 14, 2010.

Freedom Watch. Performed by Judge Andrew Napolitano. Freedom Watch. January 3, 2011.

Freedom Watch. Performed by Judge Andrew Napolitano. Feedom Watch. January 4, 2011.

Freedom Watch. Performed by Judge Andrew Napolitano. Freedom Watch. January 20, 2011.

Freedom Watch. Performed by Judge Andrew Napolitano. Freedom Watch. February 1, 2011.

Freedom Watch. Performed by Judge Andrew Napolitano. Freedom Watch. February 23, 2011.

Newman, Rick. "How Government Spending Skyrocketed." *US News.* February 9, 2011. http://money.usnews.com/money/blogs/flowchart/2011/02/09/how-government-spending-skyrocketed (accessed February 14, 2011).

"News & Sanger Sightings." *University of New York.* 2010. http://www.nyu.edu/projects/sanger/sightings/index.html (accessed February 21, 2011).

"News for Immediate Release." *California Department of Water Resources.* November 22, 2010. http://www.water.ca.gov (accessed December 16, 2010).

"NRDC Mission Statement." *National Resources Defense Council.* http://www.nrdc.org/about/mission.asp (accessed October 7, 2010).

"Obama 'Lying' About Muslim Past, Expert Says." *News Max.* October 9, 2008. http://www.newsmax.com/insidecover/pipes_obama_muslim/2008/10/09/138898.html (accessed October 10, 2008).

"Obama Organized Farrakhan's 'Million Man March'." *Now Public.* April 2, 2008. http://www.nowpublic.com/world/obama-organized-farrakhan-s-million-man-march (accessed July 11, 2011).

"Obama Underwrites Offshore Drilling." *Wall Street Journal.* August 18, 2009. http://online.wsj.com/article/SB10001424052970203863204574346610120524166.html (accessed September 22, 2011).

Obama, Barack. *Dreams From My Father: A Story of Race and Inheritance.* Random House, 2007.

O'Neill, Jim. "Soros: Republic Enemy #1." *Canada Free Press.* September 15, 2009. http://canadafreepress.com/index.php/article/14700 (accessed December 11, 2010).

"Open Society Foundations About FAQs." *Soros.* http://www.soros.org/about/faq (accessed September 22, 2011).

Orin, Deborah, and Thomas Galvin. "A to Z Guide of Clinton Scandals." *io.com.* October 16, 1996. http://www.io.com~cjburke/clinton/clinatoz.html (accessed September 2010, 2010).

Ouimette, US Navy Captain Dan. *America Wake Up!* Performed by US Navy Captain Dan Ouimette. Pensacola Civilian Club, Pensacola. February 19, 2003.

Pann, Tony. "Climategate: CEI to Sue NASA Goddard for Climate Change Fraud." *Examiner.* November 25, 2009. http://www.examiner.com/weather-n-baltimore/climategate-cei-to-sue-nasa-goddard-for-climate-change-fraud (accessed July 7, 2011).

Papst, Chris. "On Point." *Berksmont News.* December 28, 2010. http://www.berksmontnews.com/articles/2010/12/28/tri_co unty_record/opinion/doc4d1a520f56103391692486.txt (accessed July 5, 2011).

Freedom Watch. Performed by Star Parker. Freedom Watch. January 17, 2011.

—. "Star Parker: Back on Uncle Sam's Plantation." *Townhall.* February 9, 2009. http://www.townhall.com/columnists/StarParker/2009/02/0 9/back_on_uncle_sams_plantation (accessed October 28, 2010).

Freedom Watch. Performed by Ron Paul. Freedom Watch. January 19, 2011.

Pence, Mike. "Pence Claims That Obama Said Energy Costs Will Skyrocket With a Cap-and-Trade Plan." *Politi Fact.* June 10, 2009. htttp://www.politifact.com/truth-o-meter/statements/2009/jun/11/mike-pence/pence-claims-obama-said-energy-costs-will-skyrocket-with-cap-and-trade (accessed December 3, 2010).

Penner, Martin. "Number of World's Hungry Tops A Billion." *World Food Programme.* June 19, 2009. http://www.wfp.org/stories/number-world-hungry-tops-billion (accessed Decembefr 2, 2010).

Penty, Charles, and Emma Ross-Thomas. "Spanish Regional Debt Surges to Second-Quarter Record, Bank of Spain Says." *Bloomberg.* September 16, 2011. http://www.bloomberg.com/news/2011-09-16/spain-second-quarter-regions-debt-reached-12-4-percent (accessed September 19, 2011).

Perlmutt, David. "Obama Meets Working Moms." *Charlotte Observer.* April 13, 2008. http://nl.newsbank.com/nl-search/we/Archives?p_product=CO&p_theme=co&p_actio n=search&p_maxdocs=200&s_dispstring=give%20up%20 up%20a$20piece%20of%20their%20pie%20Michelle%20 Obama%20date(all)&p_field_field_advanced-0=&p_text_advanced-0= (accessed October 17, 2011).

Pietrusza, David, interview by Glenn Beck. "Calvin Coolidge Still Matters." *The Glenn Beck TV Show.* FOX News. August 13, 2010.

—. *Silent Cal's Almanack: The Homespun Wit and Wisdom of Vermont's Calvin Coolidge.* Amazon, 2008.

Seven Years In Tibet. Directed by Jean-Jacques Annaud. Performed by Brad Pitt. 1997.

Poe, Richard. "The Idiot's Guide to Chinagate." *Newsmax.* May 27, 2003. http://archive.newsmax.com/archives/articles/2003/5/26/21 4938.shtml (accessed October 26, 2010).

"Pope Benedict XVI, on Redemptive Politics Truth and Politics." *Stones Cry Out.* June 6, 2008. http://stonescryout.org/?p=370 (accessed September 18, 2011).

Prante, Gerald. "Summary of Latest Federal Individual Income Tax Data." *Tax Foundation.* July 30, 2009. http://www.taxfoundation.org/news/printer/250.html (accessed September 15, 2010).

"Profile: Craig Becker Why He Matters." *Who Runs Government.* March 2010. http://www.whorunsgov.com/Profiles/Craig_Becker (accessed February 9, 2011).

"Profile: Gil Kerlikowske Why He Matters." *Who Runs Government.* May 2009. http://www.whorunsgov.com/Profiles/Gill_Kerlikowske (accessed February 9, 2011).

"Quotes by Thomas Jefferson." *Revolutionary War and Beyond.* August 18, 1821. http://www.revolutionary-war-and-beyond.com/quotes-by-thomas-jefferson.html (accessed September 24, 2011).

Randall, Gretchen, and Tom Randall. "The Tides Foundation - Liberal Crossroads of Money and Ideas." *Capital Research Center.* December 2003. http://www.capitalresearh.org/pubs/pubs.html?id=743 (accessed December 10, 2010).

Rashid, Ahmed. "After 1,700 Years, Buddhas Fall to Taliban Dynamite." *The Telegraph.* March 12, 2001. http://www.telegraph.co.uk/news/worldnews/asia/afghanistan/1326063/After-1700-years-Buddhas-fall-to-Taliban-dynamite (accessed December 2, 2010).

Reiland, Ralph R. "Van Jones' "Green Jobs" Ruse." *The New American.* September 16, 2009. http://www.thenewamerican.com/index.php/opinion/956-ralph-reiland/1891-van-jones-green-jobs-ruse (accessed October 16, 2011).

Revkin, Andrew C. "Private* Climate Conversations on Display." *New York Times.* November 20, 2009. http://dotearth.blogs.nytimes.com/2009/11/20/private-climtae-conversations-on-display/ (accessed September 24, 2011).

"Rewriting Our History, Changing Our Traditions (Michelle Obama)." *Free Republic.* December 16, 2009. http://www.freerepublic.com/focus/news/2410091/posts (accessed September 24, 2011).

Rhodes, Celie. "What Is Keynesian Economics?" *Wise Geek.* June 14, 2011. http://www.wisegeek.com/what-is-keynesian-economics.htm (accessed July 7, 2011).

"Richard Trumka." *Discover The Networks.* http://www.discoverthenetworks.org/individualProfile.asp?indid=1630 (accessed September 19, 2011).

Romano, Lois. "John Podesta Leads Obama's Transition Team With His Usual Energy." *Washington Post.* November 25, 2008. http://www.washingtonpost.com/wp-dyn/content/article/2008/11/24/AR2008112403005.html (accessed September 15, 2011).

Rosen, Ehud. "Mapping the Orgaizational Sources of the Global Delegitimization Campaign Against Israel in the UK." *Jerusalem Center for Public Affairs.* 2010. http://.jcpa.org/text/Mapping_Delegitimization.pdf (accessed September 26, 2011).

Rosenberg, Barry. "Agencies Put Geospatial Intell Under One Roof." *Defense Systems.* October 1, 2009. http://defensesystems.com/Articles/2009/10/08/C4ISR-2-Geospatial-Intelligence.aspx?Page=1 (accessed September 24, 2011).

Rumsfeld, Donald. "EIB Interview: Donald Rumsfeld." *Rush Limbaugh.* February 8, 2011. http://www.rushlimbaugh.com/home/daily/site_020811/content/01125106.guest.html (accessed February 9, 2011).

Ryan, Paul. "Speeches and Statements: Remarks of Congressman Paul Ryan (R-WI) - As Prepared for Delivery." *House Budget Committee.* January 25, 2011. http://budget.house.gov/News/DocumentSingle.aspx?DocumentID=221249 (accessed February 8, 2011).

"S.773: Cybersecurity Act of 2009." *Open Congress.* March 24, 2010. http://www.opencongress.org/bill/111-s773/show (accessed November 23, 2010).

Saad, Lydia. "Conservatives Maintain Edge as Top Ideological Group." *Gallup.* October 26, 2009. http://www.gallup.com/poll/123854/Conservatives-Maintain-Edge-Top-Ideological-Group.aspx (accessed November 1, 2010).

Samples, John. "Testimony of John Samples, Director, Center for Representative Government On the Motor Voter Act and Voter Fraud." *U.S. Senate Committee on Rules and Administration.* Washington, DC: The Cato Institute, 2001.

Sanchez, Julian. *Obama's Surveillance Power Grab.* July 29, 2010. http://www.cato.org/pub_display.php?_id=12017 (accessed October 27, 2010).

Schilling, Chelsea. "Obama Law Tab Up to $1.7 Million." *World News Daily.* October 27, 2009. http://www.wnd.com/?pageId=114202 (accessed July 18, 2011).

Schuman, Joseph. "China Says Rare Earth Minerals Are Going to Get Rarer." *AOL News.* December 29, 2010. http://www.aolnews.com/2010/12/29/china-to-limit-exports-of-rare-earth-minerals/ (accessed September 16, 2011).

Schweizer, Peter. "Charity Donations and Liberal Hypocricy." *Live Leak.* March 26, 2009. http://www.liveleak.com/view?i=1c5_1238044128&c=1 (accessed May 14, 2011).

Senate Historical Office. "Albert A. Gore, Jr., 45th Vice President (1993-2001)." *United States Senate.* http://www.senate.gov/artandhistory/history/common/generic/VP_Albert_Gore.htm (accessed April 20, 2011).

Sessions, Jeff. "Senate Judiciary Committee U.S. Senator Jeff Sessions (R-AL) Ranking Member." *Al.com.* November 23, 2010. http://media.al.com/live/other/Dream-Alert.pdf (accessed October 1, 2011).

Shaffer, Col. Anthony, interview by Judge Andrew Napolitano. *Freedom Watch: 911 Commission Whitewash* (October 11, 2010).

Shenkman, Rick. "Interview with David Cannadine: His New Biography of Andrew Mellon." *George Mason University's History News Network.* October 8, 2006. http://hnn.us/articles/29696.html (accessed September 5, 2011).

"Simple Living." *Simple Living.* http://www.simpleliving.net/shop/item.aspx?itemid=1084 (accessed October 10, 2010).

Smiley, Gene. "The U.S. Economy in the 1920's." *Economic History Services.* February 1, 2010. http://eh.net/encyclopedia/article/Smiley.1920s.final (accessed May 9, 2011).

Smith, Lewis. "Al Gore's Inconvenient Judgment." *The Times.* October 11, 2007. http://business.timesonline.co.uk/tol/business/law/article26 33838.ece (accessed April 20, 2011).

Snyder, Alan. "President Calvin Coolidge - In Honor of a President Few Remember." *Word Press.* May 16, 2010. http://sttpp.wordpress.com/library/president-calvin-coolidge/ (accessed May 9, 2011).

"Social Media Fuels Protests in Iran, Bahrain and Yemen." *ABC News Radio.* February 15, 2011. http://abcnewsradioonline.com/world-news/social-media-fuels-protests-in-iran-bahrain-and-yemen.html (accessed February 17, 2011).

Solomon, Norman. "The Military-Industrial-Media Complex." *Fairness and Accuracy in Reporting.* July/August 2005. http://www.fair.org/index.php?page=2627 (accessed December 3, 2010).

"Soros: Hot Spot #3." *Indonesia-NYA.* November 28, 2010. http://indonesianya.wordpress.com/ (accessed December 11, 2010).

"Spain Unemployment Rate." *Trading Economics.* July 2011. http://www.tradingeconomics.com/spain/unemployment-rate (accessed September 19, 2011).

Stossel, John. "Index of Economic Freedom Lowers US Ranking." *News Max.* October 13, 2010. http://www.newsmax.com/Stossel/IndexofEconomicFreedom/2010/10/13/id/373500 (accessed December 3, 2010).

—. "Thanksgiving Was Made Possible by Privatization." *News Max.* November 23, 2010. http://www.newsmax.com/Stossel/Stossel-Thanksgiving-Pilgrims-Indians/2010/11/23/id/377959 (accessed December 3, 2010).

"Supreme Court Kelo V. New London ." *Cornell University Law School Legal Information Institute.* 2005. http://wwwl.law.cornell.edu/supct/html/04-108.ZS.html (accessed May 26, 2011).

Swaine, Jon. "Birther Row Began With Hillary Clinton." *The Telegraph.* April 27, 2011. http://www.telegraph.co.uk/news/worldnews/barackobama/8478044/Birther-row-began-with-Hillary-Clinton.html (accessed July 18, 2011).

Tarr, D.R., and A. O'Connor. "Fillibuster." *CQ Encyclopedia of American Government.* 2003. http://www.cqpress.com/incontext/SupremeCourt/fillibuster.htm (accessed September 20, 2011).

Taylor, Jason E., and Richard K. Vedder. "Stimulus by Spending Cuts: Lessons from 1946." *Cato Institute.* May/June 2010. http://www.cato.org/pubs/policy_report/v32n3/cp32n3-1.html (accessed October 31, 2010).

Tennessee Center for Policy Research. "Al Gore - Hypocrite." *Stop The ACLU.* February 26, 2007. http://www.stoptheaclu.com/2007/02/26/al-gore-hypocrite/ (accessed May 14, 2011).

"Testimony of Attorney General John Ashcroft." *The National ommission on Terrorist Attacks Upon the United States.* April 13, 2004. http://www.govinfo.library.unt.edu/911/hearings/hearing10/ashcroft_statementl.pdf (accessed May 25, 2011).

Thai, Xuan, and Ted Barrett. "Biden's Description of Obama Draws Scrutiny." *CNN Politics.* January 31, 2007. http://articles.cnn.com/2007-01-31/politics/biden.obama_1_braun-and-al-sharpton-african-american-pr (accessed October 19, 2010).

Thatcher, Margaret. "Margaret Thatcher, House of Commons Speech." *Free Republic.* November 22, 1990. http://www.freerepublic.com/focus/f-news/2562456/posts (accessed February 3, 2011).

"The Arabic Names Project: Hussein/Husayn." *Pro Hip Hop.* January 2009. http://www.prohiphop.com/2009/01/the-arabic-names-project-husseinhusayn.html (accessed July 11, 2011).

The Associated Press. "Supreme Court Strikes Down Texas Law Banning Sodomy." *The New York Times.* July 26, 2003. http://www.nytimes.com/2003/06/26/politics/26WIRE-SODO.html (accessed September 9, 2010).

"The Ed Show for Monday, December 6th, 2010, 9p Show." *MSNBC.* December 7, 2010. http://www.msnbc.msn.com/id/40557721/ (accessed September 24, 2011).

"The Quiet Revolution." *Live Journal.* February 2, 2010. http://ontd-political.livejournal.com/5261781.html (accessed July 6, 2011).

"The USA PATRIOT Act: Preserving Life and Liberty." *Department of Justice.* October 25, 2001. http://www.justice.gov/archive/ll/highlights.htm (accessed September 20, 2011).

"The Vasconcellos Project." *Politics of Trust.* htpp://www.politicsoftrust.net/board-advisors.php (accessed September 28, 2011).

The Wall Street Journal. "Chinese President Hu Disses the Dollar; Says U.S. System is a 'Product of the Past'." *Fox News.* January 17, 2011. http://www.foxnews.com/world/2011/01/17/chinas-president-calls-based-currency-product-past/ (accessed January 20, 2011).

"The World Bank About Us." *World Bank.* 2011. http://web.worldbank.org/WBSITE/EXTERNAL/EXTAB OUTUS/0,,pagePK:50004410~piPK:36602~theSitePK:297 08,00.html (accessed May 19, 2011).

Thompson, Derek. "Google's CEO: 'The Laws Are Written by Lobbyists'." *The Atlantic.* October 1, 2010. http://www.theatlantic.com/technology/archive/2010/10/go ogles-ceo-the-laws-are-written-by-lobbyists/63908/ (accessed September 23, 2011).

"Todd Stern." *Discover The Networks.* 2010. http://www.discoverthenetworks.org/Articles/SternTodd.ht ml (accessed September 20, 2011).

"Toleration - Dictionary Definition and Overview." *Word IQ.* August 2003. http://www.wordiq.com/toleration (accessed July 7, 2011).

"Top US Marginal Income Tax Rates, 1913-2003." *Truth And Politics.* http://www.truthandpolitics.org/top-rates.php (accessed May 9, 2011).

U.S. Bureau of Labor Statistics. "Unemployment in the United States, 1900-2000." *Holt Researcher.* 2000. http://researcher.hrw.com/statdata.jsp?id=1180 (accessed May 9, 2011).

"U.S. Small Business Administration FAQs: FREQUENTLY ASKED QUESTIONS." *U.S. Small Business Administration.* http://web.sba.gov/faqs/faqIndexAll.cfm?areaid=24 (accessed September 27, 2010).

"United Nations Secretariat." *United Nations.* December 28, 2010. http://www.un.org/ga/search/view_doc.asp?symbol=ST/A DM/SER.B/824 (accessed June 2, 2011).

United States Chief Counsel for Prosecution of Axis Criminality. "Nazi Conspiracy and Aggression Volume IV Document No. 1708-PS." *The Avalon Project Yale Law School.* 1946. http://avalon.law.yale.edu/it/1708-ps.asp (accessed April 30, 2011).

"US Army Corps of Engineers - Headquarters: About Us." *US Army Corps of Engineers.* 2010. http://www.usace.army.mil/about/Pages/Home.aspx (accessed October 19, 2010).

"US Inflation Calculator." *Inflation Calculator.* http://www.usinflationcalculator.com/ (accessed January 27, 2011).

Usborne, David. "Al Gore Denies He is 'Carbon Billionaire'." *The Independent.* November 4, 2009. http://www.independent.co.uk/environment/climate-change/al-gore-denies-he-is-carbon-billionaire-1814199.htm (accessed April 20, 2011).

"Value of U.S. Agricultural Trade by Fiscal Year." *USDA.* November 10, 2010. http://ers.usda.gov/Data/FATUS/index.html (accessed December 2, 2010).

"Van Jones." *Discover The Networks.* 2010. http://www.discoverthenetworks.org/individualProfile.asp?indid=2406 (accessed September 19, 2011).

Waller, J. Michael. "PLA Revises the Art of War." *Find Articles.* February 28, 2000. http://findarticles.com/p/articles/mi_m1571/is_8_16/ai_601 00207/ (accessed September 28, 2011).

Waller, Michael. "Mexico's Immigration Law: Let's Try It Here at Home." *Human Events.* May 8, 2006. http://www.humanevents.com/article.php?id=14632 (accessed November 15, 2010).

Washington, Ellis. "Gov't Imposing New Emissions Rules on Plants, Refineries." *Ellis Washington Report.* February 1, 2011. http://www.elliswashingtonreport.com/2011/02/01/govt-imposing-new-emissions-rules-plants-refineries (accessed September 19, 2011).

Washington, George. "Braddock's Defeat." *National Center.* July 18, 1755. http://www.nationalcenter.org/Braddock'sDefeat.html (accessed September 20, 2011).

—. "George Washington, Excerpt: Indian Prophecy." *God The Original Intent.* 1770. http://www.godtheoriginalintent.com/PDF%20Chapters/George%20Washington%20Indian%20Prophecy.pdf (accessed September 19, 2011).

Watson, Paul Joseph. "Soros: China Will Lead New World Order." *Info Wars.* October 28, 2009. http://www.infowars.com/soros-china-will-lead-new-world-order/ (accessed September 22, 2011).

Watts, Anthony. "Breaking News Story: CRU Has Apparently Been Hacked - Hundreds of Files." *Watts Up With That?* November 19, 2009. http://wattsupwiththat.com/2009/11/19/breaking-news-story-hadley-cru-has-apparently-been-hacked-hundreds-of-files (accessed July 7, 2011).

——. "Jo Nova Finds the Medieval Warm Period." *Watts Up With That?* December 4, 2009. http://wattsupwiththat.com/2009/12/04/jo-nova-finds-the-medieval-warm-period/ (accessed October 19, 2011).

Wealthadvisor. *Answer from WEALTHADVISOR.* April 2009. http://askville.amazon.com/federal-income-taxes-top-10%-income-earners-pay (accessed October 5, 2010).

Webb, Kevin. "Liberal, Left-Wing Assassin Swept Under The Rug." *Kevin Webb 22.* February 2011. http://www.kevinwebb22.com/politics-congressman-jay-nixon-assassination-by-left-wing-radical-gets-no-media-coverage (accessed October 14, 2011).

Freedom Watch. Performed by Matt Welch. Freedom Watch. December 17, 2010.

"What Is Network For Good?" *Network For Good.* 2011. http://support.networkforgood.org/Default.asp?a=4&q=11 (accessed May 9, 2011).

"What Is The World Trade Organization?" *World Trade Organization.* http://www.wto.org/english/thewto_e/whatis_e/tif_e/fact1_e.htm (accessed May 25, 2011).

"What Liberals Say." *AIM.* http://www.aim.org/wls/id-like-a-killer-virus-to-reduce-population-levels/ (accessed November 25, 2010).

Will, George. "Conservatives More Liberal Givers." *Real Clear Politics.* March 27, 2008. http://www.realclearpolitics.com/articles/2008/03/conservat ives_more_liberal_giv.html (accessed July 11, 2011).

Will, George F. "Carbon's Power Brokers." *The Wahington Post.* June 1, 2008. http://www.washingtonpost.com/wp-dyn/content/article/2008/-5/30/QR2008053002521.html (accessed October 28, 2010).

—. "March of the Polar Bears." *Real Clear Politics.* March 22, 2008. http://www.realclearpolitics.com/articles/2008/05/green_fu ndamentalism.html (accessed 2010 28, October).

Williams, Walter E. "Who's to Blame?" *The American Spectator.* February 2010. http://www.spectator.org/archives/2010/02/12/whos-to-blame (accessed December 3, 2010).

Wyllie, Doug. "A Madman's Manifesto: 'The Planet Does Not Need Humans'." *Police One.* September 1, 2010. http://www.policeone.com/standorr/articles/2601251-A-madmans-manifesto-The-planet-does-not-need-humans (accessed February 8, 2011).

Zeleny, Jeff, and Joseph Berger. "G.O.P. Chairman Urges Reid to Step Down Over Remarks." *The New York Times.* Januay 10, 2010. http://www.nytimes.com/2010/01/11/us/politics/11reidweb. html (accessed November 29, 2010).

NOTES

[1] (Congressional Record (Bound Edition), Volume 146 (2000), Part 12 - Social Security Benefits 2000)

[2] (Schweizer 2009)

[3] (Smith 2007, 1,2)

[4] (Senate Historical Office n.d., 3)

[5] (Coulter 2007)

[6] (Kolbert 2009)

[7] (Blume 2010)

[8] (Tennessee Center for Policy Research 2007)

[9] (Usborne 2009, 1,2)

[10] (Eilperin 2010)

[11] (Klaus 2008)

[12] (Orin and Galvin 1996)

[13] (Poe 2003)

[14] (Flight Safety Digest 1996)

[15] (Ambinder 2010)

[16] (Swaine 2011)

[17] (Schilling 2009)

[18] (Beck, Glenn Beck: Fundamental Transformation of America 2011)

[19] (Alinsky 1971, ix)

[20] (Buchanan 2009)

[21] (Democracy Corps 2010)

[22] (Friel, Cohen and Victor 2008)

[23] (The Arabic Names Project: Hussein/Husayn 2009)

[24] (A. Klein, Hamas Terrorists Make 2008 U.S. Presidential Pick 2008)

[25] (Andrea 2009)

[26] (Zeleny and Berger 2010)

[27] (Thai and Barrett 2007)

[28] (Obama Organized Farrakhan's 'Million Man March' 2008)

[29] (Obama 'Lying' About Muslim Past, Expert Says 2008)

[30] (Obama 2007, 142)

[31] (Kurtz, Obama's Radical Past 2010)

[32] (Hitchens 2008)

[33] (Aim Report 2008)

[34] (Alinsky 1971)

[35] (D'Souza, How Obama Thinks 2010)

[36] (Top US Marginal Income Tax Rates, 1913-2003 n.d.)

[37] (Chief Financial Officer, Revenue Financial Management OS:CFO:R 2009)

[38] (Beck, Glenn Beck: Meet the Radicals: Warning Signs of Revolution 2010)

[39] (Romano 2008)
[40] (O'Neill 2009)
[41] (Mishak 2009)
[42] (Van Jones 2010)
[43] (Bloom 2009)
[44] (Domenech 2010)
[45] (Dinan 2009)
[46] (Jim Wallis 2010)
[47] (John Holdren, Obama's Science Czar, Says: Forced Abortions and Mass Sterilization Needed to Save the Planet n.d.)
[48] (Mark Lloyd 2009)
[49] (Malveaux and Hornick 2009)
[50] (Todd Stern 2010)
[51] (Cass Sunstein 2010)
[52] (Profile: Craig Becker Why He Matters 2010)
[53] (Kincaid 2009)
[54] (Profile: Gil Kerlikowske Why He Matters 2009)
[55] (Michelle Obama's Old Law Firm Defends ACORN 2008)
[56] (ABC News Political Punch 2008)
[57] (Rewriting Our History, Changing Our Traditions (Michelle Obama) 2009)
[58] (Perlmutt 2008)
[59] (Meacham 2008)
[60] (D'Souza, The Roots of Obama's Rage 2010)
[61] (Meacham 2008)
[62] (D'Souza, How Obama Thinks 2010)
[63] (D'Souza, The Roots of Obama's Rage 2010)
[64] (Meacham 2008)
[65] (D'Souza, The Roots of Obama's Rage 2010)
[66] (Schweizer 2009)
[67] (Bush 2001)
[68] (J. A. Napolitano, Freedom Watch 2010)
[69] (Lonergan 2000)
[70] (Gray 1986)
[71] (Toleration - Dictionary Definition and Overview 2003)
[72] (Rhodes 2011)
[73] (Alinsky 1971)
[74] (Beck, Glenn Beck: Left's Egypt Conspiracy Accusations Lack Facts 2011)
[75] (DePaul 2010)
[76] (US Inflation Calculator n.d.)
[77] (Cover 2010)
[78] (Beck, Glenn Beck: Who Is Organizing Against Free Speech? 2010)
[79] (Lindgren 2008)
[80] (Brody 2009)

[81] (Condon 2009)
[82] (McChesney 2008)
[83] (The Ed Show for Monday, December 6th, 2010, 9p Show 2010)
[84] (The Quiet Revolution 2010)
[85] (S.773: Cybersecurity Act of 2009 2010)
[86] (Sanchez 2010)
[87] (Brayton 2010)
[88] (Garrettson 2010)
[89] (Lake 2010)
[90] (B. Folsom 2009)
[91] (A. P. Napolitano 2005)
[92] (The USA PATRIOT Act: Preserving Life and Liberty 2001)
[93] (G. Washington, Braddock's Defeat 1755)
[94] (G. Washington, George Washington, Excerpt: Indian Prophecy 1770)
[95] (Clabough, Beck's Founders' Fridays Attempts to Undo Revisionists' Damage 2010)
[96] (Jefferson n.d.)
[97] (Beck, Meet Glenn's Mentor (Repeat) 2010)
[98] (Halsall 1998)
[99] (Beck, Glenn Beck: Founders' Fridays: James Madison 2010)
[100] (Quotes by Thomas Jefferson 1821)
[101] (Beck, Glenn Beck: Republic vs. Democracy: What Did Our Founders Truly Intend? 2010)
[102] (Ibid)
[103] (Ibid)
[104] (Welch 2010)
[105] (Top US Marginal Income Tax Rates, 1913-2003 n.d.)
[106] (Chief Financial Officer, Revenue Financial Management OS:CFO:R 2009)
[107] (Luhby 2011)
[108] (Prante 2009)
[109] (E. Klein 2010)
[110] (Wealthadvisor 2009)
[111] (U.S. Small Business Administration FAQs: FREQUENTLY ASKED QUESTIONS n.d.)
[112] (Historical Highest Marginal Income Tax Rates 2009)
[113] (Top US Marginal Income Tax Rates, 1913-2003 n.d.)
[114] (Estate Tax Exemptions and Rates Over Time 2007)
[115] (Williams 2010)
[116] (Lanman and Aversa 2011)
[117] (Goodwin 1981)
[118] (Stossel, Index of Economic Freedom Lowers US Ranking 2010)
[119] (McCormack 2009)
[120] (Get It Straight: Consumer Spending is *Not* 70% of GDP 2009)
[121] (McCormack 2009)

[122] (Bloom 2009)
[123] (Stossel, Thanksgiving Was Made Possible by Privatization 2010)
[124] (Pietrusza, Calvin Coolidge Still Matters 2010)
[125] (Taylor and Vedder 2010)
[126] (Beisner and Barton 2010)
[127] (What Liberals Say n.d.)
[128] (Simple Living n.d.)
[129] (Spain Unemployment Rate 2011)
[130] (Penty and Ross-Thomas 2011)
[131] (Bullock 2007)
[132] (Wyllie 2010)
[133] (Jones, Memphis Conference "The Dream Reborn" 2008)
[134] (Reiland 2009)
[135] (G. F. Will, March of the Polar Bears 2008)
[136] (Watts, Breaking News Story: CRU Has Apparently Been Hacked - Hundreds of Files 2009)
[137] (Watts, Jo Nova Finds the Medieval Warm Period 2009)
[138] (Booker 2009)
[139] (D'Aleo 2010)
[140] (Pann 2009)
[141] (Ibid)
[142] (E. Washington 2011)
[143] (Morano 2009)
[144] (G. F. Will, March of the Polar Bears 2008)
[145] (G. F. Will, Carbon's Power Brokers 2008)
[146] (Pence 2009)
[147] (Cass Sunstein 2010)
[148] (J. A. Napolitano 2011)
[149] (J. A. Napolitano, Freedom watch 2011)
[150] (Paul 2011)
[151] (ABC Nightly News 2011)
[152] (Newman 2011)
[153] (Parker, Star Parker: Back on Uncle Sam's Plantation 2009)
[154] (Ryan 2011)
[155] (Franklin 1776)
[156] (J. A. Napolitano, Freedom Watch 2010)
[157] (J. A. Napolitano, Freedom Watch 2011)
[158] (Foundation, The Heritage 2010)
[159] (Jefferson n.d.)
[160] (Harris 2011)
[161] (A. Klein, Bill Ayers, Communist Provided Arizona Shooter's Curriculum? 2011)
[162] (Kurtz, Obama and Ayers Pushed Radicalism On Schools 2008)

[163] (Graves 2011)
[164] (Cass Sunstein 2010)
[165] (J. A. Napolitano, Freedom Watch 2011)
[166] (Kelo v. City of New London 2009)
[167] (Supreme Court Kelo V. New London 2005)
[168] (History of the United Nations 2005)
[169] (United Nations Secretariat 2010)
[170] (The World Bank About Us 2011)
[171] (International Monetary Fund n.d.)
[172] (What Is The World Trade Organization? n.d.)
[173] (The Wall Street Journal 2011)
[174] (Beck, Glenn Beck: America's Banker: How Will China Treat Deadbeat Borrowers? 2011)
[175] (Collective Bargaining Impact on State Budgets 2011)
[176] (Labor in a Global World with SEIU President Andy Stern 2007)
[177] (J. A. Napolitano, Freedom Watch 2011)
[178] (Beck, Glenn Beck: Clear Choice From National Mall 2010)
[179] (Beck, Glenn Beck: Union Protestors Promise to 'Release All Hell' 2011)
[180] (Solomon 2005)
[181] (Saad 2009)
[182] (Revkin 2009)
[183] (Murdock 2011)
[184] (Webb 2011)
[185] (Hoover 1958)
[186] (Jordan 2003)
[187] (Alinsky 1971)
[188] (Pope Benedict XVI, on Redemptive Politics Truth and Politics 2008)
[189] (Gaffney 2010)
[190] (Choudary 2010)
[191] (FBI Captured Muslim Brotherhood's Strategic Plan 2010)
[192] (American Broadcasting Companies, Inc. 2011)
[193] (Byrne 2010)
[194] (G-8 Pledges $40 Billion for 'Arab Spring' 2011)
[195] (Cravatts 2009)
[196] (Khuner 2011)
[197] (Pitt 1997)
[198] (Angle 2011)
[199] (The Associated Press 2003)
[200] (Limbaugh, Desperate Democrats Cry Racism 2010)
[201] (Parker, Freedom Watch 2011)
[202] (Green)
[203] (News & Sanger Sightings 2010)
[204] (Fletcher and Weisman 2006)
[205] (Illegal Immigration a $113 Billion a Year Drain on U.S. Taxpayers 2010)

343

[206] (Mass Immigration Reduction Act of 2001/Stealth Amnesty 2001)
[207] (M. Waller 2006)
[208] (Hatter 2010)
[209] (Samples 2001)
[210] (A. Klein, Obama Adviser: Amnesty to Ensure 'Progressive' Rule 2010)
[211] (Canfield 2010)
[212] (Bill Ayers: Any Country With a US Military Base Should Be Able To Vote In American Elections 2011)
[213] (Sessions 2010)
[214] (Clark 2010)
[215] (Adams 2010)
[216] (Allahpundit 2010)
[217] (Moran 2011)
[218] (Holzer n.d.)
[219] (J. A. Napolitano, Freedom Watch 2011)
[220] (Genova 2011)
[221] (Klusendorf 2001)
[222] (Allen 2010)
[223] (Limbaugh 2010)
[224] (Kaplan 2010)
[225] (Beck, Netroots Targets Glenn 2010)
[226] (Eaton 2011)
[227] (Thatcher 1990)
[228] (G. Will 2008)
[229] (Ham 2011)
[230] (Glenn Beck vs Fabian Socialism n.d.)
[231] (Beck, Glenn Beck: Who Are Fabian Socialists? 2010)
[232] (Glenn Beck vs Fabian Socialism n.d.)
[233] (Ibid)
[234] (Ibid)
[235] (About the Fabian Society n.d.)
[236] (Beck, Glenn Beck: Restoring History 2010)
[237] (United States Chief Counsel for Prosecution of Axis Criminality 1946)
[238] (Mataconis 2011)
[239] (Ibid)
[240] (Miller 2011)
[241] (A. Klein, Another Stunner Behind Obama's Libya Doctrine 2011)
[242] (Groves 2011)
[243] (Beck, Glenn Beck: Union Protestors Promise to 'Release All Hell' 2011)
[244] (A. Klein, Another Stunner Behind Obama's Libya Doctrine 2011)
[245] (Ibid)
[246] (McCarthy 2008)
[247] (Hoover 1958, 104)

344

[248] (Hoover 1958, 342-343)
[249] (Maoism n.d.)
[250] (Great Leap Forward n.d.)
[251] (Kurtz, Glenn Beck: Radical in Chief 2010)
[252] (Lifson 2008)
[253] (Beck, Glenn Beck: America's Stretch of Stability the Exception, Not the Norm 2010)
[254] (Hoover 1958, 365)
[255] (Schuman 2010)
[256] (J. M. Waller 2000)
[257] (Ibid)
[258] (Beck, Liberation Theology and the Political Perversion of Christianity 2010)
[259] (Balz 2010)
[260] (Clabough, U.S. Military Prepares for Economic Collapse 2010)
[261] (Gaynor 2011)
[262] (Levinson 2011)
[263] (Beck, Glenn Beck: Who Wants a Califphate in the Middle East? 2011)
[264] (James Glassman & Jared Cohen: On 2008 Alliance for Youth Movement Summit 2011)
[265] (April 6 Youth Movement 2011)
[266] (Beck, Glenn Beck: What is the Red-Green Alliance? 2011)
[267] (Social Media Fuels Protests in Iran, Bahrain and Yemen 2011)
[268] (Hume 2010)
[269] (Beres 2009)
[270] (Buruma 2007)
[271] (Andrews 2007)
[272] (Finnegan 2010)
[273] (Hamden 2008)
[274] (Beckerman 2005)
[275] (John Podesta n.d.)
[276] (Beckerman 2005)
[277] (Moyers 2007)
[278] (Rosen 2010)
[279] (Jones, Introducing The 'American Dream' Movement 2011)
[280] (Blodget 2011)
[281] (Richard Trumka n.d.)
[282] (Heilemann 2011)
[283] (Longshoremen Storm Wash. State Port, Damage RR 2011)
[284] (2008 Presidential Election Finance/Insurance/Real Estate Sector Totals to Candidates 2009)
[285] (Beck, Glenn Beck: George Soros' Mr. Potter Moment 2010)
[286] (Beck, Glenn Beck: The Puppet Master 2010)
[287] (Beck, Glenn Beck: Soros Exposed: Research on the Progressive Puppet Master 2010)

345

[288] (O'Neill 2009)
[289] (Burton and Farzad 2011)
[290] (Open Society Foundations About FAQs n.d.)
[291] (George Soros 2011)
[292] (O'Neill 2009)
[293] (J. M. Waller 2000)
[294] (O'Neill 2009)
[295] (Horowitz and Poe 2005)
[296] (Blount and Weiss 2008)
[297] (Obama Underwrites Offshore Drilling 2009)
[298] (Koch 2010)
[299] (Watson 2009)
[300] (Soros: Hot Spot #3 2010)
[301] (George Soros: Top 10 Reasons He Is Dangerous 2011)
[302] (Bruck 1995)
[303] (Bruck 1995)
[304] (Jenkins 2010)
[305] (Thompson 2010)
[306] (Allan and Warden 2011)
[307] (Lewis 2005)
[308] (Boulton 2010)
[309] (Rosenberg 2009)
[310] (American Jobs Act 2009)
[311] (Beck, Glenn Beck: Three Reasons to Be Wary of Google 2011)
[312] (Kudlow 2006)
[313] (The Vasconcellos Project n.d.)
[314] (Fuller 2010)
[315] (Beck, Truth About Church and State 2010)
[316] (Testimony of Attorney General John Ashcroft 2004)
[317] (Shaffer 2010)
[318] (Ouimette 2003)
[319] (Rumsfeld 2011)
[320] (Beck, Glenn Beck: The Revolution is Now 2010)
[321] (About the MoveOn Family of Organizations n.d.)
[322] (Apollo Alliance Background n.d.)
[323] (Ibid)
[324] (Kerpen 2009)
[325] (34 Years of Tides n.d.)
[326] (Randall and Randall 2003)
[327] (Ibid)
[328] (34 Years of Tides n.d.)
[329] (What Is Network For Good? 2011)
[330] (34 Years of Tides n.d.)

331 (Ibid)
332 (Randall and Randall 2003)
333 (Ibid)
334 (Ibid)
335 (Ibid)
336 (Ibid)
337 (NRDC Mission Statement n.d.)
338 (US Army Corps of Engineers - Headquarters: About Us 2010)
339 (Hopper 2006)
340 (Jacobs 2008)
341 (Fish and Wildlife Service 2009)
342 (Beck, Glenn Beck Quote of the Day: America Makes Nothing of Value 2010)
343 (California Department of Food and Agriculture 2010)
344 (Penner 2009)
345 (Value of U.S. Agricultural Trade by Fiscal Year 2010)
346 (News for Immediate Release 2010)
347 (Department of Water Resources California State Water Project 2011)
348 (California Department of Food and Agriculture 2010)
349 (J. A. Napolitano, Freedom Watch 2011)
350 (Glover 2011)
351 (Kurtz, Cloward-Piven Redux 2010)
352 (Dolan and Gordon 2010)
353 (McGreevy 2010)
354 (Rashid 2001)
355 (From Astronauts To The Boss, Thoughts On Shuttle 2011)
356 (Cobiella 2011)
357 (Papst 2010)
358 (Greenberg 2010)
359 (Papst 2010)
360 (Top US Marginal Income Tax Rates, 1913-2003 n.d.)
361 (U.S. Bureau of Labor Statistics 2000)
362 (Smiley 2010)
363 (Snyder 2010)
364 (Coolidge 1920)
365 (Pietrusza, Silent Cal's Almanack: The Homespun Wit and Wisdom of Vermont's Calvin Coolidge 2008)
366 (J. B. Folsom 2004)
367 (Shenkman 2006)
368 (Lord 2003)
369 (Bovard n.d.)
370 (FDR's Second Bill of Rights and the Progressive Mission 2009)
371 (Cass Sunstein 2010)
372 (Eisenhower Memorial Commission n.d.)

[373] (Tarr and O'Connor 2003)

[374] (Carter 2004)

[375] (Hume 2010)

[376] (Hilton n.d.)

[377] (Anders 2007)

[378] (Limbaugh 2010)

[379] (Beck, Glenn Beck: Indoctrination in America 2010)

[380] (Coulson 1998)

[381] (Boortz 2010)

INDEX

351

www.ingramcontent.com/pod-product-compliance
Lightning Source LLC
Chambersburg PA
CBHW060834280326
41934CB00007B/780